THE PIRATES AND THE MOUSE

THE PIRATES AND THE MOUSE

Disney's War Against the Counterculture

BOB LEVIN

FANTAGRAPHICS BOOKS

FANTAGRAPHICS BOOKS

7563 Lake City Way NE
Seattle, WA 98115 USA.

Editor: Tom Spurgeon
Editorial Liason: Gary Groth
Designers: Carrie Whitney, Preston White
Promotion by Eric Reynolds
Published by Gary Groth & Kim Thompson

First Fantagraphics Books edition: June 2003

ISBN 1-56097-530-X

Printed in Korea

Table Of Contents

Introduction:
The Voice of Revolution Raised

On February 15, 2001, a three-judge panel of the United States Court of Appeals for the Ninth Circuit unanimously affirmed a lower court's decision to deny the toy manufacturer Mattel, Inc.'s motion for an injunction to prevent the photographer Tom Forsythe from fulfilling his artistic vision through the placement of its Barbie dolls in sexually explicit positions in order "to critique the materialistic and gender-oppressive values" he believed they represented.

Bob Dylan had been right. The times, they were a-changing.

But this one had taken over thirty years.

In the first days of the 1970s, America had seemed ready to tear itself apart. The smoke from inner-city riots still seared nostrils and stung eyes. The tears shed at the funerals of JFK and Malcolm and Martin and Bobby had not dried. The heady, bonding optimism that the early gains of the civil rights movement had inspired had been corroded by unfulfilled promises and unrealized dreams into rage and threats and plans to blow up the Statue of Liberty. The expanding war in southeast Asia was a meat grinder, shredding connections and civilities, splattering the walls with the blood of parents set against children, hard-hats against freaks, hawks against doves.

It was a time for the well-considered fire-bombing of judges' homes and liquor-fueled vigilante raids on communes. For armed assaults on courthouses and vandalizing of alternative newspapers. The ambush of policemen on patrol and the brutalizing of hippies passing through town. Deans' offices were trashed by Phi Beta Kappa undergraduates and ROTC buildings and Defense Department research facilities bombed by doctoral candidates taking a break from their dissertations. Selective Service offices were at the mercy of bands of marauding nuns. The IRS was scrutinizing the accounts of leftist groups as if

1

their discrepancies could fund nuclear submarines. The FBI, through a sinister program no one had ever heard of, COINTELPRO, were bugging the same folks' walls, tapping their phones, and infiltrating their membership with spies and provocateurs. Transmission towers exploded and banks incinerated. Planes were hijacked, one a week; and people fled to Canada and Sweden, Cuba and Kathmandu. Timothy Leary got ten years for smuggling a couple ounces of pot across the border in his daughter's underwear. The White Panthers' John Sinclair got the same for giving two joints to an undercover agent. H. Rap Brown and Stokely Carmichael and Eldridge Cleaver and Angela Davis and Tom Hayden and Abbie Hoffman and Jerry Rubin and Bobby Seale and Afeni Shakur (Tupac's mother) and Reyes Tijerina were on trial for, if not their lives, substantial portions of them — and Mark Hampton and Fred Clark were executed in their beds. The U.S. military and local law enforcement agencies incarcerated demonstrators by the football stadium-full or clubbed or gunned them down on campus commons and sprayed the survivors with tear gas from assault helicopters, while the current president, Richard Nixon, vilified those left penned, bleeding, weeping, as "bums," and a future one, Ronald Reagan, led cheers for a greater "bloodbath."

A cultural war raged just as wildly as this political one. The dominant ethos of the country, which that had been ratcheted into place throughout the 1950s and early '60s, was one of muted consensus and polite conformity. (*Father*, we were reminded weekly in prime time, *Knows Best*.) Loyalty oaths, school prayers, and pledges of allegiance were mandatory, if you did not want to be spanked. The banning of *Lady Chatterley's Lover* and *Tropic of Cancer* (two percent of what were later judged the Best English Language Novels of the century), Elvis Presley not being televised below the waist, Ozzie and Harriet sleeping in separate beds, and there not being a bare nipple to be seen in Hollywood (or a pubic hair in *Playboy*) made perfect sense; to believe otherwise was to enter upon a path at whose end madness lay. It was the heyday of well-rounded, well-adjusted, crew-cut fraternity boys in penny loafers and crisply-pressed khakis, and virginal, every-hair-in-place sorority girls in saddle shoes and camel's hair coats, pairing off with mirror-image, suburban neighbors, in mirror-image suburban neighborhoods, to achieve two-car, two-point-five-kid-centered familial stability and community admiration. Financial security was the aim and deviance to be crushed like Japanese beetles on the roses.

The new nation came wild-haired, bare-footed, costumed as frontiersmen and buccaneers, Renaissance princesses and fairy sprites. It cavorted in the nude. It replaced keg parties, backyard barbecues, and the cocktail hour with marijuana, LSD, methedrine, laughing gas, mescaline, magic mushrooms, opium, STP, and anything it could find in the medicine cabinet. It had its own bone-jarring, head-rattling music, augmented by light shows that rewired any senses the music and drugs had missed. It had its own sacred texts — *The I Ching, Black Elk Speaks* — never before seen in any Sunday school in Scarsdale or New Trier; its own dietary musts (who had ever before even contemplated wrapping their tongue around tofu?); its own "far out," "mind-blowing," "mellow" language. "Come together," it sang. Pick up the "good vibrations." "Wear," it pains me to remember, "flowers in your hair." It lived on over 2000 rural communes and it operated over 5000 cheese-selling, baguette-vending, taxi-driving urban collectives. And it took to sex like it was grabbing M&M's from a bowl.

Each of these dislodgments was met by the prevailing-standards bearers as if not only the country was at stake but all of western civilization. Resistance was a must — or lions would be feeding on Billy Graham at half-time of the Rose Bowl while the rest of us burned. The young people at the center of this struggle were either one of the noblest, most courageous, most morally committed generations in our nation's history, clear-sighted harbingers of a new civilization that would, in the judgment of one social analyst (Theodore Roszak), save us from "the final consolidation of a technocratic totalitarianism" and bring about, in that of another (Charles Reich), "a higher reason, a more human community, and a new and liberated individual... a renewed relationship of man to himself, to other men, to society, to nature and to the land"; or they were a pack of unkempt, foul-smelling, disruptive, obscene, vicious, self-indulgent, spoiled brats who needed to be taught the most serious of lessons (A Majority of Everybody Else).

"For the first time since 1776," Harrison E. Salisbury, editor of the Op-Ed page of the *New York Times*, summarized, "the true and authentic voice of revolution was raised in the U.S.A." Before this voice was stilled, our society would be transformed. And one of the most inflammatory incitements within this revolt would be a comic book.

Chapter One:
Fascism Lost the War

Draw a mouse. Go to jail.

For the Honorable Albert C. Wollenberg, Judge of the Federal District Court for the Northern District of California, on June 27, 1979 — after nearly a decade of litigation, after appeals to the Ninth Circuit and the United States Supreme Court, after the amassing of a 2500-page court file, after the contentions of some of the finest attorneys within his jurisdiction — that was the proposition he was expected to implement.

Wollenberg was a bald, fleshy-faced man, with black-framed, no-nonsense, Clark Kent glasses. He was seventy-nine years old and a member of a German-Jewish family prominent in San Francisco since the Gold Rush. A graduate of UC Berkeley and its law school, Boalt Hall, he had been a federal prosecutor for seven years and a successful attorney in private practice for thirteen more. As a two-term Republican assemblyman and Chairman of the Ways and Means Committee, he had helped enact the legislative program of his close friend, Governor Earl Warren. Warren had named him a Superior Court judge in 1947. Eisenhower had elevated him to the federal bench in April 1958. He had upheld the constitutionality of a statute making it a crime for a union official to be a member of the Communist Party, but he had also ruled that draft boards could not change a man's status simply because he had protested the Vietnam War. He considered himself to have a "conservative bent," but his reputation was that of a thoughtful, tolerant man.

On one side of this thought-testing, tolerance-probing case was the plaintiff. Walt Disney Productions. The moving party. The aggrieved innocent. In fifty years, it had sprung in boot-strap-lifted, grindstone-nosed, wheel-shouldered, inspirational storybook fashion from a commercial art venture in Kansas City built on free desk space and $500 worth of office supplies to a globe-spanning entertainment conglomerate. Its good-hearted, uplifting, family-oriented fare drew upon those values — patriotism and puritanism, consumerism and conformity — that the cultural revolution had called into question and simultaneously fed them back to a needing-to-be-reassured public, bringing it $750,000,000 a year. On the other side was the defendant. The malfeasant. The willful violator of the injunction he, Judge Wollenberg, had granted and the Court of Appeal and Supreme Court had sustained. Whose career's trajectory, though tracking the direct opposite of Disney's stratospheric ascent, was, in its commitment to a free-spirited, convention-defying, bluenose-shocking, light-out-for-the-territory view of the personal and public good, just as resolutely mythic-American.

In 1963, the *San Francisco Chronicle* had made Dan O'Neill, a skinny, bespectacled, twenty-one-year-old college dropout — five colleges by his own count — the youngest syndicated cartoonist in American newspaper history.[1] Within a few months, his strip, "Odd Bodkins," whose quirky humor, philosophical joustings, and positions on political and social issues would make it unlike anything on a mainstream comics page before or since, was in forty papers, including the *Chicago Daily News*, the *Los Angeles Times*, and the *Washington Post*; and he had been the subject of a feature article in *Newsweek* and lauded as the voice of "the post-'Peanuts' generation."[2] Within a few years after that, his provocations had caused almost every paper to drop him and the *Chron* to fire him for a second, third or fourth — accounts vary — and apparently final time.

O'Neill had drawn from this experience the lesson that what America truly needed was the destruction of Walt Disney. Taking this mission upon himself,

~~~~~~

[1] The source of this distinction is O'Neill. However, since the very first information he provided me, that the day following his birth, on April 21, 1942, Hitler invaded Russia ("I showed up and fascism lost the war") could be disproved through research requiring no more than one arm's reach across my desk ("Early in the morning of June 22, 1941, German forces struck across the border of the Soviet Union..." Gerhard L. Weinberg. *A World at Arms*), I learned — and now warn all who press on — not to lean too heavily upon his allegations for support. He is a man unhobbled by factual restraints when a touch of moon-dust will enliven life's dance. He is a story-teller in its most noble of manifestations, relating to the world through re-worked lines and remodeled anecdotes, more devoted to achieving the most affecting of tellings than the exactly replicated, always less satisfying what-was. To quote his attorney in the above proceeding, "You don't talk to Dan if what you're interested in is some Kantean discourse addressing the abstract nature of truth. He's Irish." It is surprising how often this explanation, uttered by others, surfaces to account for some quirk in O'Neill and, uttered by him, characters within his work.

That disclaimer expressed, now let me say that R.C. Harvey, the estimable comic historian, who has researched the subject, says, "The youngest I could find was twenty-three, twenty-four or twenty-five, so he might be."

[2] At its peak, O'Neill says, "Odd Bodkins" was in 375 papers, whose combined circulation of 55,000,000 earned him $5000 a week. I have confirmation it was in 75-to-100, with a circulation of 20,000,000 — which still isn't boiled potatoes — and he was earning not quite one-tenth that.

he rounded up a rag-tag band of rogue cartoonists, the Air Pirates, named after a group of evil-doers who had bedeviled Mickey Mouse in the 1930s, and launched a comic book in which a number of Disney characters, particularly — and most notoriously — Mickey, engaged in ultra-un-Disneylike behavior. Now he stood before the bar, thirty-eight-years-old, essentially unemployed, with total assets of seven dollars, a 1963 Mercury convertible, a banjo, and the baggy gray suit he was wearing. Disney, which already had a $190,000 judgment against him, sought to have him fined another $10,000 and imprisoned for six months.

Chapter Two:
San Francisco Loves Lunatics

Nevada City, a town of 2880, lies in the Sierra foothills, two and a half hours east and north of San Francisco. Its style mixes the Wild West, hippies gone to the hills, and yuppies on the rise. It is full of dogwood and wood-frame Victorians, white and trim as prize ducks. The Gold Rush made it, for a minute, California's third largest city. About those days, a current promotional brochure boasts "Nevada City was wild and wooly... Gambling saloons arose in splendor and numbers and were thronged. Liquor was plentiful and fights were common. Claims were jumped and murders committed. Brothels and opium dens were not uncommon." While this history remains a selling point, contemporary real estate agents are more likely to boast of a proximity to recreational activities and the low rate of juvenile crime. Newcomers, though, are warned in the small print to select garden plants "that are fire and deer resistant, cold hardy and drought tolerant." Toughness is a good idea if you plan to linger.

Dan O'Neill does not have a phone, so it took a series of messages left at various locales and a couple confirmatory notes to set a date to talk. When we had, I cleared my calendar and, with my wife Adele, found a bed-and-breakfast by scribbling down phone numbers from a *Best of...* guide, while supporting our local independent bookstores by clogging an aisle at Barnes & Noble. The woman who took my call made customary inquiry: How did we hear of them? What time would we arrive? Why did we visit? "Anniversary? Get-away weekend? Our wild flowers are in bloom."

"I'm writing about a local cartoonist," I said.

"We have a considerable artists' colony," she said. "Charles Schulz's son lives here. Who are you writing about?"

"Dan O'Neill," I said.

She hadn't heard of him.

I told her about "Odd Bodkins."

She hadn't heard of it.

I told her about the Air Pirates, Disney, the litigation, in phrases that always drew V-sign body language from my friends.

"And what is your position?" she said, the temperature in her voice dropping below when it might have been my anniversary.

Periodically, I must remind myself Berkeley is not the world. I do that even when I enter El Sobrante. "Well, I am an attorney," I said, adroitly realigning as if my left foot had skidded on an icy slick, "but I haven't studied the decision. I'm not sure where I'll come out."

"I think stealing another person's creations is terrible. We have a close friend who worked for Walt Disney, and he says he was a lovely man. What's the point of what this fellow was doing?"

I mentioned the First Amendment and parody.

"What?"

"Parody. Satire. Like... Did you ever read *MAD* magazine?"

"I saw a copy once. I thought it was... weird."

"Don't lose our room," Adele said.

"Disney represented a lot of what the Pirates thought was wrong with America. So to make fun of him, they drew like him."

"Well, that's awful. It'd be like drawing Snoopy, that wonderful dog that everyone loves, and making him perform obscene acts."

"You've got it," I said.

When we'd hung up, Adele said. "From now on, with the happy villagers, maybe stick to golden poppies. Unless you want to get O'Neill lynched."

Four different sporting events were on four different television sets in the saloon's four corners. O'Neill bought us each a sugary, non-alcoholic, caffeine-laced drink over ice ("Speed in a bottle," he assured me) and led us onto the patio where he could smoke. He wore an olive-green, rolled-brim cowboy hat, scuffed boots, faded denim jacket, faded denim shirt, jeans. He had a blue bandana tied around his neck. His eyes, behind rimless glasses, were paler blue than his denim. The crow's feet in the corners were deeply etched. He had shaggy, grey-brown, collar-length hair, bushy eyebrows, a mustache that had adorned "WANTED" posters from Deadwood to Dodge. His voice was gravelly and deep.

"The first O'Neills showed up here in '51 from Australia, where they'd been shipped as convicts. My mother's family [O'Donnells] came 'round the Horn after the Famine. Back in Ireland, the same names in the same families have been marrying each other for hundreds of years. A goofy bunch. Irish history has the O'Neills down for Armenians for, like, twenty minutes. Then two horses, everything sharp, all the women, and a couple of dogs were missing. They got them all, took off, and eventually turned into Norse raiders who took over the top of Ireland. It was like Florida compared to where they'd lived. The

O'Neills have been 50,000 years in a fog bank. There's no way to get a suntan on us. We have to marry Indians if we want one.

"My old man [Hugh D. O'Neill, Jr.][3] fought with Pappy Boyington. He was one of the first volunteer night fighters. Volunteer meant you were going to die. The first squadron he was with went into Africa. The skipper was a drunk. He kept the young kid pilots awake all night drinking with him. Proved what a man he was and the kids'd go out on dawn patrol and fly into a mountain. They lost three pilots in the African campaign and eighteen more because of this guy. My father complained; the next thing he knew, he was transferred to a desk in nowhere. He heard there was this volunteer outfit so he got into that. Nobody'd ever been night fighters before. They had an early form of radar that didn't work, but they put a great big wooden hump on the Corsair with nothing in it that looked like a secret weapon. They got to Bougainville; and, one night, Halloween, he caught a Jap bomber against the moon. That was Washing Machine Charlie. Every night he'd come over. The Marines just had the beach. The rest of the island was Japanese. The Marines couldn't get any sleep so they couldn't fight. So he nailed him. The next night, he was up there; and, every fifteen minutes, you have to clear your guns at altitude or they'll ice up. He's flying around in the dark and fires a few rounds. Pfft! Blows up another one. He'd've run into it if he hadn't shot it down. That convinced the Japanese there really was some secret weapon, so they stopped Washing Machine Charlie. Everybody got some sleep and took Guadalcanal. The gunfight that pivoted the war.[4]

"He stayed in twenty-eight years[5] — through the Pacific, Korea, flying close air support at the Quinchon Reservoir when MacArthur, the dodo, got the Marines trapped after intelligence told him it was surrounded by millions of Red Chinese. The walls of the house are covered with Distinguished Flying Crosses and Purple Hearts and presidential commendations. He was a mighty warrior. He retired when they thought he was going to die of a heart condition. He put his machine gun down and got a doctorate in educational psychology [from the University of Oklahoma] and taught at USF. Around 1960, he and my mother [Marian] moved up here. She was a fashion illustrator and artist."

---

[3] O'Neill, his father and grandfather bore the same moniker. Within the family, they sport the *noms-de-rail* "Wheatie," "Boysie" and "Pat."

[4] The battle for Guadalcanal lasted from October 1942 until February 1943. The landing on Bougainville was eleven months after that. Weinberg, *supra*.

[5] In a subsequent conversation, O'Neill recounted a story about his father's first command, which involved another officer coming home drunk with a huge erection, trying to jump his wife, missing the bed, hitting the floor, and rending his joy stick asunder. You get the feeling every time you talk to O'Neill you could get stories of this splendor. (Having had several conversations with O'Neill since I wrote this, Adele suggests I replace "could" with "must.")

While his father was in the Navy, O'Neill lived — again, by his count — in seventeen states. (The experience, he once said, left him with "the ability to be completely at home in a strange situation and completely ill at ease in a stable one.") He was in and out of schools — about two a year — "always the new boy and always in fights," suspended or expelled every semester of high school, beginning with Maryknoll Missionary, a seminary, when he was fifteen. He eventually graduated from St. Joseph's, a private, Catholic school in Alameda, after the public school system and he severed relationships over his pumping 4,000,000 cubic feet of ferrous sulphide through the ventilation system at Oakland High School, shutting the place for two weeks. "Huey Newton, fifteen years later, upstairs at the O'Farrell Theater,[6] he goes, 'You're the Dan O'Neill that blew up Oakland High?' He grabbed me and danced me around the room. 'God, that was the only vacation I had in my life.'[7] He wanted me to edit the Black Panther paper. I said, 'I got to tell you this, Huey, before somebody else does. I'm a honkie. You take me into headquarters, they'll notice.'"

By the time O'Neill reached high school, the publication of Jack Kerouac's *On the Road* had set the beatnik scene, centered just across the Bay Bridge in San Francisco, front and center in the imaginations of those teenagers unsatisfied by images of game-winning touchdowns, student council presidencies, or slow dancing to "Silhouette" with Arlene Sullivan on *American Bandstand*. (Well, maybe Arlene lingered in the picture.) He and his friends swapped their button-down Oxfords for sweatshirts and their belt-in-the-back caps for berets, bulked up their goatees with burnt cork, and began hanging at the jazz clubs and coffee houses of Broadway and Grant Avenue.

Prodded by "The Big Folk Scare of 1958," touched off by the Kingston Trio's hit recording of "Tom Dooley," O'Neill augmented his social allure by

---

[6] The O'Farrell was owned by O'Neill's friends Jim and Artie Mitchell, San Francisco pornography impresarios. (*Behind the Green Door,* which cost $60,000 and earned $10-$50,000,000 — accounts vary — was their most celebrated work.) Sons of an Okie card shark from the oil refinery-soaked suburb of Antioch, through their commitment to free speech (particularly in the more erotic sub-genres), sexual openness (especially when captured for posterity in living color), and consciousness expansion (predominantly of the jam-it-down-your-gullet, snuff-it-up-your-nose class), the Mitchells had emerged as mutant avatars of the counterculture in certain circles. Their theater, whose inner office walls O'Neill's drawings decorated, was a major partying point for celebrities, artists, socialites, and politicos — including some judges and at least one future San Francisco District Attorney — and would become, in the words of Hunter S. Thompson, who served a tour as its "night manager," "The Carnegie Hall of public sex in America."

[7] Newton may have had a touch of the blarney himself, since, according to his biographer, Hugh Pearson, he was expelled from every public high school in Oakland, which must have left him some moments of leisure.

teaching himself the banjo. (The final push in this direction had come at a party when the girls he had drawn with a piano-interpretation of "Johnny B. Goode" deserted him for a fellow with a guitar and two chords at his command.) Soon he was gigging around Northern California, at clubs like the Drinking Gourd and Copy Cat, in a group called The Highgraders. His musical career peaked in 1963, when he was hired for the neo-Dixieland house band at the Red Garter on Broadway. "I had the peppermint vest," he says, "the stupid bow tie, the white pants. All these young Republicans from Stanford and me."

O'Neill had been drawing cartoons since he was four. With his father overseas, it was something he could do that pleased his artist mother. Walt Kelly's anti-establishment "Pogo" was a major influence. So were the Disney comics. "Especially the Ducks. That one guy [Carl Barks] wrote Everyman stories. They could have been Shakespeare. This guy, doing two pages a day for forty years for Western Publications[8] in a closet somewhere; and Disney doesn't even know what he's doing." His favorite Barks story concerned an April Fool's joke. In the foreground of a long shot of the town dump, where the nephews have gone to find a wallet with which to fool Uncle Donald, lies a discarded copy of *Mein Kampf.* "A clue," O'Neill says, "to where this life of mine was going. See, something about fascists does it to me. When the McCarthy hearings were on, we had the only television in Oklahoma, so all the kids were over; and they interrupted *Time for Beanie,* and twenty-five of us became anti-fascists at that moment. If it'd been a left-winger, I'd probably be in the White House. I'd've been worse than Reagan."

In 1956, Orr Kelly, a *Chronicle* reporter, left that paper in order to start his own weekly, *The Berkeley Review.* He lacked an editorial cartoonist; and his assistant editor, a friend of O'Neill's mother, recommended him. He worked there six years; and, in 1961, after his family moved to Nevada City, he began "Odd Bodkins," a daily strip, for the Nevada County *Nugget.* His second installment depicted a little man in a bottle. "I'm tremendously virile," he said. "Women have locked me up, but last night they forgot to make sure the cork was tight." The next panel showed an empty bottle, followed by off-stage screams: "Stop him!" "Catch him!" "Rape!" Then a female arm jammed the man back in. "Well, the staff, all Catholic, complained to the priest; and I was denounced from the pulpit. Alpha Hardware dropped $400 worth of advertising, which was a lot of money then. It looks like I'm out of business in a week; but the printer, Charley Adler, from the German family that rode bicycles on the high wire, told the publisher, "Run the strip or I won't print your paper.

---

[8] Western was licensed by Disney to publish comics based upon its characters, which it did in a joint venture with Dell Comics until 1962, after which they were published through Gold Key and Whitman.

And I'll call every other printer in the West and they won't either."

While at the *Review,* through Kelly, O'Neill had met Bob Bastian, the editorial cartoonist for the *Chronicle.* "Whadya want, kid?" Bastian said. "'Your job," O'Neill said. "Here's how you get it," Bastian said. "Go back to school. Get on the newspaper. Get in the yearbook. Get published. Publish, publish, publish." Five years later, about to be married, his future wife pregnant, unemployed except for his strip, O'Neill sent brochures to 500 newspapers — or ninety three, accounts vary — offering them "Odd Bodkins" for five dollars a week. His only reply came from an editor in Santa Cruz who told him that for what O'Neill was asking he could get "Peanuts." "How?" asked O'Neill. "The syndicate." "'What's a syndicate?" When the editor told him the *Chronicle* had one, O'Neill took his strip to Bastian. "He said, 'Great,' and took it to the editor. They said, 'Don't call us. We'll call you.' I figured, that's it. Two weeks later, they called. I put the phone back on the receiver so hard it broke. They didn't know I was twenty-one. From the cynicism they were seeing, they thought I was thirty. After the contracts were signed, they asked me to John's Grill for lunch. Oh, boy, big time! 'How old are you?' 'Twenty-one.' They choked. 'Oh God, it's too late.'"

"I showed up," O'Neill told Gary Groth, *The Comics Journal*'s editor, in an unpublished interview from the mid-1980s, "with a three-piece suit and a gold watch; and my editors said, 'Hey, that's all wrong, kid. You have to be a character like Emperor Norton. San Francisco loves lunatics.' It was a business, and I was a commodity." By the time he left — long-haired, beaded, buck-skinned, and often accompanied by Barney, an Irish setter with one wooden leg — he had won a permanent place in the city's lore (and many of its citizens' hearts); and the paper had been rattled as though by a 7.0 temblor.

The *Chronicle* O'Neill joined had been shaped by its brilliant and controversial executive editor Scott Newhall. Newhall had been hired out of college, in 1934, as a fill-in photographer. He became a reporter after losing a leg to an infection contracted in Mexico — according to O'Neill, after being bitten by an insect while covering a story. However, Newall's widow has written the precipitating event — in what amounts to one of the few times an O'Neill version of history has been topped — was when her husband kicked a horse in the course of a frustrating search for a lost Aztec gold mine, and it kicked him back.

In 1952, when Newall assumed his managerial position, the *Chron* was losing a circulation war with William Randolph Hearst's *Examiner* 350,000 to 170,000. By the time Newhall resigned, in 1971, the *Ex* could only survive by begging its rival into a joint profit- and cost-sharing agreement. Newhall had won his campaign by assembling a staff of writer/columnists — Terrence O'Flaherty, Herb Caen, Charles McCabe, Stanton Delaplane, Ralph Gleason, Art Hoppe, Lucius Beebe — whose work and names may not have traveled far beyond the Bay Area but whose personalities and style — literate, amusing, hedonistic, tolerant — reflected and helped shape its way of being. Newhall may have undervalued solemnity enough to cause the Ben Bradlee character in *All the President's Men* to quip, "Send it to the *Chronicle*. They'll print anything"; but his paper was lively — when the *Examiner* inveighed against the evils of topless bars, Newhall wrote, "What this city needs is not fewer topless bars but more topless newspapers" — and more attuned to its readers' subconscious desires than many, more journalistically worthy tomes. And the profits his attitudes reaped leveraged him room for editorial positions his conservative Republican publisher, Charles Thierot, might have otherwise scotched.

The *Chron's* social world, however, was built upon cocktails and Frank Sinatra-as-role-model and weekends at tennis ranches in Carmel Valley. Its standard bearers had grown up in the Depression and been adults through two wars. Their view of the good life was represented by Caen's Jaguar, "The White Rat": eye-catching, costly, and impossible to maintain. Though Caen was friendly, Hoppe happy to pen an introduction to O'Neill's first book, and the six-foot-one, 240-pound McCabe amenable enough to occasionally growl an acknowledgment from his customary seat at Gino & Carlo's bar, it was not a scene into which O'Neill comfortably fit.

He had no community of cartoonists to bond with either. The competition for a limited number of slots in an ever-diminishing number of newspapers kept practitioners wary of newcomers. Aside from Bastian, he didn't even know another cartoonist. And when he met one, it wasn't always a Kodak Moment. "There'd be this guy," he told Groth, "and he's all beat up and worn out, eighty-two or eighty-three, and he's got a pencil in his hand; and you're saying, 'Hey, that's my future — if I'm lucky and don't get hit by a bus.'"

O'Neill found comfort two doors down from where he banjo-ed. In 1964, following the death of his wife's father, he had asked Caen what might cheer her up. "The Committee," Caen said.

A troupe of improvisational comedians which had spun off from Chicago's legendary Second City, the Committee ran on Broadway from 1963-73. Its humor was more political than its predecessor, but (or, perhaps, because of that) it developed fewer stars. (While the Second City boasted Alan Arkin, Shelly Berman, Mike Nichols and Elaine May as alums, the Committee's best known graduate was Peter Bonerz, who played Jerry, the dentist, on the original *Bob Newhart Show*.) At its peak, it had two theaters in San Francisco, one in L.A., and a road company. It was also known for running one of its actors for mayor and leading a well-ahead-of-its-time campaign to legalize marijuana.

The O'Neills fell from their chairs, laughing. The next morning he went back and found a cast member out front working on a Harley. "I had been doing the strip for a year, and it was a mess. I had 127 characters going every which way. I didn't know what I was doing. So I told him, 'You have a moral obligation to take me in. You guys are funny every day, and that's what I have to be.'"

He stayed nine years. He progressed "from the lobby, to the kitchen, to the Green Room, penetrating the sacred councils of satire. I didn't understand a thing they were saying, but something sank in. I don't know what. How to stay up all night. How to ingest exotic substances." Someone would say, "Here's an improv. problem"; and he would solve it on paper. He learned how to build scenes and how to create characters who would be themselves, independent of who he was.

The Committee also introduced him to Lenny Bruce. "They held me up by the scruff of the neck. 'This is Dan O'Neill. He's a cartoonist.' Lenny looks at me. 'I'm a cartoonist too.' And he draws one of my characters on a napkin. Now, Lenny Bruce is wearing a blue suit, and I'm wearing a blue suit. He's got black shoes on, and I've got black shoes on. He's got a tie, and I've got a tie. But his blue suit doesn't have any lapels. His tie is a string tie. His shoes are sharp, little, pointy dancing shoes. I've got wing tips. I've got a big knit tie. My lapels go from here to Christmas. So I'm not quite on the beam. And he draws my character, except coming out of his center is a huge penis that swells to the size of a basketball; and he's got an anguished look on his face, and he's going, 'There's no hole in it!' He read me as a San Francisco Irish Catholic, oppressed, suppressed, depressed, repressed, like a book. Acid didn't do anything compared to what that did to me."[9]

The early "Odd Bodkins" strips usually had two characters in dialogue.[10] The construction was set-up (one panel), exposition/interplay (middle panel/s), punch line (last panel). Sometimes the subject of one strip carried over into the next, but there was no connective, narrative line.

The two primary characters were short: waistless but with arms and legs; neckless but with mouth and eyes; only one had a nose. ("Potatoes with hands and feet," their creator called them.) Neither appeared clothed, but no sexual organs showed. One wore glasses, and his torso was white. The other did not,

[9] In 1961, when the City and County of San Francisco prosecuted Bruce for using the word "cocksucker" in his act at the Jazz Workshop, the assistant district attorney who tried the case was Albert Wollenberg, Jr. Bruce was acquitted.

[10] My points of reference for this section – prior commitments having rendered me unable to chain myself to a microfilm machine scouring old newspapers – are three collections: *Buy This Odd Bodkins Book*, *Hear the Sound of My Feet Walking, Drown the Sound of My Voice Talking*, *The Collected Unconscience of Odd Bodkins*. While out of print, all can be found, with persistence, on line, at used book stores, or through dealers' catalogues.

The search, even if unsuccessful, may have rewards. My most prized involved the rare book collection at UC's Bancroft Library. Its catalogue claimed an O'Neill title I didn't recognize. (It had it wrong.) I submitted my request slip and waited at a polished wood table, surrounded by Victorian period oils. The room was silent but for the tap of computer keyboards, the turn of another page. I was handed a cardboard folio which contained two dozen UG comics, some obscure, some ordinary. There, amidst the PhDs pouring over arcane manuscripts and esoteric texts, I perused S. Clay Wilson's *Pork*. It was all I could do to refrain from elbowing the scholar beside me, "Look at the *schlong* on that one!"

and his torso was black. Neither had a name, but the former came to be called Hugh. (The latter would disappear and be replaced by Fred the Bird, son of a progressive mother who had not taught him to fly.) Neither had a distinct personality; but one assumes they were "human" since the strip's non-human characters — a turtle, a rabbit, a talking lamp, a bat-winged hamburger snatcher — look like what you would expect, if one takes the verisimilitude of the bat-winged hamburger snatcher on faith.[11]

Each frame was essentially an empty chamber, occupied only by the speaking (and listening) "human" or rabbit or lamp. Background details, establishing place or influencing mood, are rare. If the strip requires a phone, there will be a phone (and perhaps a table for it to sit on) but never anything else — never a hooked rug or Utrillo print or ficus plant. There is no cross-hatching or shading. Once in a long while, a "WHAP" or "SPLAT" hovers in the air.

The rudimentary visuals establish "Odd Bodkins" as a humor strip. There are the funny-looking humans, the talking animals, the fairy godfather in his wizard's hat. (Humor strips — see "Li'l Abner"— can be drawn elaborately; dramatic or action strips cannot be drawn minimally.) The stripped-down style announces, too, that the humor will be modern, intelligent, "hip." It links to "Peanuts"[12] or "The Wizard of Id." (Slipping off the comics page to establish intellectual clout, it also connects to Beckett's emptiness, to Pinter's sparsity.) But drawing only goes so far in establishing a strip's character. The rest must come from words.[13]

These early ones were not particularly disturbing. True, there was none of the cloying sentiment of "Happiness is a warm puppy" or the haven't-we-all-been-there humor of Lucy pulling away the football. O'Neill was more likely to moan a wish "to hide from organized happiness" or seek laughs from more pointed topics: a dove-of-peace whose health insurance has been canceled; a turtle whose shell has been repossessed. And even in his strip's infancy, refer-ences were creeping in to Watts and Vietnam and rabid anti-Communists (in the person of a 100% American Dog). But while this may have been daring

---

[11] One etymologist attributes the name "Odd Bodkins" to O'Neill's inability to draw figures. O'Neill has written it was a Saxon term for a short sword used "mainly for stabbing people in the back while smiling at their front" — a definition, at least the sword part of which, the *OED* con-firms.

[12] O'Neill credits his career as a cartoonist to Charles Schulz. "Before Schulz, cartoonists had to be artists. After him, newspapers could shrink strips in half and double the count. Schulz opened the door for bad artists, like me, doing postage stamps."

[13] Words are primary with O'Neill. When Adele asked why someone, who admittedly couldn't draw well, chose cartooning as a profession, he said, "Art is just a way to save words. Instead of talking about 'Here we are in Spain,' I can draw it. It saves a lot of trees."

on a newspaper comics page, where readers still expected to wash their Wheatina down with nothing spicier than "Blondie," it was well below the levels of engagement open to editorial cartoonists, Jules Feiffer, or even the *MAD* of a decade before.

But, in hindsight, some of these strips hold a prickly prescience. In the first collection's opener, O'Neill's black spokespotato inveighs against people who waste his time. What, Hugh asks, would you do if they didn't? "Save the world," he replies. In the last strip, Hugh is building a brick wall. "If you want to get ahead in this society...," he says. He notices a brick sticking out, tries to tap it back into place, and has the entire wall collapse. The last panel shows a pile of bricks from which extends a voice balloon. "You have to bury yourself in your work."

By O'Neill's second collection, his efforts as a savior had dislodged several bricks. The dominant visual symbol is a road upon which most of the action occurs. We are on a never-ending journey. Hugh focuses the quest in the opening panel by asking, "Where is God?" His subsequent reasoning — since God is everywhere and it would be "inconvenient" to be inside everything, we must be inside him: ergo, "That isn't the sky!! That's God's stomach lining!!" — sets the tone for how it will be conducted.

While no increase in O'Neill's ability to render human anatomy is evident, he no longer shies from other visual efforts. Panels dazzle with their action, jolt by their misproportions, unnerve through startling composition. The sun and moon, regular presences, occasionally converse with one another, more often oddly hover, discombobulating but benign. Backgrounds careen in constant flux. The sky shifts from white to black and back again. Sometimes a series of lines parallel the horizon; sometimes they arc; sometimes they fragment the sky kaleidoscopically. Craggy mountain ranges mutate into pyramids or cones. Trees and flowers pop up from nowhere and vanish. Word balloons — entire sequences of panels, in fact — turn from white to black. Sounds like SMASH and OUCH, rendered three-dimensionally, threaten to blow apart the page.

The strips are no longer one gag and out. But no narratives like these ever before resided beside "Mary Worth." The adventures include an assault by a runaway gingerbread man and an encounter with O'Neill's old bottle-dwelling friend, now hiding from the bomb and computerized society. Extended sequences record Hugh's dismay that there is no word for "non-tickle" and Fred's belief that people are falling off the edge of a flat world, despite all claims to the contrary by "some Italian [who] discover[ed] a country most people would have left alone." The strip's language — here and there sprouting a "far out," a "bring down," and, most tellingly, a veritable bouquet of "stoned"s (as in, "Gee, I wish I was...) — indicates O'Neill's tilt toward the counterculture. The volume's climactic episode, in which Hugh and Fred escape the 100% American Dog (revealed not only as the reincarnation of

Hitler but a close friend of the Nixons) by popping a "magic cookie" which transports them to the safety of a hallucinatory castle, suggests he has executed a 10.0s-across-the-board plunge into it.

The other aspect of O'Neill's growth is captured by the collection's most powerful piece: "Stomp the Frog." Hugh and Fred meet a bushy-mustached, pistol-cannon-slingshot-firing fellow who explains violence is necessary for change and change is necessary for life. But while violent, he will not hurt anyone. He only wishes to express his rage at the thought of 2,000,000 years of human life being wiped out in a nuclear winter. The episode, in which this fellow manages to identify himself both with the despair, isolation and hope of his entire generation and with The Four Horseman of the Apocalypse, ends with him walking off into the distance and Christ crucified upon a telephone pole.

Weaving between the holocaust and the hallucinatory is a repeatedly voiced theme. O'Neill derides a puppet character who, whenever his strings are cut, reties them. He warns against being "realistic to the point of helpless." He deplores those who have been "chained to death" by allowing those who loved them to "load [them] down with chains." Such advocacy was a lodestar for outsiders coming of age in this time. It asserted the value of the self against the threat of mass conformity. It rallied those who feared their individuality would be trampled beneath the sensibly shod feet of legions of organization men in grey flannel suits. It was a warning against what Aldous Huxley termed "the nightmare of swarming indistinguishable sameness." It sided with D.H. Lawrence's call: "Instead of chopping yourself down to fit the world, chop the world down to fit yourself."[14]

In his strip's final year, O'Neill's creativity and daring soared. I doubt any cartoonist has ever worked so far ahead — and afoul — of the beliefs and sensibilities of the majority of his audience. Three decades later, recalling the times, the pressures, the various cadences being called, the conflicting marches' destinations, I doff my hat; I shake my head. "Wow!" I mouth.

The strips shimmer with shade and shadow. They pop with surreal details. They play against actual landscapes — albeit ones whose topography places them closer to "Krazy Kat" than the Hudson River School. They exist beneath planetary conjunctions that forecast futures outlandish in the extreme.

O'Neill now takes full advantage of his medium. He tweaks his audience's nose with Superman recumbent across four panels, blowing dope. He pummels it with political grotesques: The Gross National Product (a Stars-and-Stripes-clad, belching pig); The Great Unwashed (an obese, hairy behemoth crying out hungri-

---

[14] This attitude was succinctly expressed by an aspiring jazz pianist of my acquaintance, in the summer of 1960, explaining why he wasn't going to college: "Shit, man, you mean be a-everybody?" a motto I co-opted for a pivotal moment in my novel, *The Best Ride to New York*. Alfred, its original utterer, by the time I last ran into him, twenty years ago, had already been a junkie, Black Muslim, and successful Philadelphia session player.

ly for a color TV, garbage disposal, washer-dryer); the top-hatted, frock-coated Big Opinion. ("I am not a mere opinion," he proclaims to Hugh and Fred, whom he has just trampled, "I am a value.") O'Neill is freest — and wackiest — with his lettering. He varies sizes and styles, using a half-dozen different fonts inside a single panel. Sometimes a panel is entirely words. Sometimes it takes the form of a book title, eye chart, blackboard lesson, traffic sign. Sometimes — if God or the universe is speaking — and both God and the universe spoke through O'Neill in those days — a word balloon will descend from the panel's top with no picture attached.

One of O'Neill's niftiest devices (borrowed from Saul Steinberg, one imagines) played with comics being a blend of word and picture by making the latter of the former. He will plant, as a three-dimensional object in his first panel, the word RIGHT which, when viewed in his fourth panel after Hugh and Fred have passed it by, shows as WRONG to make the point that what you see depends on your perspective. He will have Hugh and Fred run toward LOVE, only to have it devoured when they arrive by a crocodile (another Steinbergian salute) representing FEAR. He will show them staring warily, head-on at SEX and DEATH, two things they fear to look behind.

The text now reveals O'Neill as an unabashed partisan. He is for drugs and motorcycles. He is against the war and the Highway Patrol. He also ponders matters of the spiritual and moral. Here is a personal Top Ten of *pensées* he dropped along the way:

Hostility is a Loco Motive. Don't step in front of it.

To see or Nazi. That is the question.

Shooting at us is their way of telling us to grow up.

(Politics is) a system designed for the mentally deficient. It keeps them perpetually employed.

Although dominant, the military is not the highest form of existence.

The God of the Puritans (was) a paranoid of some note in the cosmos.

The larvae stage of dirt is people.

The English sparrow proves that some people will eat anything.

(If) God isn't the exclusive property of the Christians, maybe the Christians aren't the exclusive people of God.

Dying in a war is kind of dumb. On the other hand, I have four fingers and a thumb. (This last was rendered on a series of Burma Shave-like signs in outer space.)[15]

Hugh and Fred now ventured into ever-longer, ever-stranger narratives. At one point, having learned the atmosphere of Mars is half-gasoline, they reason

---

[15] George Meyer, whom *The New Yorker* credits with the comic excellence of *The Simpsons*, says his favorite line in the entire show was Homer's calling alcohol "the cause of — and solution to — all of life's problems." When I read that, I had already struck O'Neill's "There isn't a problem in the world a bottle won't solve [or]... cause," from my list of contenders.

that General Injuns, purveyor of the smog-producing internal combustion engine, must be laying the groundwork for a Martian invasion by making Earth's atmosphere suitable for them. The General's henchman, the tommy-gun toting Mr. Sparky (who resembles J. Edgar Hoover) construes Fred and Hugh's attack on the automobile as proof they are "pinko, 5th columnist wingy-dingys." They are rescued by Norton the Motorcycle, who whisks them to a Montana ghost town, where they meet the King of the Outlaws, Five-Dollar Bill O'Brady (who looks like Abraham Lincoln). He agrees over a couple of jugs to join their counter-invasion of Mars, which they reach on Norton (fueled by a magic cookie), after avoiding an attack by a Giant Space Bunny. They are received by The Magician, ordered into The Mushroom ("the only treatment for the cop generation"), taught "Politics is Poopadoodle," and turned over to The History Bee. He reveals that Mars launched its attack in the seventeenth century by introducing the idea that man must compete and exploit in order to attain the wealth and status that demonstrate his worth to God.

Well, after dying, and a sojourn in an underworld ruled by Pluto (who looks like Pluto) and his advisor, Virgo the Rat (Mickey Mouse), Hugh, Fred and Bill return to earth. But O'Neill abruptly drops them from the strip for Rollo, a grumpy, staff-clutching "pilgrim," who wanders across a landscape ravaged by nuclear explosions, seas foaming with detergent, air clogged with styrofoam, and Richard Nixon as President — and pals up with Bucky the Bug (a mostly-forgotten Disney creation of the early 1930s). At the end, Rollo leaves Bucky with a paradox. Hope is a problem because it gets in the way of reality. We should give up hope and accept. But we can't accept reality because we have hope.

These strips hit like a John Coltrane solo. The feeling that results is of a man at work, a great talent with great things on his mind, searching, seeking, reaching, who will give you everything he has — reason, humor, pain — who will hold nothing back to move you. It is true that, at times, the craziness seems overwhelming. Bill Blackbeard, former director of the San Francisco Academy of Comic Art, once wrote that "Odd Bodkins'"s "consistently hard to decipher... philosophical bent" made it unique. "In fact, the whole strip was odd." The critic David Roach said, "[T]he writing is completely mad... frankly unreadable. Far, far too many drugs." O'Neill recognized the problem. "What is going on in this comic strip?" he wrote in one installment. "The author no longer understands..." But it was only through this madness he could engage the America that assaulted his senses, outraged his conscience, thrust his nerve endings into sockets and turned on the juice. He fired back with everything at his disposal. He hoped that people would listen — would straighten up — would change. Then, when they did not, he had cast off sufficient tethers that he was prepared for further flight.

The major problem O'Neill faced was that when a cartoonist went to work for a syndicate, he signed over the rights to his strip. If he did not sign, he did not work. If he signed — and caused the syndicate trouble — it fired him and brought in someone else to carry on his creation.[16]

For O'Neill, the issue was not academic. His nature and his view of his professional responsibilities pushed for confrontations. His work *required* confrontations. An O'Neill without confrontations would be Cézanne without lop-sided apples, Renoir lacking fleshy nudes. Government, he believed, was an enemy of the people; and artists were expressions of a people's soul. So artists were the enemies of government and government the enemy of art. "Politicians," he says, "are liars, thieves and killers. They get elected, and the only thing between them and the tax payers' money is the cartoonist. He is the only cop on the block."[17]

Even O'Neill's development as a draftsman pushed the envelope. His editors protested his evolving style because they feared that papers would complain they were not getting the strip for which they had contracted. "I didn't say anything for a couple weeks," O'Neill remembers. "Then a horizon line appeared. A couple weeks later it bumped up. A hill was there. A tree grew. The sun came out, and there was light and shadows. I gradually filled it up and expanded. That period got hung in the DeYoung Museum as the best use of black and white since Herriman. Even beat 'Dick Tracy.' That was cool."

The strip's increased verbal pugnaciousness resolved less well. When O'Neill had been hired, he had been told, "No politics, no religion, no sex." He was forbidden to offend advertisers. He was not allowed to mention brand names. "I couldn't say Kleenex. I had to say 'tith-yoo.' 'Tith-yoo.' Jesus Christ! Nobody knows what 'tith-yoo' is." For seven years, he fought his editors. For seven years, they told him not to do things; and he did them. The result was that "Odd Bodkins" lost ninety percent of its readers, and O'Neill's income dropped to under $200 a month.

O'Neill says the *Chronicle* fired him for the first time in 1964, following a swipe he took at Barry Goldwater. "That cost me forty papers and $60,000 in royalties." The second came when he took on the Vietnam War. "My editors were going, 'There isn't one.' 'Well, how do you explain this third draft notice I got? How come all my friends are over there?' I was down on everything from

---

[16] Stuart Dodds, the Chronicle Syndicate's sales manager, says this was theoretically true but that, in practice, the clause was usually applied to older cartoonists with established strips whose ill health necessitated bringing someone in to continue them. "It could not have happened with 'Odd Bodkins,'" Dodd says, "for no one but Dan could do it."

[17] In acting upon this attitude, O'Neill honors a grand, ancestral tradition. "Words," Declan Kilbred, professor of Anglo-Irish Literature at University College, Dublin, has written, "were the only weapons available to a disarmed people who had sought, over centuries, to expose the differences between official pretense and actual reality." And adding pictures supplements the firepower.

the KKK to Smokey the Bear. I don't think I missed anybody. You got to remember, this is the United States. Practically ninety percent of your friends and neighbors are right-wing, fundamentalist, un-Christian, Nazi-bastard, racist dogs. No one sunk the Mayflower when we had the chance, and we are stuck with those attitudes."

The war was a constant source of friction. When he had been hired, O'Neill had agreed to submit nine "roughs" a week, from which six final strips were to be selected. Now he stopped submitting alternates, turned in those he did submit only at the last moment to make alterations difficult, and amped up his work's volatility. (At his most testy, O'Neill would lace his strip with Morse-coded obscenities. On one occasion, Stanleigh Arnold, the *Chronicle's* Sunday and features editor, an ex-Navy man, caught and changed one offensive oath to a more moderate dot-and-dashing. O'Neill then exploded at this tampering with his copy.) When he refused his editors' pleas to tone his strip down, O'Neill says, they began changing his punch lines, printing it with someone else's lettering and writing that made no sense. "One episode they did that; and I'm screaming over the phone from Jenner to Dolly, the Dragon Lady, Scott Newhall's Chinese secretary, 'You've put your fingers in my brain for the last time. This is war. I'm coming down for Scott's leg.' So I'm on my motorcycle. I'm furious. It's white-hot. It usually takes two hours to get to San Francisco, and I'm there in forty-five minutes with my chain saw. I get into the elevator; and, somewhere between the first and second floor, I lose it. I'm starting to laugh. I'm going to blow the scene. But I've been trained by actors: you start the scene; you finish it. The door's going to open, so I lower my hat, because if I make eye contact with one living soul, I'm going to laugh so hard I'm going to ruin the whole thing. I put on my fury face. I'm gonna keep my eyes down, start up the saw, hold it in the air where I can't hurt anybody, and saw up the first thing I bump into. I walk down the hallway. Vrrr! I bump into something. I wave the saw around, giving people time to get out of the way; and I come down... Vvvvooo! I've just sawed the City Desk in half, and Abe Melinkoff is sitting there. The saw went between his legs, and the most feared editor in the West is a broken man. He was the Number Four editor; and Number One, Two and Three hated him. They were so happy he was busted up they gave me a $600-a-month raise."[18]

On November 2, 1969, the *Chronicle* fired O'Neill in, he says, retaliation for his continued expression of his political views. (It claimed it desired only to

～～～～～～～～～～～～～～～～～～～～～～～～～～～～～～～～

[18] Carl Nolte, a reporter/editor at the *Chronicle* since 1961, says, "O'Neill says he cut Melinkoff's desk in half with a chain saw? Wow! Too bad it isn't true. Good story, though." When I reported his denial to O'Neill, he re-swore its veracity, comparing it to the time Mark Twain nailed a *Chron* editor who was trying to avoid him into his own office.

remove a "relatively obscure strip... in order to accommodate a nationally known one" — "Miss Peach.") O'Neill says the *Chron* received 15,000 phone calls an hour and 25,000 letters a day in protest. Contemporary press accounts document "a stampede of letters," "a blizzard of phone calls," 150 pickets, and a lead editorial in UC Berkeley's *Daily Californian* demanding "Odd Bodkins'" reinstatement. Stan Arnold reported spending most of his day "fending off outraged proponents of this offbeat comic strip." Veteran newspaper men were quoted as having never seen a response to a feature's cancellation that equaled this one.

The *Chronicle* not only reinstated "Odd Bodkins," but it devoted a full page to running the installments its readers had missed. Then it attempted to revive the strip's syndication with a promotional brochure that capitalized on the cancellation by quoting extracts from the outcry it had provoked: "Return 'Odd Bodkins' or I shall be compelled to drive my motorcycle through your city room"; "Without 'Odd Bodkins,' the city's suicide rate will rise"; "If we don't get 'Odd Bodkins' back, we're going to break every window in Miss Peach's school"; "You have retarded the evolution of mankind"; "This is a CRIME!"; "My teenage daughter let out a shriek of despair"; "How could you remove the best comic strip of all time?"; "Have you gone mad?"; "It's no longer worthwhile to go out in the morning and steal the paper from the neighbors." Only canceling "Peanuts," the editors wrote to potential customers, could have drawn a comparable reaction. (They also suspected — but did not say — that a friend of O'Neill's who taught creative writing at USF had given his students an assignment for extra credit.) "[I]f you are willing to accept controversy as a price of an intensely loyal audience...," Arnold said, "you should try this comic."

Then Herb Caen told O'Neill a source within the Bohemian Club,[19] a San Francisco-based bastion of wealthy businessmen and Republican politicians, had reported over-hearing President Nixon, on whose Enemies List O'Neill says he roosted, order Thierot to get rid of him.[20] The publisher replied he'd try again in six months. He didn't think O'Neill's supporters would rise again. Neither did O'Neill.

"I thought about it. They got my copyright. They're gonna throw me out

<hr/>

[19] The Club has been the object of speculation from all sides of the political spectrum. In January 2002, for instance, a thirty-seven year old "Phantom Patriot," in a bullet-proof vest and skeleton mask, was arrested on the grounds of its 2000-acre retreat near Monte Rio, armed with a double-barreled assault rifle, two-foot long sword, .45 caliber pistol, crossbow, knife, and bomb-launcher, seeking revenge for the child abuse and human sacrifices he believed regularly carried out there.

[20] The Enemies List, the creation of Nixon's Chief Counsel, Charles W. "Chuck" Colson, a self-proclaimed "flag-waving, kick 'em-in-the-nuts, anti-press, anti-liberal, Nixon fanatic," had over 200 members, including Edward Kennedy, Jane Fonda, Bella Abzug, James Reston, Steve McQueen, Joe Namath, and the president of Yale University. I never came up with a complete roster. I never saw O'Neill's name on any of the partials — but he certainly merited inclusion.

with nothing. I got six months left. What am I gonna do? I still loved the damn strip. It was what I did in the world that the world needed. It didn't need a hod carrier; and I was a lousy private detective, a terrible cowboy, and only an okay bartender. Taking my comic strip away would be like losing my arms and legs. You put a lot of years into something you become the person who does that."

O'Neill contacted John Reynolds, "a great lawyer, who had a picture in his office of Eleanor Roosevelt with her arm around him. That's how Irish he was." "Who was responsible for the contents of a comic strip," he asked, "the copyright owner or the artist?" "'The owner," Reynolds said. "'If there is a copyright violation in the strip, who pays?" "They do." O'Neill then plucked twenty-eight secondary Disney characters — Grandpa Beetle, the Big Bad Wolf, Practical Pig — from his comic books and slowly fed them into his strip. "Then I did a strip about George Jackson in San Quentin: 'They're going to lynch that guy!'; and they threw me out as predicted."

The *Chronicle's* view is that O'Neill self-garrotted. He continued to miss deadlines, and his repeated outrages alienated the liberals who should have been his core audience and sabotaged all efforts to market him. In February 1970, Arnold sent O'Neill a heartfelt letter embracing "Odd Bodkins'" potential to promote "compassion, accommodation and understanding" but lamenting its author's tendency to burn rather than extend bridges. The editor was especially offended by O'Neill's portrayal of Lincoln. How, he asked, could the *Chron* "disseminate a feature that vilified a gentle man who personified [what]... 'Odd Bodkins' was supposed to represent... We could sell it possibly to a few Southern sheets [who]... still look upon Lincoln as the devil, but we don't want that trade."

In late November, the *Chronicle's* axe fell again. Interviewed by Van Amburg, a local TV news anchorman, O'Neill seemed to take this latest severing serenely. It might be time, he said, for him to give up being a "large scale" cartoonist and try something different. "Who knows," he said, "maybe I can get into the penitentiary like some of my friends."

But, Amburg re-assured his viewers, there was no cause for alarm. O'Neill only planned to do a comic book.

Chapter Three:
Bad Taste Would Be Blood Dripping

One day in early 1933, Harry Wildenberg, the sales manager for Eastern Color Printing, which turned out the Sunday comics sections for a number of newspapers, had a revelation. The standard newspaper page which, when doubled over, had produced the tabloid, if doubled again, resulted in a book. If he filled this book (he would call it *Funnies on Parade*) with reprints of the more popular Sunday comics ("Joe Palooka," "The Bungle Family"), he might peddle it to corporations for use as a promotional giveaway. Proctor and Gamble ordered a million. So did Gulf Oil. Then one of Wildenberg's salesmen, Max Charles ("M.C.") Gaines decided to stick price tags on the covers and see if people would pay newsstands a dime for them.

There had been similar ventures. Not long after the first newspaper comic strip appeared, in 1896, some of the most popular ("The Yellow Kid," "Mutt and Jeff") were collected and published in book form. In 1922, an eight-and-a-half-inch by ten-inch, twenty-four page magazine, *Comics Monthly*, which featured a different black-and-white strip each issue ("Barney Google," "Polly and Her Pals") had a seven-month run. In 1929, *The Funnies*, a weekly tabloid featuring original strips with recurring characters ("Frosty Ayres," "Bunk Buford"), lasted nine — or thirty-six, accounts vary. But it was through the efforts of Gaines and Wildenberg that, in the words of arts journalist Roger Sabin, "the first modern comic book" was born.[21]

---

[21] This honor is a matter of dispute. Michael Barrier and Martin Williams consider *Famous Funnies* — see below — to be "the first true comic book in the modern sense." Jules Feiffer ("the first regularly scheduled comic book"), George Perry and Alan Aldridge ("the first comic book to be deliberately directed at the magazine-and-newspaper-buying public"), Ron Goulart ("the first regularly

Gaines tried to interest George Delacorte, a successful publisher of pulp magazines — as well as *Modern Screen* and *Ballyhoo* — who had published *The Funnies* (and whose Dell Publishing would become a major comic book publisher), in Eastern's experiment; but Delacorte dropped his option after financing and selling out a modest 35,000-copy first printing. Eastern, then, decided to go it alone. It acquired rights to more strips ("Hairbreadth Harry," "Tailspin Tommy") and, in July 1934 — or May, accounts differ[22]— published *Famous Funnies*, which quickly became a monthly. The first issue sold out — but lost $4,000. However, by its seventh issue, it was clearing $2,500; and its circulation would eventually approach 400,000 — or 1,000,000, accounts vary — copies a month.

Famous Funnies' success sparked a rash of new books (*Century of Comics, Toyland Funnies*). Gaines, who had parted from Wildenberg, acquired the right to reprint Percy Crosby's philosophical-little kid strip, "Skippy," and made him the first character to have his own book — with a 500,000-copy first printing. Soon other syndicates began utilizing their strips to publish comics, and other would-be publishers signed up as yet unspoken-for strips for their books: United Feature's *Tip Top* ("Li'l Abner," "The Captain & the Kids"); McKay Corporation's *King Comics* ("Mandrake," "The Little King *")*; Delacourt's *Popular Comics* ("Dick Tracy," "Little Orphan Annie"). When the public's demand began to exceed the number of existing strips, publishers began contracting for original material.[23]

The foremost feature of this industry was its lack of quality. The governing philosophy was: rake in the most dimes at the least cost. This was achieved by giving the public what it wanted as cheaply as possible, as quickly as possible, and, when it lost interest, giving it something else. The approach influenced custom and procedure in several ways. The first was the "studio" or "shop" approach to production. Basically, the book came off an assembly line in which

published comic book in the standard format"), and Ron Frantz ("the first commercially produced comic book") concur. Coulton Waugh, however, goes along with Sabin, calling *Funnies on Parade* "the first comic book of the modern type." Les Daniels hedges his bets, saying of *Parade* "The comic book was born" and calling *Famous* "the first recognizable comic book to enjoy retail sales." Jim Steranko votes for a "Mutt and Jeff" collection in 1911; and Robert L. Beerbohm, slapping down *The Adventures of Obadiah Oddbuck,* from 1842, trumps them all.

[22] It was customary for comics to be dated months in advance of their actual release to allow them a longer shelf life in case a next issue was not forthcoming and an unalert reader might wander by.

[23] According to Sabin, the "first all-original comic book with recurring characters" was *New Comics* (1935). Barrier and Williams credit Major Malcolm Wheeler-Nicholson's *New Fun* with being "the first comic book made up entirely of new material." Goulart and Frantz concur. The others are silent on this issue.

the page passed from person to person, with each performing a specific task — writing, penciling, inking, coloring, lettering — so no individual could pursue an independent artistic vision or establish an identity in the public eye upon which he might capitalize during future salary negotiations.

Second was an ingrained disrespect for the product. Comics books were printed with cheap ink on cheap paper. They were designed to be thrown away. If they weren't, without special precautions, they fell apart. They were not kept in print — as if no one coming upon a character for the first time would be interested in learning anything else about him — or as if one story about a character was just as good as any other. The original artwork was more likely to be used to mop up coffee spills than saved for posterity. While newspaper strips or gag cartoons were the subject of gallery shows, memorialized in book form, and even discussed in learned journals, no such honors fell upon comics. Coulton Waugh, an English-born cartoonist — he replaced Milt Caniff on "Dickie Dare" — captured the general feeling in his *The Comics,* published in 1947, the first book on the subject. Towards its end, having primarily concerned himself with the great newspaper strips, Waugh cast an eye on their lowly bastard cousins. "So raw," he wrote, "so purely ugly." Such "soulless emptiness" and "outrageous vulgarity," presented upon a paper "like sand in cooking."

Not surprisingly, the creators of comic books, most of whom were high school graduates at best, mostly young, mostly poor, often the children of first- or second-generation immigrants, laboring within a culture where the definition of quality remained within the grasp of aesthete-equivalents of Cabots and Lowells, were not apt to view themselves as producing work of value. (If it is true, as Marcel Duchamp said, that art is anything an artist says it is, it is equally true that it is not art unless some artist anoints it.) For the most part, they would rather have been doing strips or magazine illustrations, where the pay was better and the social prestige higher. They viewed comic books as a way to get by until their careers moved upwards or, if they had already abandoned that hope, as a way to put roofs over heads, bread upon tables, and bottles in pockets.

Finally, the artists had few rights. They were paid by how much they produced, not how good it was. (Fifty cents a page for writers was about the going rate; artists got more, but it took them longer.) With few exceptions, they owned no part of their output. The publishing companies owned the original artwork and any subsidiary characters created as part of an ongoing series. And if you created your own character and brought it to a publisher, you signed it over in order to be published. The result was an almost total stifling of individual initiative.

Despite all this, comic books became phenomenally successful. There were rip-roaring western comics, heart-pounding adventure comics, sassy teenager comics, cute talking-animal comics. (*Walt Disney's Comics and Stories* debuted in 1940.) But comic books received their biggest boost from a character who, when released, had already put twenty-six rejection slips in the pockets of his creators, two Cleveland teenagers: Jerry Siegel, who wrote; Joe Shuster, who drew. Superman had been modeled on the hero of Philip Wylie's 1930 novel, *Gladiator*, with a touch of Samson and Doc Savage thrown in. He had been designed as a newspaper strip but first appeared in public in 1938 in *Action* No. 1, having been recommended to the publishers J.S. Liebowitz and Harry Donnenfeld by the ubiquitous Max Gaines for their company DC (Detective Comics). Soon Superman had his own book and was selling 1,400,000 copies a month.[24] His success ushered in a wave of superheroes: Batman (the second most popular, selling 800,000 comics a month); Captain America; Captain Marvel; Flash; Green Arrow; Green Lantern; Hawkman; the Human Torch; Sub-Mariner; Wonder Woman — all of whom came into being by the end of 1941.

In 1940, there had been sixty comic books on the stands; by 1941, there were 168. World War II — and the enlistment of the superheroes in the fight against the Axis — brought comic books to the apex of their popularity. By 1943, 25,000,000 — or 15,000,000, accounts vary — comic books were being sold each month. Hundreds of thousands were sent to servicemen, and on military posts comic books out-sold *Life, Reader's Digest*, and *The Saturday Evening Post* ten to one. The basis of this appeal, the historian William W. Savage, Jr. writes, was that since comics were ostensibly designed for children, their creators weren't restrained by the same standards or considerations they would have been if their work had aimed for an adult audience. Artists could splay upon the page — through distortion or exaggeration, rage or calculation, frustration or desire, consciously or not — more extreme imagery than Hollywood movies or pulp magazines could deliver. The result was the demonizing of Germans and Japanese through the graphic depiction of bizarre scenes of torture or violence, merged with a barely restrained sexuality — lots of scantily clad women strung up to be branded or whipped by slant-eyed fiends and swastika-laden madmen — that would remain staples in comic book marketing.

After the war, as public interest in superheroes declined, the industry explored new genres to attract readers. The first to succeed was the "true crime" comic. The most successful, *Crime Does Not Pay*, sold as many as 1,500,000 copies an issue, over half to adults. By 1948, there were thirty-eight crime comics, representing nearly twenty-five percent — or fifteen percent, accounts vary — of all books on the market. As their popularity began to wane, that of "romance" comics surged. The first — and most successful — *Young Romance*, debuted in 1947. Two years later, there were 120 — and almost half their readers were over eighteen. In fact, surveys from the late 1940s show that, while over ninety percent of all children, ages six to eleven, read comics, and eighty-five percent of those twelve to seventeen did; so did forty-one percent of all men and twenty-eight percent of all

[24] *Time*, by comparison, sold 700,000 copies an issue.

women between the ages of eighteen and thirty.

In 1947, M.C. Gaines was killed in a boating accident. His twenty-seven-year-old son, William M. Gaines, a divorced NYU student hoping to become a high school chemistry teacher, found himself the head of his father's Educational Comics — sometimes called Entertaining Comics — best known for *Picture Stories from the Bible*, which was still leaping off Hebrew school shelves when I commenced attendance in 1951. M.C. had believed in the instructive possibilities of comic books, but the public seemed to be finding guidance elsewhere; and E.C. — sometimes called EC — was $100,000 in debt. Beginning with his April 1950 release of *Crypt of Terror* (soon renamed *Tales from the Crypt*), quickly followed by *The Vault of Horror* and *The Haunt of Fear*, Bill Gaines corrected his father's error, reversed his family's fortunes — and brought the horror comic front and center. Within three years, 130 of the rotting-corpse-rich little rascals were filling racks from coast to coast.

E.C.s were in a class by themselves. (No less an authority than Stephen King, in *Danse Macabre,* though he stumbled over the titles — *Tales from the Vault,* for instance — called them "the epitome of horror.") By 1952, Gaines had added to his line-up the equally outstanding — and frequently just as grisly — *Weird Science, Weird Fantasy, Crime SuspenStories, Shock SuspenStories, Frontline Combat, Two-Fisted Tales,* and, in the words of Les Daniels, "the most extrordinary comic book ever... and one unparalleled in its effect on the national consciousness": *MAD*. At their peak, they sold more than 1,500,000 copies a month. (By its sixth issue, *MAD* was selling 500,000 copies a month itself.)

E.C.'s stable of artists — Harvey Kurtzman, Al Feldstein, Bill Elder, Jack Davis, Wally Wood, Joe Orlando, Johnny Craig, Jack Kamen, Bernie Krigstein, George Evans, Reed Crandall, Al Williamson, John Severin, Graham "Ghastly" Ingels — forgive me for going on; but I was a card-carrying E.C. Fan Addict,[25] and the work of these men obsessed me into adulthood.[26] Gaines gave them free rein to exercise their talents — and obsessions. He also, virtually alone in the industry, let them sign their stories and establish identities with their readers. (Disney, for instance, kept the names of its great creators, such as Floyd Gottfredson, who made Mickey Mouse's comic strip notable, and Carl Barks, the genius of the Duck books, secret for decades.) E.C. stories were more literate, better researched, and vastly more original than any of their competitors'. They were anti-war, opposed to racial and religious discrimination, and against

[25] E.C. organized its official fan club in November 1953. By June 1954, it had 17,000 members. (By way of comparison – and to demonstrate our elite-hood — the Captain Marvel fan club, a decade earlier, had over 500,000.) For a quarter, we received a bronze pin, a membership card, an arm patch, and a certificate suitable for framing — all of mine, deeply regrettably, lost.

[26] See: Levin. "Remembrances of a Fan Addict Past," *The Comics Journal,* March 1988.

censorship and Joe McCarthy, positioning themselves where few "respectable" publications, let alone other comic book publishers, dared — or cared — to stand. And through lively letter pages, self-mocking promotional campaigns, and a generally we're-all-in-it-together editorial tone, E.C. fostered a community of spirit that existed nowhere else in the field.

But what truly made E.C. great was — no surprise — the horror and the sex. The husband who incinerated his wife with tanning lamps and the one who froze his into a block of ice. The wife who stashed her husband's hacked-up remains in Mason jars and the one who used their butcher shop's display trays for hers. The man who was eaten by piranha in his bubble bath and the one who slid down the firehouse pole honed razor sharp and the one who fed himself to dogs. The woman who was steamed by the billboard's smoke ring and the one rotted by her perfume and the one whose face was ripped from her cranial bones. The legions of voluptuous, filmily clad maidens menaced by the multi-tentacled and gelatinous, the wild-eyed and razor-wielding, the saliva-flecked and fanged. The space colonist — my personal favorite — who held fifty beautiful women in suspended animation and thawed them, one at a time, like Sara Lees.[27] The images seared themselves into the brain. I meet people today who cannot remember if Moby Dick was harpooner or harpooned but can recall panels from E.C.s with excruciating particularity.

But such excellence could not endure.

The comic book had been under attack almost since its birth. Most adults viewed it, Martin Barker wrote in *A Haunt of Fears*, "as, at best, a marginal, silly medium suitable only for children or, at worst, as a dangerous, inciting medium suitable for no one." The first major anti-comics campaign kicked off in May 1940, when a piece by Sterling North in the *Chicago Daily News* was picked up by forty other papers — and then had 25,000,000 copies reprinted for dissemination by churches and schools. North's thesis was that comic books were trash that filled children's minds and blocked them from developing an interest in finer literature. (While comics were selling in the millions, a successful children's book might sell 5,000 copies.) That became the focus of the debate in comic books' first years. Did they suck children into an inescapable, sensibility-stultifying sewer or did they, as their supporters claimed, foster an interest in reading that would naturally lead to a devouring of *Summa Theologica*? (Comic book publishers also tried, unsuccessfully, to defuse their opponents' arguments by turning out adaptations of great works of literature, biographies of important historical figures, and narratives recounting the lives of the saints.) No firm conclusions were reached; but the

[27] See: Levin. "Sex and the Single 11-Year-Old," *Comics Journal*, Dec. 1997, for further humiliating revelations. (Note: I did not say "*With* a Single 11-Year-Old," as an over-eager friend from abroad once put it, introducing me and my work, through mis-translation, to his woman-friend. Good Lord, the look she gave me.)

debate died down during World War II, when comic books so patriotically participated in the war effort.

However, after V-J Day, the issue reappeared in altered garb. In those postwar years, along with fears of UFOs and the Red Menace, a specter of Juvenile Delinquency swept the land. Organizations like the National Congress of Parents and Teachers, the Committee on the Evaluation of Comic Books, and the Catholic Church's National Office of Decent Literature — which maintained a list of objectionable comics that was never made public out of a fear that impressionable youths would utilize it as a study guide — launched a campaign premised on the belief that this ten-cent torrent of mayhem and libido had turned our young people from the straight and narrow. Newspapers and magazines spread word of the threat. Symposiums and debates and "decency" advocates led to organized comic book burnings and angry mothers picketing newsstands and abandoning fully loaded shopping carts at the check-out counters of groceries that refused to stop selling the offending works.[28] (Sterling North, taking another look at comics, found them more depraved than ever. He prescribed regular doses of Frank Merriwell and the Rover Boys as a cure.) States and municipalities banned books too rich in gore or flesh through laws that were usually struck down by courts or vetoed by governors more sensitive to the First Amendment.

The point man of the anti-comics attack was Fredric Wertham, M.D. Born in 1895 in Germany as Friedrich I. Wertheimer, he had come to the United States, following post-graduate studies in Paris and London, to work at the psychiatric clinic of Johns Hopkins University's School of Medicine. The photos on his book jackets lodge him in an observer's mind somewhere between John Carradine in *Revenge of the Zombies* and Captain Marvel's arch-foe Dr. Sivana. His face is bony and sharply angled, his lips tight and unsmiling, his thin hair precisely brushed and parted. He wears a banker's double-breasted, pin-striped suit; his eyeglass frames are dark and unforgiving. But Wertham's life was not entirely punitive and repressive. His major area of professional interest was the impact of social factors upon individual psyches. He worked with alcoholics, poor children, convicted felons. He established the first "free" psychiatric clinic in Harlem. His testimony on the damaging effects of segregation led the state of Delaware to integrate its schools — and helped influence the United States Supreme Court, in *Brown vs. Topeka Board of Education*, to strike down "separate but equal" public facilities. He was a close friend of Clarence Darrow. This was not a bad list of credits to place before St. Peter; but when it came to comic books — which Wertham damned at every opportunity — if you were a non-felonious, non-sexually deviant, pre-ado-

[28] Les Daniels, writing in 1971, when Women's Liberation's novelty was rubbing male nerves the rawest, emphasizes this aspect of the forces of repression. His account of the fight, in *Comix*, is replete with references to "outraged womanhood," "mothers," and "the feminist movement." (He also blames women for Prohibition.)

lescent, card-carrying E.C. Fan-Addict — the man deserved a circle in Hell below Vlad the Impaler.

Wertham first went after comic books with an article in the *Saturday Evening Post* in 1948. His *magnum opus, Seduction of the Innocent,* appeared in 1954, having been excerpted the year before in *Ladies Home Journal.* "A billion times a year," he wrote, "an American child sits down to pore over a comic book." Ninety million comics a month streamed toward children,[29] and less than twenty percent of them were to his liking. (Wertham approved of *Walt Disney Comics and Stories,* though he even faulted it for scenes of violence and racial insensitivity.) The rest bludgeoned their readers' minds into moral jelly. They destroyed feelings of conscience, mercy, sympathy, trust, charity, loyalty. They fostered contempt for the law, police, all authority. They were how-to manuals for the commission of criminal acts. They encouraged drug abuse, sado-masochistic masturbation fantasies, homosexuality (Batman and Robin were prime offenders here), lesbianism (Wonder Woman), and racial superiority (Superman). There was, he concluded — citing much anecdotal evidence and not a single objective study — "significant correlation" between comic books and "the more serious forms of juvenile delinquency."[30]

In April 1954, a United States Senate subcommittee, chaired by Estes Kefauver of Tennessee, opened formal hearings into the problem. Kefauver had gained national attention with his televised investigation of organized crime in 1950.[31] Having lost the 1952 Democratic presidential nomination to Illinois Governor Adlai Stevenson, he hoped this new campaign would fuel his run in 1956. The hearings lasted three days. Witnesses included pro- and anti-comics

[29] Wertham kept the source of his numbers confidential. Other estimates place comic book sales in the early '50s at half his figure.

[30] Legend has it that *Seduction* was printed with a detailed index of all the comic books to which Wertham objected but that his publisher sent representatives with razor blades to stores to excise them lest they fall into the wrong hands. In truth, what was severed, most likely due to a fear of libel suits, was a "Bibliographical Note" that merely listed who published the books Wertham abhorred.

[31] As part of that investigation, people who worked in the juvenile crime field had been polled about comic books. Sixty percent said they were not a contributing factor to the problem and seventy percent said banning them would have no effect.

[32] Gaines argued that there was no proof comic books harmed anyone and that if you cleaned them up, no one would buy them; and children would find other ways to gratify their appetites. The highlight of his testimony — affected, he later claimed, by his over-use of Dexedrine-rich diet pills — was his defense of the cover of *Crime Suspenstories* #22, on which an axe-murderer held aloft the severed head of a young woman. Of course the cover was in "good taste," Gaines insisted. "Bad taste" would have been showing the head lifted higher so you could see blood dripping from the ruptured vessels.

"experts" (among whom was Wertham), publishers (including Gaines), retailers, distributors, and former investigators-into or legislators-on comic books.[32]

The hearings were not a neutral search for truth. A national reputation could not stand supported by a phalanx of buxom blondes lashed to posts waiting to be whipped. A presidential campaign would not flow smoothly along a carpet of dismembered corpses, luridly colored, graphically displayed. The committee's conclusions were known in advance and the witnesses paraded only to underscore them. Amy Kiste Nyberg, in her thorough study, *Seal of Approval*, instructs its "intention... was to force [or frighten] the publishers into adopting a self-regulating code like the film industry." And on March 5, 1955, it issued its report,[33] saying that while no causal relationship between comic books and juvenile crime had been established, the danger comics posed was so severe that the industry should take "precautionary" measures.

Meanwhile, in September 1954, the publishers, at Gaines's urging, had incorporated the Comic Magazines Association of America.[34] Gaines hoped the Association would fund a study into the effect of comic books on behavior and enlist the American Civil Liberties Union to fight for its right to free expression. But the CMAA became dominated by companies whose output was far PTA-friendlier than E.C.'s. Fearful of triggering an even greater public outcry and not at all unhappy if their kinkier competitors took it in the teeth, they established a Comics Code Authority, with a $100,000 annual budget, to regulate comic book content. It would screen every book — first, the script; then, the penciled artwork; finally, the finished pages — and award a Seal of Approval to those it endorsed. After Wertham refused an offer to chair this committee, the position went to Charles F. Murphy, a former New York City judge. He filled the other five seats with women — because of their "sensitivity" — including a librarian, a social worker, and an English professor.

The Comic Book Code of 1954 mandated that good must always defeat evil. Comics could neither portray criminals nor criminal acts sympathetically. They could not show disrespect for the law or established authority. They could not depict "brutal" torture, "gruesome" crimes, or "excessive" use of guns or knives. The words "crime," "horror" and "terror" were stricken from covers. Comics could not contain scenes of depravity, lust, masochism, or sadism. Cannibals, ghouls, vampires, werewolves, and zombies were banished. Obscenity, profanity, smut, and vulgarity were banned. References to physical afflictions were to be avoided. Slang and bad grammar were discouraged, religious and racial slurs forbidden, nudity

[33] Kefauver requested that the report be illustrated with offensive comic book panels, but the Government Printing Office refused because it felt them "unsuitable" for an official publication.

[34] In the late 1940s, an earlier body, the Association of Comic Magazine Publishers, had failed in its attempts at self-regulation when many large publishers refused to join because they did not want to be tainted by affiliating with their less savory brethren; and many small publishers declined because of the cost.

and "suggestive" bodily alignments outlawed. All styles of dress had to be "reasonably" acceptable to the general public. A woman's "physical qualities" could not be exaggerated. Divorce could not be portrayed favorably. No scenes of sexual violence, sexual abnormality, or illicit sexual activity could appear. Respect for parents and for moral and honorable behavior was to be fostered. The positive nature of family life and the sanctity of marriage were to be emphasized. The "baser" emotions could not be stimulated.

Dell, the largest publisher, which produced one-third of all comics — including the Disney titles — refused to submit its books for approval, saying they were already "clean and wholesome." Gilbertson, which published the *Classics Illustrated* line of literary adaptations, refused, saying its books weren't comics. Gaines tried to continue E.C. without the seal, but distributors refused to carry his books. After unsuccessful attempts to develop a code-friendly line of comics and some "picto-fiction," twenty-five cent-magazines that skirted it entirely, he pulled the plug on everything, except *MAD*.[35] And about a dozen other publishers, including Ace, Avon, Comic Media, Eastern Color, Quality, Sterling, and United Features, folded.

Between 1952 and 1956, the number of comic book titles declined from 635 to 250 and their combined circulation to 35,000,000. The major companies that remained, Dell, Gilbertson, DC (*Superman, Batman*), Harvey (*Casper, Richie Rich),* Archie (*Archie, Jughead),* and Charlton (undistinguished war, western and romance books) presided over a domain of pap. I and the other members of my E.C. klavern moved on to the works of Ray Bradbury and Mickey Spillane. I do not recall any decline of juvenile delinquency being celebrated in the land following this reformation — but I cannot deny there was a dramatic drop-off in UFO sightings.

By the decade's end, the comic book industry had begun a recovery in terms of sales, if not quality, when DC resurrected some of its former stars (Flash, Green Lantern, Aquaman, Hawkman, the Atom) and revamped some others (Superman, Wonder Woman). (In 1959, according to Nyberg, the sale of all titles nationwide totaled 600,000,000, a figure — and I read it twice — I find hard to believe since it exceeds sales during comics' Golden Age.) Among those that had struggled through the lean years and now sought to capitalize on the fat was a man in his mid-thirties, with the mustache and mentality of a carnival barker, who had been in the business almost since its inception.

In 1939, at the age of seventeen, Stanley Lieber had been hired as a go-fer by Martin Goodman, the husband of a cousin, for his new business. Goodman, a publisher of pulp magazines *(Star Detective, Marvel Science Stories)* had expanded into

---

[35] Wertham took to the pages of *Reader's Digest* to rail against *MAD* as just another "crime comic." According to Ted White, DeWitt Wallace, the *Digest's* publisher, received so many protest letters that he picked up a copy and was sufficiently amused to apologize and ban Wertham's future writings from his magazine.

comic books. His company, Timely Comics, soon birthed Captain America, the Human Torch, and Sub-Mariner; but, after the war, its business had declined severely. Timely transmuted into, first, Marvel Comics, then Atlas, then Marvel again; and the man who emerged as its chief writer-editor-art director, preserving his given name for the great novels he still expected to write, was now known as Stan Lee.

To keep Marvel afloat, Lee had attempted to revive Timely's great heroes. He tried western books. He tried romance. He even tried *World's Greatest Songs*, with Eddie Fisher on the cover; but, by 1957, he had been forced to cancel most of his titles and lay off most of his staff. Then, Jack Kirby, who, with his partner Joe Simon, had created Captain America — and, among other comics, *Young Romance* — returned to Marvel and helped it establish a roster of modestly successful, non-sexual, non-violent sci-fi, mystery, and monster books — which included such characters as the ever-popular Grothu, the Giant Ant Eater. And in November 1961, inspired by the sales figures of DC's Justice League of America, which had debuted eleven months earlier, Lee introduced Marvel's own superhero team. *The Fantastic Four* inaugurated a run of books that transformed the industry — and provided it with an *éclat* absent since the days of E.C.: *The Incredible Hulk, The Amazing Spider Man, Dr. Strange, Daredevil, Iron Man, Thor, The X-Men, The Avengers, The Silver Surfer.* At its peak, in 1968, Marvel was selling 50,000,000 comics a year.

Marvel's great conceptual breakthrough was the humanized superhero. Lee abolished secret identities. He demanded "love." He demanded "pathos." And he insisted upon heroes with "feet of clay." His company's new creations and their need to make a living, trouble getting dates, parental conflicts, and — sometimes the "clay" ran ego-high — their uncertainties about existing in a world in which heroes could transform overnight into villains and villains into heroes, a world in which they could even *die* — enabled readers to identify with them in ways that they could not with their earlier caped-and-masked counterparts.

Marvel augmented its textual leaps with visuals that struck with the impact of a Bristol board Armory Show. Lee allowed his artists unmatched freedom in developing characters, shaping stories, and dramatically delivering them. Kirby had always been known for his "explosive, kinetic" style, but his pages now surged and seethed as if subterranean dynamos were powering them. Jim Steranko, a magician/escape artist-turned-illustrator, infused his work with color-experimentation, photo collage, optical illusions, and startling page layouts. And Steve Ditko's "trippy" swashes, swirls, and visual distortions — and whose most noted character, Dr. Strange, even lodged in Bohemia-central Greenwich Village — caught the attention of that developing corner of the market certain it knew what "Lucy in the Sky with Diamonds" was *really* about.

Finally, Lee wrapped Marvel's comics within a self-proclaimed "universe," with its own past, present and future, and stories that occurred within all three frames of time. Characters appeared in each others' books. Story lines, which ran for months, interconnected, took on mystical dimensions, and played out in relation to the history and rules that this universe had established for itself. Besides proving to be a great way to sell comic books — you had to buy a heckova lot of issues to keep up with what was going on — this provided a *gravitas* comics had previously lacked. This need for knowledge, this dimension of thought showed respect — and provided rewards — for an intelligent, informed readership; and readers responded with passionate commitment. The essayist Geoffrey O'Brien, in his marvelous evocation of the '60s, *Dream Time,* describes what it was like for a group of Harvard undergraduates, of which he was one, to have been a fan. Stan Lee, he wrote, "had transformed Marvel Comics into a crucial cultural enterprise... [It was] like watching *The Odyssey* being written."

Lee created a community devoted to Marvel's books. By tagging himself, his artists and writers with folksy, just-us-guys nicknames, he made his company seem part of the family. His in-jokey, us-against-them editorials, which praised readers for demonstrating the intelligence and sophistication necessary to appreciate such quality work, strengthened these bonds. His lively Letters-to-the-Editor pages, which printed correspondents' complete addresses — another industry first — enabled readers to contact one other and reinforce each others' obsessions directly. His Merry Marvel Marching Society fan club established an official umbrella under which they could huddle. Soon Marvel had a public clamoring so loudly for its product, it could unload unsold back issues for two-thirds over cover price, leaving private dealers to sell hard-to-get numbers for mark-ups far above that.

In February 1968, a twenty-four-year-old former illustrator for the American Greeting Cards Company, Robert Crumb, rolled down Haight Street, selling *Zap* #1 out of a baby carriage. If all of Russian literature may be said to have crawled out from beneath Gogol's *Overcoat,* then all of underground comics — *Insect Fear, Young Lust, The Fabulous Furry Freak Brothers, Tits & Clits, Trashman, Binky Brown Meets the Holy Virgin Mary* — clambered down from his perambulator.

One evening the previous January, Crumb had stepped into a Cleveland bar on his way home from work. Two fellows were leaving for San Francisco. Without a word to his employer — or, for that matter, his wife — and with seven dollars in his pocket — Crumb, who had recognized "kindred spirits" in the LSD-spiked

[36] This behavior was not uncommon. What is now known as the '60s did not emerge in most of the United States until sometime between the police riots at the Democratic convention in August 1968 and Woodstock a year later. But if you were young and non-traditionally bent, what had filtered back to you from the Bay Area made you want to take a look. I came in October 1967, when two fellows with whom I was in VISTA working for a legal aid office in Chicago and — not incidentally — hanging on to draft deferments until we turned twenty-six — took an unauthorized leave and needed a third to split a non-stop drive. We stayed three days and zoomed back. One I spent with Adele, whom I had dated in college and hadn't seen since she'd dumped me for a fellow who was *this* close to a recording contract with Folkways. He'd ended up apprenticing to a goat herder; and she'd come out to San Francisco State where she'd studied Samuel Beckett, danced all night to the Grateful Dead, and been engaged to a German count. She took me for a picnic on Mt. Tam: cheese; wine; bread; a joint. Man, I thought, some people live like this. And some are in Chicago being called "White motherfucker" by their clients. A year later, when my tour was up, I returned.

rock show posters that were a signature component of the Bay Area scene, asked to come along.[36]

In San Francisco, Crumb met Don Donahue, a UC Berkeley drop-out who had been active in fringe creative circles since reading Oscar Lewis's *Bay Area Bohemia* while in high school and deciding a life devoted to art, poetry and sex was not without appeal. Crumb was seeking a publisher for a comic book of his creation, and Donahue announced he was one — on the basis of one issue of an eight-page newspaper, *Mama-Daddie*, whose near-entire run had been impounded by its printer because of too many sexual organs rampant. Donahue swapped a used tape recorder to Charles Plymell, a "second-tier" Beat poet of his acquaintance, and Plymell ran off 5,000 copies on his Multilith.[37]

The counterculture was still defining itself then, establishing its own institutions and badges of identity, ruling what to include within its borders, deciding what to hang on its walls, stuff in its backpacks, lay upon its coffee tables and shelves. It had newspapers — *The Los Angeles Free Press, The Berkeley Barb, The East Village Other* — and some of these had comic strips — "Captain High," "Suzie Slumgodess" [sic] — but, until Crumb-Donahue, it had no Wildenberg-Gaines to make the next conceptual leap. No one had yet seen if a comic book would fit.[38]

Zap presented itself as a twenty-page, black-and-white comic.[39] The cover, augmented by yellow and blue, showed a blocky 1930s vintage auto, designed and engineered not far from the Toonerville Trolley. Its tires were bulbous and patched. Its radiator spouted a geyser. Its headlights were half-lidded eyes. Its license plate (@*!!!) was a cartoon-speak oath. The driver was a bald man with a white beard several times as long as his head. Beside him, a woman wore a flower pot as a hat. Three peculiar children huddled around her; and, behind them, from the dark, a pair of eyes peered. The woman is saying, "I wish someone could tell me what 'Diddy-wah-diddy' means." The man is saying, "If you don't know by now, lady, don't *mess* with it." The cover says "Fair Warning: For Adult Intellectuals Only." It says "Zap Comics are Squinchy Comics" (as if anyone knows what "squinchy" means).

<hr />

[37] Plymell has recalled the run as less but concedes that whoever was there was probably too drugged to count.

[38] Strict constructionists will argue that there had been earlier UGs: Jack ("Jaxon") Jackson's *God Nose*; Frank ("Foolbert Sturgeon") Stack's *Adventures of Jesus*; Joel Beck's *Lenny of Laredo*. But these came, went, and nothing followed. *Après Zap, le déluge.* (An earlier *Zap* had been contracted for the year prior by Brian Zahn, the publisher of Philadelphia's underground paper *Yarrowstalks*; but he had grown queasy about the cover — a naked man with his cock plugged into an electric socket — and Crumb had never provided an alternative.)

[39] A later edition added four pages of strips that originally appeared in *EVO*.

A reader who turned the page was welcomed by a lunatic raving that this comic book was part of his plan to revenge himself upon his enemies and that "You've read too much already... I have you right where I want you... So, Kitchy-Koo, you bastards." Several short-on-the-linear "stories" followed. "Whiteman" portrayed a middle-aged man, beset by headaches, constipation and indigestion, obsessed with sex, stifling rage, hiding fears. "Mr. Natural Visits the City" delivered the message "The Whole Universe is Completely Insane." "I'm a Ding Dong Daddy" wordlessly ran a sappy-looking fellow through a variety of stock cartoon poses before blasting him into a constellation of stars. "Ultra Super Modernistic Comics" strung together a number of oddly shaped panels depicting eyeballs, lightning, a robot, a rose. There was not one superhero, funny animal or ghoul; but there were references to "speed freaks," "acid," "bringdowns," "Polacks," "niggers," "shit," multiple nipples and one vagina. Any doubt where *Zap* was coming from — or what additives had produced it — were laid to rest by the full-page back cover "advertisement," where three formerly "boring, uptight... alienated, frustrated," middle-class, young Americans testified to the value of turning on. "AMAZING RESULTS. See for Yourself. Help Others. Available in every major city from coast to coast."

Zap sold out its first printing in four months.

By 1970, significant UG publishers operated in New York, Chicago, and Milwaukee. But the Bay Area remained the movement's center. Many of the largest and most successful publishers were there: Donahue's Apex Novelties; The Print Mint of Don and Alice Shenkar and Bob and Peggy Rita; Rip Off Press, which was owned and operated by a group of transplanted-Texans, including the cartoonist Gilbert Shelton; and Ron Turner's Last Gasp Eco-Funnies — as well as several smaller ones, like future film director Terry Zwigoff's Golden Gate Publishing. So too, drawn by the weather and the area's tolerance of offbeat lifestyles, were many of the leading cartoonists: Kim Deitch, Justin Green, Rick Griffin, Bill Griffith, Rory Hayes, Victor Moscoso, Trina Robbins, Spain Rodriguez, and S. Clay ("The Man Who Put the UGH in Underground") Wilson. Together, they had taken a discredited — no, never-credited — art form and shown it could be a vehicle for exciting work.

The UG world could not have differed more from that of traditional comic books. If it took notice of the Comics Code Authority at all, it was as a checklist to discover additional conventions to defy. Since mainstream outlets would not handle its comics, the UG developed its own distribution system, relying on independent book stores, record stores, and, most heavily, "head" shops, purveyors of psychedelic posters, rolling papers, hash pipes, and black lights. ("People needed to be told what to read," Donahue recalls, "You bought your bong; you picked up your comics.") Distribution could be even less formal than that. As Turner explained, "You'd find guys at your doorstep that had a Volkswagen full of incense and roach clips and they'd say, 'I hear you got comics.' So you'd trade them for incense or, you know, whatever, and they'd go off. Or maybe they'd say, "Look, I haven't got any money but I'll be back in a month...' It was all very trusting. We could have cared less about money. It was evil as long as you had enough to live."

Most importantly, the creators, not the publishers, were supreme. They penciled, inked, and lettered their own books. They wrote the stories, cast the characters, chose the angles of viewing, the lighting and shadows, the flashbacks and cuts that shaped the telling. They set their own schedules and worked their own pace. (Since one could live comfortably on $300 a month, including dope, and income could be augmented with food stamps, Medi-Cal, and an employable significant other, this pace was not exhaustive.) They owned their artwork and copyrights. Their books remained in print, and they received royalties on sales. And they controlled their content.

The exercise of this control was what made the UGs' impact cataclysmic. The cartoonists quickly recognized that they could say or draw anything. They unleashed upon their pages unbridled imaginations and uninhibited ids, turn-your-stomach grotesqueries and in-your-face raunch. Their philosophy, in the words of UG chroniclers Patrick Rosenkranz and Hugo Van Baren, was: "[N]othing [is] so sacred that it should be left unknown..." They celebrated drugs — non-prescription, all varieties, all dosages. They reveled in sex — oral, anal, bestial, incestual. They attacked the war — but filled their pages with the bloodiest of images. They attacked racism — but gloried in racial offenses. They brokered in defilement and groped for transcendence. They rolled in gutters and spoke of bliss. They played out their dreams, their cravings, their fantasies, their fears. They showed people the inner recesses of their minds, adding, as Ron Turner put it, "the power of vision to that of cognitive thought." It was as if they believed that tossing down a dose of their most scorching incitements would flush the pipes of the American mindset and clear its way to satori.

One of the appeals of the comic book for these artists was that it was a "people's" art form. Comics could be cheaply produced, inexpensively disseminated, and easily understood. They would not be hoarded by collectors or frozen in museums or require deciphering by experts. And the artists found an audience eager to embrace them. Print runs of 15-20-30,000 copies sold out;[40] a half-dozen companies were selling 100,000 comics a month each; some *books* sold 100,000 copies; some series sold in the millions.[41]

The counterculture had arisen, in part, from the realization that much of what your parents had told you was bad felt damn good; and much of what

[40] For a normal 15,000 print run, the artist received $1000; the printer got $1500; and there was about another $1500 in costs. Thus, if the book sold over 8,000 copies, at half-a-buck apiece, it made money. If there were profits, the artist received fifty percent.

[41] By way of comparison, the *Barb* had an 85,000 circulation, *EVO* 65,000, and the *Freep* 95,000. *Newsweek* had 2,000,000 readers; the *Wall Street Journal* and *Rolling Stone* had 300,000; and the sex-tabloid *Screw,* which first appeared in 1969, had 100,000.

they'd said was good could get you killed damn quick. The UGs delivered this message in unexpurgated, unmodulated, exhortative fashion. Artist and audience shared the same vision, cozied, for the most part, in the same extreme corner of the country's cultural divide.[42] (What kind of world view was it, they asked, "straight" comic books were pushing, when superheroes "could fight and kill, but not fuck?") "We are so blessedly outrageous," the UGs sang. "We are having so much fun. How can you imagine the future is not ours?" They were, commentators wrote, "the perfect medium to express defiance of social norms," the ideal way "to explore the wild dreams and wild desires which seem to have no place in our predominately rationalistic and materialistic society." There was no better way "to demonstrate... disdain of conservative taste than to pervert what the public perceived as children's entertainment" — to transform the once disturbance-free, innocence-protected world of funny books into a free-fire zone where all holy bovines were fair and easily bloodied game.

And if your aim was the perversion of children's entertainment — in order to expose its lies and hypocrisy — to eliminate it as a force for the stifling of dissenting impulses — to extinguish its ability to mold impressionable minds into obedient cogs serving the corporate state — what better place to begin than with the company that had carried out more of this indoctrination than any other in your lifetime?

---

[42] As to who this audience was, an EVO survey showed that seventy-one percent of its readers attended college and thirteen percent graduate school. Ninety-eight percent smoked marijuana and seventy-seven percent took LSD. My surmise is that the UG readership was slightly lower on the educational scale and slightly higher, hard as this is to believe, on the zonked.

Chapter Four:
What If We Dropped More Pianos?

The cartoonists who would form the core of the Air Pirates, Dan O'Neill, Ted Richards, Bobby London, Gary Hallgren, and Shary Flenniken, met at the 1970 Sky River Rock Festival and Lighter Than Air Fair.

The fair proclaimed itself "America's first multi-day, outdoor rock concert." It had begun two years earlier, after promoters who had drawn 3000 people to a field near Seattle to witness a piano being dropped from a helicopter, followed by a Country Joe and the Fish concert, wondered how many people they might attract if they booked more bands. (It is perhaps fortunate for American culture they were not so piped they wondered, Hmmm, how many would come if we dropped more pianos?)

To put this meeting into its proper sociopolitical context, it should be noted that four months earlier, on April 30, President Nixon's announcement of the invasion of Cambodia had led to demonstrations that closed 500 college campuses and touched off over two dozen clashes with police, 200 bomb alarms, thirty damaged ROTC buildings, and the torching of the Isle Vista branch of the Bank of America. In sixteen states, the National Guard was called out. At Kent State, Ohio Guardsmen shot and killed four student protestors. At Jackson State, Mississippi state troopers killed two and wounded a dozen. At Buffalo, a dozen were shot; and at New Mexico, ten were bayoneted. In New York City, construction workers attacked anti-war demonstrators, injuring thirty. And according to pollsters, three-quarters of the country opposed the anti-war protests and would deny those arrested in connection with them the protection of the Bill of Rights.[43]

[43] Fifty-eight percent blamed the students for what happened at Kent State and only eleven percent the Guardsmen.

1970 was also the year which saw three SDS members killed by the bomb they were assembling in a Greenwich Village townhouse, two Catholic priests arrested for plotting to kidnap Henry Kissinger, and Jonathan Jackson's efforts to free his older brother, George, from San Quentin result in four deaths, including the younger Jackson and the Marin County Superior Court judge he had taken hostage. The same weekend as the fair, police killed two and injured seventy at a Chicano anti-war rally in Los Angeles.

The fair had been envisioned as a bucolic demonstration of people's ability to "come together and live and love... and enjoy life in the manner they saw fit"; but its roaring campfires, 3:00 a.m. drumming, and the accompanying howl springing from thousands of throats turned others' thoughts from Eden to *The Inferno*. It ran from August 28 through September 8 and drew 20,000 freaks, bikers and straights to a 160-acre farm north of Washougal, Washington, near the Skykomish River. Its sponsor was the Hydra Collective of the Seattle Liberation Front, an anti-war group whose leadership included Hillary Clinton's future guru on "the politics of meaning." It featured live music by Red Bone, the Youngbloods, and Country Joe. There was nude swimming; free rice and vegetables courtesy of The Hog Farm; concession stands selling fifteen-cent hot dogs, twenty-cent cups of soup, dollar tabs of LSD, thirty-five cent mescaline, and marijuana lids for eight-to-ten dollars; a table for drug donations for the bands; several days of cold rain; several acres of cold rain-resultant mud; one drowning; several rapes; several births; a long-smouldering, foul-smelling garbage dump; and, according to neighbors who had unsuccessfully sought court orders to strangle the entire event in its crib, "more than a few bizarre sexual exploits" performed *al fresco*.

O'Neill says he already knew Richards, who had looked him up after reading about him in *Rolling Stone* and wondering how someone who drew so badly warranted such attention. Richards isn't sure where he met O'Neill. As for "Odd Bodkins," though, "I straight took to it. His rendering skills were limited, but the storytelling and interpretations — the tunneling, the flights, the landscapes — were exceptional. He was stretching the high notes, scales and rhythms. Only later did I learn the effort that went into making it seem effortless."

Richards was a strapping, six-foot-two, 180-pound, twenty-four-year-old. His father, orphaned in the midst of the Depression at age fourteen, had escaped the Pennsylvania coal mines by joining the army. He had won the Silver Star after parachuting into Normandy with the 101st Airborne, become a Sergeant Major Green Beret, and authored the military's manual on hand-to-hand combat. Into his forties, he still enjoyed a bar brawl. Richards's mother was from Eufala, Alabama. She was a portrait sketcher and tale-teller, steeped in the works of Southern writers, and could recite Uncle Remus from memory. "I was devastated," Richards says, "when I read *The Great Santini*. That was *my* story."

Richards had been "seeing" cartoons since he was five. His favorite strips were "Pogo," "Peanuts," and Jimmy Hatlo's "They'll Do It Every Time." His favorite comic books were *Superboy, Uncle Scrooge,* and *Walt Disney's Comics and Stories.* He had always been "Class Artist"; but, on the army bases of the South where he grew up, art was a seasonal activity, usually limited to turning out turkeys for Thanksgiving and Santa Claus for Christmas. The rest of the year, he played baseball, football, and worked on self-designed science projects, like building model airplanes that flew. Drawn to "application," not homework, he quit school in 1965 to play electric bass in a Beatles-Stones cover band. Then, with the draft closing in, he enlisted in the Air Force.

He served two and a half years before receiving a general discharge for (accurately) suspected but unproven marijuana use. For most of his tour, he was stationed at Fort Benning, where he was part of the base "literati." They read books, watched *Star Trek* and ran computer programs for the entire squadron, which included the Strategic Air Command, whose nuclear armed planes, constantly heading for and being pulled back from targets in the Soviet Union, had inspired *Dr. Strangelove.* "The theater it played was packed with G.I.s every night," Richards says, "until they ran it out of town. We thought that and *For a Few Dollars More* were the two greatest movies ever made."

Richards was working for a finance company in Cincinnati and mulling over college when the counterculture exploded. The upheaval looked like more fun than either alternative, so he bought his ticket by writing a series of articles on the plight of the city's Appalachian whites and poor blacks for an underground paper, the *Independent Eye.* When a rift developed between staff and management, he split with a faction that established the rival *Clean City Express.* From October 1969 until May 1970, he served as cartoonist, reporter, editor, publisher, and "the guy who drove to the printer's. We got up to about a 25,000 circulation, limited by what we could fit in my car."

Richards came to the Bay Area in June 1970, hoping to break into professional cartooning. "The standard syndicates were closed off," he says, "but the alternative press allowed easy entree; and if your strip got popular, you could get a comic." He found work pasting up pages and drawing cartoons for the Berkeley *Tribe,* which had been formed by ex-*Barb* staffers — including Detroit Annie, Sgt. Pepper, Aloma Sue, and Egbert Souse — who had felt exploited by its parsimonious owner, Max Scherr. The *Tribe,* whose circulation eventually reached 35,000, did not pay contributors but gave each a stack of papers to sell. For Richards, who had no formal training as a cartoonist, the experience was valuable if somewhat circumscribed since, with the UG press, "all you had to draw was pigs and Nixon."

Robert Keith London, who, at twenty, was the youngest Pirate, also worked for the *Tribe.* (His general world view was expressed by a doobie he had drawn for a front page shortly before the fair, captioned "Smoke Lotsa Dope.") He had been born in the Brighton Beach section of Brooklyn, near

Coney Island, but grew up in eastern Queens. His father, a physician, worked for the Vicks Company; and his mother, who had trained to be an opera singer, had sung with swing bands. After graduating Martin Van Buren High School, London had attended college on Long Island but dropped out before finishing. He had shoulder-length brown hair, a splotchy beard, over-sized, wire-rimmed glasses and colored his roots with cowboy hats and boots.

London had been drawing cartoons since he was four. He was a fan of E.C. ("Thimble Theatre") Segar, Bud ("Mutt and Jeff") Fisher, Billy ("Barney Google") DeBeck and the comedians Groucho Marx, W.C. Fields, and Stan Laurel. He had been fired from the old line-leftist *Guardian* for an irreverent drawing of a Joan Baez-like folk singer fucking a dollar sign and had split from the more contemporary, underground New York *Rat* and Chicago *Seed* when they fell under the control of orthodoxies whose line he would not toe. "They wanted me to draw communist propaganda," he told S.C. Ringgenberg twenty-five years later. "I considered myself to be a cartoonist [not]... a pair of hands for the counterculture."[44]

London had come to California, hoping to convince Gilbert Shelton, whom he had met in New York, to have Rip Off publish a comic about a character he was developing: Dirty Duck, a cigar-smoking, pornography-smitten, sixty-nine year old, who lusted after the teenage hippie-chick Annie Rat. London had modeled Annie on his girlfriend and received the idea for Dirty Duck while sitting by a pond and recognizing how much the birds on it did not act like Disney's.

Gary Hallgren was twenty-five. He had gold-rimmed aviator glasses, a trim mustache, a puppy-dog face, and wavy, shoulder-length brown hair. Born in Seattle, he had grown up in small towns around Puget Sound — Sequim, Port Townsend, Ferndale. His father, who worked as a Linotype operator for newspapers, had served as a Gunner's Mate in the Pacific in World War II and again during the Korean conflict. He had met his wife, a telephone operator, at a USO dance in San Diego.

Hallgren began his education in a two-room schoolhouse with one other first-grader. "I always drew pictures," he says, "and I was always in trouble for doodling, instead of paying attention." He progressed from cars, through trucks and airplanes, to people. His favorite newspaper strips were "Snuffy Smith," "Bringing Up Father," "Pogo." His favorite comic book characters were Donald Duck and Uncle Scrooge. He had a B.A. from Western

---

[44] The *Rat* was taken over by radical feminists in 1969. Historians do not identify any such clear re-invention of the *Seed*, but all UG papers found themselves increasingly pressured to adapt rigorously restricted views in furtherance of the struggle. The *Tribe*, by the way, was no ideological cupcake. It favored a People's Militia, "responsible" bombings, and the murder of policemen. Before its demise in 1971, it had adapted a political philosophy rarely espoused this side of Kim Il Sung.

Washington State College in Bellingham, where he had majored in painting and design while planning to become a commercial artist.

During high school, Hallgren had worked in his art teacher's sign painting shop. Sign painting was a thriving business at that time in that area, with each town fostering its own style; and Hallgren brought his particular "cartoon sensibility" to the field. In college, he worked for Bellingham's best company; and, after graduation, newly married and in need of income, he stayed on. But shortly after completing his union apprenticeship, he was fired. "I don't know if my employer didn't want to pay me more," Hallgren says, "or if he was sick of having this long-haired freak on his payroll." In 1969, he formed a partnership with Doug Fast, an Art Institute of Seattle graduate, whose art nouveau/psychedelic style he admired. Their company, Splendid Sign, was located near a houseboat colony on Lake Union in downtown Seattle

O'Neill says he met Hallgren after spending four hours waiting in the rain to learn who had done the superb brushwork he had spotted on the side of a van parked behind the fair's stage. Hallgren says they met when he was summoned to the media tent for one of the most memorable moments of his life. "I had always considered newspaper cartoonists super straight, like Charles Schulz; and there he was, looking like the ultimate underground cartoonist, hunched over, working on his daily strip, his hat keeping off the rain. 'Hi,' he said, 'I'm Dan O'Neill. I'm on mescaline. What're you on?'"

Shary Flenniken was an admiral's daughter. She had lived in Norfolk, San Diego, Kodiak, Alaska, and the Canal Zone before her family settled in Seattle when she was nine. Her father had been the best cartoonist in the U.S. Naval Academy's Class of 1932. He had won *his* Silver Star during World War II as a submariner and also served in Korea. Her mother had been a drama major at Mary Washington College in Fredericksburg, Virginia, and both her parents were superb storytellers. She had two older sisters, one of whom had died of rheumatic fever at age eleven in 1948.

"I read," Flenniken says, "from the minute I learned how. Fairy tales. *Little Women.* Obscure children's books passed down by my sisters." By the time she was fifteen, she also drew regularly. "I was left alone a lot, so I would stay up all night, drawing and painting in the kitchen. And do that for the next forty years." She painted flowers with opaque watercolors. She did pen-and-ink drawings of Italian marble cutters and teenage boys smoking under street lamps. (The latter, her first sale, brought $15 at a street fair.) She did a collage of the Kennedy brothers playing football with soldiers in Vietnam, on which she dripped human blood that she obtained from her dentist. "But I wasn't doing it because I thought of it as a career. I did it because it was fun."

After graduating high school in 1968, Flenniken cast her lot with her times by running away from home in pursuit of an iron sculptor she had known for two weeks. ("I don't know what I was thinking. Do other people have brains at that age? I was a complete ditz.") She found him in Vermont, encumbered by a five-year-old son and an eight-and-one-half-months pregnant wife. She returned to Seattle where the family mantra became "What can we do with Shary?" The answer was: Ship her to Key Largo, where her sister had given up a folk-singing career to dive for sunken treasure. There, Flenniken became friendly with one of the few women at Cornell's School of Veterinary Medicine. She accompanied her to Ithaca, where Flenniken enlisted in the anti-war movement. Back in Seattle, she enrolled at a commercial art school; but the lure of designing soda pop ads paled beside that of putting her body on the line at rallies, demonstrations, protests, and riots in the service of causes that ranged from ending the war to regaining fishing rights for Indians. When the opportunity arose to both draw and further the revolution by working for the underground paper *Sabot* (formerly the Seattle *War-Whoop and Battle Cry*), she seized it.

Sabot was putting out a daily paper at the Fair from the back of a truck on a mimeograph machine run by a dwarf named Maury. The combination of a dwarf, a mimeograph machine, and the dark-haired, blue-eyed Flenniken proved quite the draw. O'Neill, Richards, London, and Hallgren all ended up asking to draw for the paper — and crashing in her geodesic dome (or so Flenniken told Robert Boyd in her *Comics Journal* interview. Hallgren says he only met O'Neill at the Festival).

After the fair, the garbage pit still smoking in their rear view mirrors, the group dispersed. Hallgren returned to Splendid Sign. Richards joined Flenniken at *Sabot*, doing paste-ups, drawing cartoons, learning about pens, improving his inking. He was developing a character, Dopin' Dan, based on his military experiences; and he pressed his enthusiasm for comics upon her, encouraging her to think in terms of sustained cartoon narratives, instructing her how this was accomplished.

O'Neill gave London a ride back to the Bay Area. During a stop at his studio in Marin County, O'Neill proposed they team up with the others and form a comic book company. London was impressed by the studio but not the proposal. He went back to New York, failed to make up with an old girlfriend, and returned. He was depressed, living in an Oakland slum, not knowing what to do with his life when O'Neill reappeared. "'Give up,' he told me," London says. "'Just say, 'Yes.' He needed me to convince the others to do comics with him if it was going to work, because I was the only one who had his act together. I was the only other one with chops."

London resisted for a couple weeks. Then he hitchhiked to Jenner and moved in with O'Neill. In exchange for room and board, he helped with "Odd Bodkins." He learned the cartoon business by first-hand observation and studied classic strips like George Herriman's "Krazy Kat." He also worked on "Dirty Duck." The last two weeks of "Odd Bodkins," O'Neill says, he gave London space at the bottom for it, an homage to "Krazy," which had begun within another strip Herriman was doing. "I lettered and no one recognized the drawing was different." (London says these strips were never published.)

They also discussed the comic book company. While O'Neill was aware of the UGs, he was not close to any of the artists or impressed by their work. He had been an established cartoonist when they appeared, and none of them approached his credits or experience. Crumb had drawn greeting cards. Wilson, Green and Robbins were fine arts majors turned off by academia. Moscoso and Griffin made rock show posters. Shelton had drawn for a college humor magazine. "All these guys doing dick jokes and calling themselves underground cartoonists. You could count the number of them who could draw and write on one hand." (For their part, O'Neill says, when he turned to comics, the UG cartoonists referred to him as "that jive-ass motherfucker from the *Chronicle.*") He was also much less enmeshed in the counterculture life than they. "I never bonded to that Haight-Ashbury scene. In the Beats, there was a working intelligence trying to change the world into a better place. The hippie thing had no intelligence to it and got negative real fast. It trashed out on heroin and methedrine, and most of the people who started it fled to the country. I was coming from there to go to San Francisco. We passed each other on the way."

O'Neill envisioned a co-operatively owned, counterculture publishing empire. It would turn out regular, monthly comic books, unlike the customary UG approach when a book's next issue seemed less dependent upon the calendar than the drug of the day, zodiac propitiousness, or "You know, man, like whatever." ("Everybody else was putting out one book a year and having coffee and cheese and wine parties," O'Neill once said — dietary habits which suggest he was speaking of a different group of UG cartoonists than is generally depicted in the literature — "and talking about what great work they're doing.") Each cartoonist would be expected to produce a page a day. They would work on some books jointly — *Air Pirates Funnies*, which became their flagship vehicle, for example — but each would also do his own books, where individual vision could be pursued without outside editorial interference.

The communal aspect promised O'Neill the camaraderie his past life as a cartoonist lacked. Drawing "Odd Bodkins," he had felt isolated — a freak, even. Now he would unite with and take strength from others like himself. "The dream was to have a studio where people are working together, and they're happy, and they like each other. Suddenly everyone would feel normal." He had been expelled from the *Chronicle.* The others had been excluded from the existing camps within the underground. They seemed a good fit. "One tired, beat-up pro," was how he saw it, "and a bunch of brand new amateurs who were ready to go. You know, tigers."

London still had one reservation: O'Neill wanted to continue his use of Walt Disney characters. London told Ringgenberg he objected. "No way. I am not using other people's characters. I do not want to engage in any copyright infringements... I had created my own characters and I wanted to pursue that." But O'Neill said his lawyers had told him that Disney's copyrights on certain characters had expired, leaving them in the public domain and available for use. And a parody of others would be protected by the First Amendment. London's reaction was, "Look, the guy was a syndicated cartoonist, so when he said he had lawyers, I believed he had lawyers." Besides, by now, he wanted to do a comic book. "Finally, I said, 'Okay, I'll give you the studio if you give me *Dirty Duck.*'"

On December 31, 1970, London flew to Seattle to bring the others back. Richards met him at the airport; and, as if seeking a living *leitmotif* for what was to transpire, the two welcomed in the new year by attending an all-hippie vaudeville show.

Around the time of London's departure, O'Neill made an independent foray into the UG world. His point of entry was Co. & Sons, a San Francisco publishing house owned and operated by John Bagley. O'Neill says several publishers had asked him to do a comic, "But I went with the weakest to get some parity, to try to keep them all alive, not just one."

Bagley was a man no survivor of the era mentions without rolling his eyes. Though few indictable specifics are ever pronounced, it is understood he was a world class character and rogue. There are references to a lavish loft with beautiful women lolling about. There are hints of financing from dubious sources. There are remembrances of O'Neill screaming at Bagley for more money and Bagley screaming at O'Neill for additional pages. Bagley's curtain-closing act was to announce a mysterious, fatal disease for himself and vanish. In the nut bowl of life, even macadamias regarded him with awe.

Co. & Sons published three issues of *Dan O'Neill's Comics and Stories* — the title, a play upon *Walt Disney's Comics and Stories,* underscoring O'Neill's continued fixation. The covers show, in numerical order, Practical Pig shooting The Big Bad Wolf, Bucky Bug shooting Practical, and Mickey Mouse tossing a grenade at Bucky. The books were almost entirely reprinted strips from the last months of "Odd Bodkins," supplemented by a Hallgren one-pager, some early London, and miscellaneous, original O'Neill. (That his debut in a forum that permitted him unfettered artistic expression resulted in Jocko Cuntsocker, a character who fornicates with chickens, may have struck some as less than encouraging.)

Dating these books is difficult. The covers say "January 1948," "December 1947," and "November 1949," which, as guides go, suggest they were hired off the Blind and Addled portion of the board. (O'Neill says he dated them for "my favorite years in comics.") I place them between late 1970 and mid-1971, though if one is to give credence to O'Neill's story — see below — that he didn't regain his rights to "Odd Bodkins" until mid-1972 — none could have been published before then without litigation from the *Chron.* But Hallgren's story bears a 1971 copyright; London, who thinks they were run off before the Pirates' studio assembled, recalls seeing page proofs while in Jenner; and Richards believes the first was done before he arrived and, later, "I woke up one morning and the other two were there." Finally, the back covers of the last two issues solicit subscriptions for *Air Pirates Funnies*, and, by 1972, it must have been clear that book was not going to appear again soon.[45]

Shortly after arriving in Seattle, London looked up Flenniken. "My father was dying," she recalls. "I was incredibly depressed. I was completely lost. And when Bobby arrived, I felt I was meant to be with him."

Flenniken was living in a "political collective" that consisted of herself and her five-foot-four, 200-pound housemate who had a crush on Richards. Seattle, with its Wobblie past and Seattle Seven-present,[46] was a hot bed of political — and sexual — action. Each collective in town seemed to be trying to outdo every other in proving itself the most liberated. One removed all bedroom and bathroom doors to foster openness. In another, after a member was raped and the men called for revenge, the idea was voted down by the other women because it was "sexist."

London joined the *ménage*. But after two months, his relationship with Flenniken imploded, and she moved out. He remained in Seattle, working on "Dirty Duck," a half page of which Shelton published in the *Free Press* beneath his own "Fat Freddy's Cat." He wanted more; but London received a letter from O'Neill, "Come on down, and let's get rich."

Richards had met Hallgren shortly before Christmas when, attracted by Splendid Sign's work, he had walked into the shop and introduced himself. When London arrived, he brought him to Hallgren's home where they made an indelible impression. "I was appalled at their 'street' manners," Hallgren recalls, "picking up an elaborate gingerbread house I'd made and insisting it was time to eat it." London, who feared involvement in the group might interfere with his own professional aspirations, but who also feared being left out and left behind, put O'Neill's idea of a comic book company to the other two.

Richards, whose goal had been comics all along, was eager to become involved. So was Hallgren. He had fantasized about living in San Francisco since seeing his first rock show posters. He had also toyed with the idea of becoming a cartoonist, and the quality of the work being done in the UGs had strengthened

---

[45] Why Disney never sued for these copyright infringements is also a mystery. It may be that one of the benefits of the underground's haphazard distribution system was that they flew below its legal department's radar.

[46] The Seven — formerly the Seattle Eight, but one of them had disappeared — had been charged in April 1970 with leading a rock-throwing, window-smashing, paint-splashing mob of 2000 in an assault on the federal court building. The trial judge had declared a mistrial in December but cited all of the defendants for contempt, eventually jailing six of them.

this desire. And he believed that, in order to survive, Splendid Sign had to become more "businesslike," a commitment his partner refused to make.[47]

Hallgren had already achieved his first professional cartoonist credit. The owner of Seattle's largest comic book store, Underground Art — a fellow actually named "Art" — for whom he had painted a Crumb-like design on the refrigerator of the houseboat where he resided — had asked him to contribute to a comic he planned to publish. He had S. Clay Wilson ensconced in a hotel churning out the feature story, and he needed back-up. Hallgren delivered, but the book never appeared, most likely because it had been planned only as a means for Art to acquire original pages by Wilson.

To assess their proposed venture's potential, Hallgren, London and Richards hitched a ride to San Francisco in a bread truck full of hippies. O'Neill, who was temporarily quartered in the O'Farrell's projection room, lodged them at his parents' apartment. One night, early in their stay, Hallgren asked London, "Bobby, what are we doing here?"

"Gary, we're going to draw comics and become famous," London said.

It made sense to Hallgren. He had been feeling "rudderless," so the idea of joining with someone self-assured, professionally experienced, and as self-directed as O'Neill appealed to him. And he was impressed by the boldness of O'Neill's ideas. "Becoming cartoonist revolutionaries and starting our own company was radical thinking to someone who was just a lowly draftsman. Plus, I had the corroboration of Ted and Bobby. I thought their work showed a lot of potential. So I figured I had nothing to lose."

Hallgren returned to Seattle. He tried to sell his share of Splendid Sign, "But the concept was too much for my partner, so I just left; and it devolved." He packed everything he owned into a 1948 truck, which didn't run but with which he couldn't bear to part. He hitched it to the back of his 1960 Studebaker Hawk — later rented to George Lucas for use in *American Graffiti* — and moved down with his wife, "An abuse of her sensibilities I probably wouldn't go through again." The loaded-to-its-axle truck provided an Okies-fleeing-the-Dust-Bowl aura to their embarkation. It also threatened to burn out the Studie's motor going uphill; and they had to pick up a hippie hitchhiker to man the brake, so they weren't run over by it going down.

In late April, Flenniken came to Berkeley to visit friends. The hitchhiker *she* picked up was planning to call upon a girlfriend there on his way to Costa Rica. The girlfriend lived in an all-macrobiotic household — more welcoming a recommendation for some in this era than an AAA oval — and Flenniken moved in. She and London re-connected, and he invited her to join the group. But initially, she told Boyd, "It was just kind of like 'Bring your girlfriend along,' not like a working thing."

---

[47] Doug Fast was not entirely ill-equipped for the world of commerce. He went on to do a memorable set of ads for Rainier Beer and design the Starbucks logo. He is now art director for a prominent Seattle advertising agency.

Chapter Five:
A Lifestyle of Their Own

Shortly before Flenniken arrived, the Pirates had sublet two rooms — one tiny, one big — from an electronic music group on the second floor of a warehouse at 740 Harrison Street in San Francisco. The building, which no longer exists, was so unimposing that visitors were surprised to learn it bore an address. The neighborhood was rich in body shops, radiator repair, and discount fabric but light on other amenities. Southbound 101, slicing by at rooftop level, provided urban white noise.

The Pirates slept in sleeping bags and shared a bathroom in what had been a darkroom. They had no kitchen. To shower, they had to walk several blocks to Glide Memorial Church and hope no man of the cloth was lathering up. The rent was cheap, but they needed an advance from Last Gasp's Turner to pay it. Living there were: O'Neill, who had been divorced that year, leaving his wife with a boy, six, and a girl, five; O'Neill's girlfriend of the moment; Richards; his occasional girlfriend; and London and Flenniken. Hallgren stayed over from time to time, but, "As a former business owner, I was a man of means compared to most underground cartoonists." He rented a house in Lagunitas, in north Marin, from which his wife would ship the others an occasional home-cooked meal.

It was welcome — except by O'Neill, who had a bias against health food. ("Health food is cheap food with soy sauce," he once wrote.) Usually, the Pirates depended on Turner to drop by with CARE packages of Oreos or pork buns, which, according to London, in terms of epicurean, if not numerical, accuracy, they'd fall upon "like The Three Stooges." Without outside intervention, they had to walk a mile to a restaurant. "By the time you got back," O'Neill says, "your dinner was wasted because you were hungry again."

London recalls Harrison Street as "a zoo." Hallgren terms it "A bit much. An emotionally charged place with a lot of paranoia, elation, megalomania, and psychodrama. Not exactly in touch with reality." Richards repeatedly clashed with O'Neill, with whom he had, by most accounts, at least two fistfights. (O'Neill once described a disagreement "over how to draw a tree," thus: "He knocked me across the room. I bounced off the wall and landed with a knee in his throat, a knee in his crotch, two punches in his kidneys and bit him in the stomach before he hit the ground." Not only did Gilbert and Sullivan get along better, so did Robinson and LaMotta.) Richards also came to dislike Flenniken, whom he considered a spoiled brat and referred to derogatorily as "The General's Daughter." Actually, says Flenniken, Richards disliked anyone he perceived as being from a higher social class. "Ted was very Maoist. You know, 'You're a scholar. You should be put in a training camp.'" For his part, Richards says their life "seemed very normal. It was a strange period and an exciting time, calling for artistic courage from everyone; and I thought, 'This is okay.' There were weeks of close camaraderie and times of falling out like any family." He also says only one of these out-fallings caused him to deck O'Neill.[48]

Zoo or not, Harrison Street was where most of the work on the collaborative Air Pirates comics occurred. "Everyone was drawing," London says. "All our energy was going into those books." Flenniken's view is also upbeat. Sure, she told Boyd, Richards, Hallgren and London were "mean, competitive assholes... just butts" who, like most UG cartoonists, viewed the field as "a guy thing." They mocked her work and hogged the best supplies. (Her breakthrough occurred when she was allotted something besides a paper bag to draw on.) But O'Neill was supportive. At one point, he stopped her when she was about to walk out for good with what she still refers to as "The Speech." "He told me 'You can't leave. We need you. The world needs women to do this work. You have something valuable to contribute.'" She developed artistically and professionally, and she enjoyed the communality. It was "really, really fun. We were living, eating, fucking, everything together." They would sit around, smoke dope, and come up with wild ideas for their company.

The wildest were O'Neill's. He knew that becoming moguls required

[48] Four years later, Richards struck the most celebrated blow in UG history. To kick off the publication of Mark James Estren's *A History of Underground Comics*, Straight Arrow Books threw a party in the grotto of Wilfred "Satty" Podreich, a German-born psychedelic collage artist, who, untroubled by Zoning Board compliance, had excavated the basement of his Marina District house into an enormous, multi-compartmentalized cave. Satty had filled his home with discarded furniture, old books, dolls, mannequins, a human skull. Entire regions were accessible only by ladder. In 1982, drunk, he fell from one, sustaining injuries that killed him.

The party was not entirely festive. Many UG cartoonists resented *History* since, for one thing, they had been told that unless they allowed uncompensated reproduction of their work, they would not be mentioned in it; and, as the evening wound on, Richards clocked the guest of honor. Richards now says, it was "a nice punch, not intended to maim," motivated by "a flirtatious wife," rather than a disagreement over creators' rights.

more than product. They would need a better distribution system than the UGs relied on. But O'Neill's alternatives seemed to stem more from the six pounds of hashish Hallgren had brought with him than the Harvard B-School case system. One involved dropping comic books from blimps. Another was to hire winos to dress as policemen and sell them on street corners.

The younger Pirates were, in the words of someone who knew them then, "Hell-bent on learning the cartoonist trade and succeeding in it as a life work." They looked up to O'Neill, listened to him, and believed in him. He had succeeded in the newspaper business, and they had not. He was respected by the underground, and they weren't. Hanging with him provided social and professional cachet. But O'Neill, while he enjoyed the admiration and the power derived from having this mini-army to command, had already walked away from a prestigious, financially successful career. He had other priorities, other demons prodding him — other dragons to slay.

To realize his goals, O'Neill instituted a training program that relied heavily on the group's mutual self-education. He considered himself a good writer but inept visually. ("I had a very weak line. Either that or palsy.") Hallgren, on the other hand, was a graphic whiz. "A God," Flenniken calls him. "Exceptionally talented," says Richards. "His rendering and lettering were as skilled as most professionals." London had a wonderful comic sensibility and the ability to communicate the loftiest ideas to a mass audience. Richards brought blue collar grit and a wised-up, big-city-embittered point-of-view ("I mean, I'd already run an underground paper in the middle of right wing Cincinnati") to their work. "Ted was a great gut-level reader of situations," Flenniken says, "and it was cool to listen to him cut someone else up — but not you." Flenniken provided, besides her own considerable artistic skills, a dose of bubble-popping, feminine cynicism to the testosterone that floated in the air. She viewed the others as lurching off, overloaded with self-importance and short on common sense. "'What's going to happen if you go to jail?' I'd ask. I'd been to jail. It's not pretty. It's stupid. I was scared. A little bit. Not enough to care."

O'Neill planned for them to develop their craft by copying the masters. He stocked a reference library with copies of *Uncle Scrooge*, *Little Lulu*, and *Felix the Cat* by swapping original "Odd Bodkins" dailies to Gary Arlington, an ex-record store clerk who, in 1968, had opened the San Francisco Comic Book Company, the country's first comic book store. The Pirates then tried to duplicate these works. They used different tools — crowquill pens, rapidographs, brushes — to hone skills and develop hand-eye co-ordination. One of O'Neill's girlfriends, Annie Marino, a photographer for the Mitchells often credited with the idea for "art" porn films, would bring in a 16 mm. projector and screen classic comedies, so they could learn to structure scenes.

And O'Neill incorporated improvisational techniques he'd learned at The Committee into the training. He might assign a story in the style of a particular cartoonist — "Mary Had a Little Lamb," say, as done by Otto Messmer. Or he might have someone assume the role of an enemy of Mickey Mouse — O'Neill was usually The Phantom Blot; Hallgren, Black Pete;[49] London, Sylvester Shyster; and Richards, The Big Bad Wolf — begin a story with his character, introduce someone else's, and turn the page over to him. "I'd say, 'Okay, I'm going up ahead, Bobby, and you've got to drag the story to where Mickey meets a gorilla playing a piano on a bridge.'" Once Hallgren took a weekend off, so O'Neill killed his character. "He gets back, and I left him in the water with a bomb dropping. How's he gonna get out of that? So Hallgren's got these pages of him diving real deep, and the bomb coming down, and this shark coming, and the shark eats the bomb, and it goes off and blows it up, but he gets away. I taught him to run out on the studio." The goal, though, was not to top the other guy or draw him into a corner but to create an integrated work that made everyone look good. They learned to subsume individual style and ego to the common weal. They learned discipline. They learned to meet deadlines. They tried — this is Flenniken to Boyd again — "to get along on paper. Not fuck each other up and compete."

Sometimes the games spilled off the page. O'Neill liked to put on his Phantom Blot outfit and tear down alleys on his Norton, with an Indian buddy aboard firing arrows with paint-filled light bulbs as tips at billboards. "THONK! BLOT! The winos were getting terrified. 'I don't think I'll drink this stuff any more.'" When people got used to his play-acting, he'd put someone else in the suit. "Oh, cut it out, O'Neill." "Cut what out? I'm over here." Or he'd climb onto a deck built across the warehouse's beams and painted blue to blend in with the ceiling. When guests arrived, he'd pop his head out so it floated, disembodied, like the Cheshire Cat.

However offbeat the approach, whatever success the Pirates achieved collectively was due to O'Neill. Flenniken lauds his gift for making people feel they were coming together in what was both a noble cause and a huge party. "Professionally," she adds, "he was an inspiration. All you have in this business are a blank piece of paper and a pen. The magic happens at the point your mind sees something and your hand gets it down. Dan's imagination and mechanics were incredible." And Hallgren commends his ability to focus each of them on the task at hand. "He let our minds float productively between reality and fantasy by maintaining the legend that something marvelous was coming out. When each artist decided to broaden his focus and not be

[49] Black Pete was originally known as Pegleg Pete, but, I have been told, a name change was effected because Disney did not wish to offend amputees. This sensitivity, as we shall see, did not extend to certain other groups.

Disney-oriented, a lot more conflicts developed. He provided serious cartoon mentoring, of which no one ever gets enough."

O'Neill has said the Air Pirates were born out of the "revolutionary fervor" of the times. "Those were the '60s, and it was everybody's duty to smash the state. And we smashed a lot of it; but, you know, they smashed us back." Still, the specific planks of his platform are elusive. Indeed, he is capable of saying within the same interview that the entire group was "very political" and that "None of us had a political thought..." Testimony from his cadre-mates is equally undispositive. Hallgren calls O'Neill and Richards "very much political" but says he was totally unaware politically until awakened by O'Neill to the implications of Disney's power. His initial participation, he says, stemmed from a commitment only to "good, clean, satirical fun." Richards says that while he resented Disney's "corporate seizure of the American narrative," he, too, thought the idea was just "good, sporting fun." Flenniken says London was extremely political. London says he was entirely apolitical and that even O'Neill's first Disney drawings were "spontaneous and non-political. There were no campfire ghost stories about the Evil Disney Empire." But, he does say, O'Neill, Richards and Flenniken were "into being radicals to the extent of, you know, 'Screw the system. We'll publish ourselves.'" It may be that "politics" was not an issue in any doctrinaire, how-to-pull-the-lever (or where-to-plant-the-bomb) sense but that simply living and working as UG cartoonists was a political statement. Certainly, every UG book that appeared could be counted as another vote against the war and for drugs.[50] "The main point," O'Neill also says, "was to buck corporate thinking. We just didn't like bullshit."

According to London, while working on *Air Pirates Funnies* #1, O'Neill showed him two panels of a story called "The Mouse" — and there, again, was Mickey. This presented a twofold problem — one moral, one practical. While the counterculture was built on defying convention, its ethic favored the perfection of individual style over ripping off someone else's.[51] Plus, Disney was known to vigorously protect its property through litigation. London told Ringgenberg that, because he still believed in O'Neill's lawyers, he went along with the idea; but the others thought he was "crazy," and "a real row developed [that]... split... the group."

Flenniken denies anyone had reservations about anything the group was doing. "Dan would say it; Bobby'd interpret it; Gary'd swallow it; and Ted'd buy

---

[50] The choices people made on these issues in those years were not without danger. For instance, statistical analyses now show that a failure to do sufficient drugs as a youth put you severely at risk for ending up, thirty years later, a Republican on the House Judiciary Committee.

[51] Both Victor Moscoso and Rick Griffin had preceded the Pirates in using Disney characters in their comics. Moscoso had even once hoped to work for Disney until, Rosenkranz and Van Baren tell us, "the fascist realities of Disney's politics became apparent to him..."

it — because it was the best party in town." She says they all believed that Disney was fronting "for the military-industrial complex; and there was this incredible disillusionment with — and outrage at — '50s America, which the Mouse represented. It had all been blown apart by the war. Everyone was totally on board. We thought, 'We are going to freak the fuck out of these guys.'" Hallgren says he came to like the idea of taking on Disney because it was "way too powerful and all-encompassing culturally." And Richards says he believed they would be "helping the people regain access to their own stories." Disney had appropriated, emasculated and sugar-coated not only America's folklore, but the world's fairy tales and myths. The Pirates aimed to restore their bite.

In August 1970, the Air Pirates moved a few blocks south to 560 Fourth Street, a twenty-five-foot tall, forty-foot wide, former firehouse which Francis Ford Coppola's film production company, American Zoetrope, used for storage. O'Neill and London discovered it when they smelled toxic fumes emanating from some plastic sculpture inside. Ignoring the possibilities of the odor as portent, O'Neill asked Coppola, who was in the process of finishing *The Godfather* and presumably had more important matters on his mind than background checks on prospective tenants, about renting it. O'Neill then paid the $400 a month he requested with an advance wrangled from Bagley for London's *Dirty Duck* #1.

The Pirates' new residence had a kitchen, shower, bathroom, balcony, ping-pong table, desks to set drawing boards on, and movie props to play with: masks; jumpsuits; bottles for the test tube babies in George Lucas's *THX-1138*, in which the Pirates stored brown rice. They also were in close proximity to Coppola's media van full of costly electronic equipment which, Hallgren relates, O'Neill once commandeered to convoy the group to visit a friend "who lived up an incomprehensible series of switchback roads in rural Marin. There, fortunately, memory deserts me."

At one point, by O'Neill's count, seventeen people lived in the warehouse. Hallgren, now separated from his wife, had moved in. So had a number of UG cartoonists. There was Willy Murphy, an ex-J. Walter Thompson employee and creator of "Those Wonderful Vegetable Heads." (He would die of bronchial pneumonia five years later.) There was Larry ("Dr. Atomic") Todd, an art major at Syracuse, who, upon his arrival, grabbed a mattress, some draperies, erected "a private zone," and emerged some days later with a six-foot-long, paper maché hash pipe. (Todd later spent ten years painting murals for carnival rides, until a mild stroke turned his creative efforts back toward cartooning, glass-blowing, and tattoos.) And Sheridan Anderson, an exceptional sign-painter and master of show-card lettering, who would author a wonderful comic about fly-fishing. (He died early of cirrhosis of the liver.) And Gary King, about whom O'Neill says, "He was sixteen, this ugly little thing with red hair, wearing a blanket. He had been tossed out of school for drawing cartoons, and his teacher brought him to us in despair"; and whom Hallgren calls, "The most obnoxious, hostile kid I ever came across." (King moved to Seattle and was last heard of working as a bartender.) There was Bill Plympton, who was either "The world's first gay cartoonist" (O'Neill), "A guy who liked to draw cheesecake" (Hallgren), or the Bill Plympton "Who does a lot of animation advertising work in New York City" (Flenniken).[52] There was Vaughn Bodé, who had edited the New York cartoon tabloid *Gothic Blimp Works* and created Cheech Wizard. (He died of auto-erotic strangulation in 1975.) And Scott Judge, a superb satirist who suffered from "stage fright" when it came to actually publishing. (He returned to Bellingham and became a scrimshaw artist.) And Kent Robertson, who, under an Arab pseudonym, did a comic book, *The New Gravity*, which was almost entirely text. (He is also deceased — or maybe not — accounts vary.) There were two non-cartoonist pals of Richards, Trucker Joe Barreca and Gerry Weinerstein, a.k.a Gerry Tambourine, a.k.a The Purple Panhandler, who would don a purple cap and purple tuxedo and beg at the train station to raise grocery money for the household. (He became a clown for Ringling Brothers.) And there was "Barney Steel," who took his name from a bar down the Peninsula. The author of *Armageddon Comics,* he is recalled by Turner, his publisher, as an ex-Navy SEAL of the jump-in-the-ocean-with-a-forty-pound-pack-on-your-back-and-swim-two-miles-to-meet-another-SEAL-with-a-pack-on-his-back-so-you-can-put-them-together-and-have-a-nuclear-bomb school. ("A very dangerous guy. He could kill you with either hand.")[53] And there was still room to squeeze in the occasional cartoonist-groupie.[54]

London says, "Compared to Fourth Street, Harrison Street was restrained." Aside from himself, no one worked. Richards "wouldn't get out of his sleeping bag." Hallgren "had pimp's disease and was trying to become the Roving Rogue of North Beach."[55] O'Neill had "pulled the first of his major disappearing acts" that would absent him for days. Increasingly fearful of being sued by Disney and feeling completely lost, London says he finished *Air Pirates* #2 himself. Then, while O'Neill was away, he suggested to the others they omit Disney

~~~~~~

[52] This Plympton's official bio. says he moved to New York from Portland in 1968 and mentions no Bay Area interlude. He did not respond to an inquiry designed to resolve this dispute.

[53] London says the other cartoonists hung out at Fourth Street but did not live there. Instead, O'Neill was "bringing in winos and heroin addicts, trying to integrate them into the group." Hallgren says most of the other cartoonists never lived in the warehouse except briefly. "O'Neill did bring in some strange people that had dubious talents and personalities. Winos and junkies they may have been, but they weren't your *average* winos and junkies."

[54] Richards, according to Flenniken, boasted that his drawing table attracted the most because they could tell he had "the biggest dick." Richards denies such popularity. "I wish," he says, "but there weren't many around."

[55] And Hallgren denies meriting that appellation.

characters from the third issue and feature Roger Rabbit — about whom more later — a character O'Neill had recently created. He was "soundly hooted down"; so, wired on caffeine, he knocked off twenty-four pages and completed *Dirty Duck* in two weeks to keep them from being evicted.

Hallgren agrees O'Neill's leadership was faltering. His ideas were becoming more bizarre, and the other Pirates' disagreements grew more heated as he spun out of control. And the cartoonists O'Neill was recruiting often seemed a bad fit, personality- and style-wise. "They didn't work in the 'big foot' style. They weren't interested in humor books."

Richards concurs that work became secondary to "a lot of fooling around." O'Neill's escalating emotional problems were causing the group to lose direction; and when he was there, the two of them were often at each other's throats. Offered a contract by Last Gasp for a Dopin' Dan book, Richards put his efforts there. "A cultural and artistic statement about Disney needed to be made; but Mickey Mouse was never a major part of my lexicon, and you could not make a living being a Disney parodist. I thought the way to defeat Disney's grip on the public's imagination was to develop better characters and create better stories." He had built his skills and perfected his style, and he was confident there was an audience for what he had to say.

They had not been living the healthiest of lifestyles.[56] O'Neill was reveling in his still-bankable celebrity and the license of the age. "He knew everybody; everybody knew him," one old friend recalls. "People were in and out of that warehouse all the time. All these women wanted to get laid by Danny O'Neill. Almost damn near stood in line. All this alternative shit going on. He was plugged in. He was seriously taken over by it."

"We had thirty cents a day to live on," O'Neill told Artie Romero in 1978, "but we were so high on what we were doing, it didn't matter." And what they were doing, he told Groth, "Was what everybody was doing. A lot

---

[56] Much of the Pirates' off-campus socializing centered around the shop of Errol Hendra, a red-bearded ex-merchant seaman from New Zealand. Hendra shot the photostats and negatives used for the offset printing of most of the psychedelic and comic art of the period. His place was wall-to-wall posters, with Hell's Angels, rock stars, UG cartoonists, dope dealers – and, sometimes, the Sheriff of San Francisco — hanging out in the darkroom, sitting on the water bed (itemized as a depreciable "water-storage facility" on Hendra's IRS returns), joking, bantering, smoking weed, playing out the dramas Hendra liked to set in motion like he was the ring-master of a bedlamite circus.

Hendra, who lived in a shabby neighborhood near the Mission, was known to carry large sums of cash. One evening, two men with ski masks and automatic rifles arrived to relieve him of it and other items of interest he was assumed to have on hand. Hendra tried to escape by shinnying down a drainpipe and fell three stories to the sidewalk, fracturing his spine. His last years were spent in hospitals and rest homes, calling for friends to spring him. But, as one says, "There was no place to spring him to."

of drugs, sleeping with everybody, breaking every taboo we would find."[57]
"I was amazed they got anything done," Turner said. "They had a lifestyle all their own." They had gone through Hallgren's hashish — and more — in O'Neill's term, "like squirrels. Smoking bad Mexican pot was nothing. It was just rev-o-lu-tion-ary, and you were cool. But it's no substitute for food, and we were all stretched out. Didn't have anything to eat. Didn't have anything to cook anything to eat." They were also doing their share of cocaine and assorted psychedelics. The result, O'Neill says, was that he, Hallgren and London were hospitalized from malnutrition and/or exhaustion.[58]

In O'Neill's case "exhaustion" was a euphemism. Divorced, broke, waiting for Disney's hammer to fall, constantly pumped on heavyweight, mind-altering drugs, he was, as Richards phrased it, "under a lot of pressure for a guy his age. He was a genius cartoonist but high-strung, and it was frightening to see someone you respected behaving like he was." At one point, enraged by something no one can recall, screaming "Bullshit! Bullshit!" he busted up the place with a baseball bat, clobbering drawing boards, tearing up copy, while the others looked on dumb-founded and terrified. A friend had to bring him to his beach house before he calmed.

Another time, he broke down more completely. After a fight with Richards, London told Ringgenberg, O'Neill hopped on his motorcycle and vanished.[59] Flenniken recalls the disappearance but does not say a fight contributed. She relates O'Neill tied a doll to her hair, informed her "This is what they did to Irish women. Hung their babies," and had to be hauled out of San Francisco Bay by the Coast Guard when he tried to swim to Ireland. The psychiatric ward only released him after another patient suggested he take up smoking and look normal.

---

[57] Most precise behavioral data on O'Neill has been lost to the shadows of time. I thought I was about to dredge up a barge-full when, at an art gallery opening where I was updating a friend on my work, a strikingly handsome, red-headed woman beside us exclaimed, "Dan O'Neill! Is he still alive? I dated him thirty years ago." She handed me a card. "Call me. I'll tell indiscreet stories."

The card came from the English and American Literature Department of a prestigious Ivy League university. The Internet identified my potential source as equally impressive in the feminist/gender/Derrida/Lacan racket. Great! I thought, if there is one thing my book lacks, it is Lacan. But when I phoned, her coals had cooled. While she'd "adored him to death" — he was "sweet," "charming," "a great storyteller" ("Dan's thoroughly Irish," she reminded me) — she had no facts to report, except how he was in bed, which, I am sure we all agree, has no place in a work of this nature.

[58] London says he was the only one hospitalized — with anemia and a 106-degree fever — because he was the only one working. Hallgren says he was never inside a hospital in San Francisco, except once for strep throat. "Maybe that's what O'Neill is thinking of." He adds, "If Dan was as organized in a business sense as in the confabulation department, we'd all be millionaires."

[59] In a revisionist mood, London now suspects O'Neill's disappearance entailed no more than shack-ing up with a girlfriend in North Beach.

One evening, smoking hash on the warehouse roof, the Pirates heard a sharp CRACK! — followed by a loud, deep bass rumble — from the northeast, where the Moscone Center now stands but which was then several bulldozed blocks of urban renewal-sculpted *faux*-Dresden. An earthquake big enough to levitate Chryslers had hurled an enormous wave of dust into the air. The wave — and the quake beneath it — were rolling directly at them. They had time to pass the bowl once and think, "Well, are we dead yet?" But the entire razed area was landfill. The future majestic Moscone Center sat on frigging jello, while their funky ex-firehouse lit on solid rock. The instant the wave seemed about to pluck out their hearts, it hit bedrock and crashed.

It was like... Like, maybe, they were being signaled that they grooved in this perfect, harmonized spot: observant of all; knowing about all; and immune from all. Or, maybe... Maybe, man, the instruct was that they... we... everyone was part of a wave and that some waves had not hit their rocks yet; but that all waves eventually would. That was the trouble with damn readings. You could never be sure which was on the money. The only thing you knew for sure of at any moment was the quality of that moment. Which was, in this case: "What a fucking rush!"

By November 1971, unable to pay rent, they were out of the warehouse. London and Flenniken, who would marry that New Year's Eve, moved to Abbey Street, near Mission Dolores. O'Neill and Hallgren took flats on Osgood Alley in North Beach. Richards ("Hey, I'd had a job where I wore a suit and tie. I knew how to rent an apartment") found a place with Murphy and Todd at 17th and Noe.

During the seven months the Air Pirates were together, Weathermen bombed a restroom inside the U.S. Capitol building, causing $300,000 worth of damage; Assistant Attorney General (now Supreme Court Chief Justice) William Rehnquist declared "qualified martial law" in Washington, D.C. as 12,000 anti-war demonstrators were arrested (the charges against most were later dropped); 190 Selective Service offices were ransacked; in one of 140 protest bombings, an Army research center at the University of Wisconsin was destroyed, resulting in one death and three injuries; the Pentagon Papers were released; thirty-one prisoners and nine hostages were killed by law-enforcement personnel following a four-day siege at Attica Prison; and George Jackson was shot dead trying to escape San Quentin, an attempt that left two other convicts and three guards with their throats slit.

In this period, the Air Pirates published 15-20,000 copies of two thirty-two-page issues of *Air Pirates Funnies,* cover-dated July and August 1971, retailing for fifty cents, and appearing about six weeks apart.[60] Both were identified

---

[60] London's *Dirty Duck* and *Merton of the Movement* and much of Richards's *Dopin' Dan* #1 and Hallgren's *Tortoise and the Hare* were also completed. None were released, however, until 1972, so their discussion will be deferred.

as publications of Hell Comics ("If you're looking for laughs, go to Hell"), whose logo mimicked Dell Comics, but the actual publisher was shrouded in secrecy. When the books appeared, the *Free Press* reported that they had been turned out by "some basement press in Los Angeles"; but, in truth, the Pirates had turned to the buccaneer-bearded, ex-j.c. football lineman and heavyweight wrestler, with a B.A. in psychology from Fresno State, who had been slipping them pork buns and checks.

Ron Turner had come to comics through radical politics. While in graduate school at San Francisco State, working with the Third World Liberation Front on the strike that virtually shut down the campus in 1968, he had met Rod Frieland, a printer who alternated paying jobs with free work for leftist groups. Frieland introduced Turner to the Berkeley Ecology Center — the nation's first — which was seeking to raise funds and people's awareness of ecological issues. Turner, who had been an UG fan since spending hours entranced by a single issue of *Zap* at a party while ripped, thought he had the vehicle. "Besides, I was sick of meetings. I said, 'Leave me alone, and I'll put out something that'll cut through all this shit and communicate with youth.'"

Turner bought his comics at Gary Arlington's store, which had developed into a veritable Mermaid Tavern for the UG, and Arlington introduced him to cartoonists eager to contribute to his new venture. Then, with funds put up by a supportive dope dealer and both Arlington and Don Donahue retained as "advisors" for $25 apiece, he was ready for business.

Last Gasp's first comic, *Slow Death*, with work by Crumb, Shelton and Kim Deitch, was published in time for Earth Day, April 22, 1970. Its second, *It Ain't Me, Babe*, featured Trina Robbins, Willie Mendes, and Michelle Brand in the first all-women's anthology and took up the feminist cause. Then came *Skull Comics*, a horror book (Turner had been an E.C. fan); *Slow Death* #2; and Crumb's *Mr. Natural*. By mid-1971, Last Gasp was a full-fledged, legally incorporated publishing company, operating out of Turner's garage on Tenth Street in Berkeley; and he was recruiting artists to do books.

Turner knew O'Neill from "Odd Bodkins" as "an inventive and brilliant political cartoonist — and very funny." The two met through the People's Nickelodeon Cinema, which put on a midnight show every Tuesday at the O'Farrell. Admission was five cents; and the show featured the Nicklettes, an eleven-women comedy troupe, most of whom worked at the theater, performing such numbers as "There's No Job Like a Blow Job." (Other entertainment included the comic Don Novello — pre-Father Guido Sarducci — the not-yet-famous Tubes, yo-yo contests, John Wayne serials, and experimental films from the San Francisco Art Institute.) The Nicklettes were modeled on the Cockettes, another San Francisco *outré* institution, a group of "gender-bending" men, women and babies who put on their own midnight musicals, like *Tinsel Tots in a Hot Coma* and became best known for their film *Tricia's Wedding* in which Ms. Nixon was portrayed by a transvestite — and their New York opening, about which Clive Barnes said in the *Times:* "Having no talent is not enough." Turner had published a Cockettes paper doll book, and O'Neill was involved with a Nicklette. Through such mutuality of interests, Turner learned O'Neill was planning a three-part comic book series featuring Mickey Mouse.[61]

Turner agreed to publish the books, paying for all three issues in advance. He wanted them out before Disney could gather itself to sue, and O'Neill promised to proceed with all due haste. However, desiring to keep alive the image of the Air Pirates as an incipient, independent publishing empire, he insisted that the fictitious "Hell" be identified as the publisher. Turner, happy to operate off-camera, agreed; and the Pirates promised never to reveal his contribution.

"I was happy I had a part to play," Turner now says. "They were very bright and very brave, putting their names on the line, not hiding a thing. It was a stark attack on the establishment at a time when it was important to show people they needn't fear taking on the powers that be."

Each issue of the Pirates' books was marked "Adults Only," an admonition somewhat subverted by the solicitation of "legal adults" to subscribe for younger relatives in order to provide them "classic comedy and artwork that's been suppressed for generations." As was customary with UGs, only the covers were in color. The first, by London, showed Mickey Mouse piloting an open-cockpitted, propellor-powered plane with two sacks labeled "Dope" tied to its fuselage. (The image had been lifted from the cover of a Big Little Book, *Mickey the Mail Pilot*, with the word "Dope" having replaced the original "Mail.") The second, by Hallgren, had Mickey and Minnie on horseback, hands raised, confronted by a bat-winged, green-cloaked figure with a revolver in his right hand and the "Dope" sacks in his left. The contents were generic UG: sex, drugs, and revolutionary politics. (The least of these was politics. In fact, #1's back cover instructed: "And always remember, kids, politics is pigshit.")

Hallgren contributed two pieces to the first issue: a one-page story where toddlers smoked pot amidst references to U.S. soldiers fighting in Laos, oil spills, and drug busts; and "Keyhole Komix,"a longer effort, in which Donald Duck and Goofy spy on Minnie Mouse in her bath. In the second, he put an eight-page spin on "The Tortoise and the Hare," a Disney Oscar-winning cartoon from 1934, which featured Nepalese temple ball (hashish)-engendered visions of a cast of hundreds singing the Bonzo Dog Band's "The Stork has Brought a Son and Daughter to Mr. & Mrs. Mickey Mouse." London had eighteen pages of Dirty Duck trying to get into Annie Rat's pants, spiced with

[61] This connection also brought O'Neill and his girlfriend to Turner's as housemates. The tenancy terminated when he came home to find one of their domestic squabbles had reduced his furniture to kindling.

allusions to S&M and unflattering references to both hippies and the police; and a one-pager on Merton of the Movement's adventures with five pounds of hashish. Richards had some Dopin' Dan strips — dope-smoking and the fragging of officers predominated — and a lengthier narrative about a Bud Fisher-ish Zeke Wolf, whose efforts to scarf down the Three Little Pigs[62] are interfered with when he is declared An Enemy of the People.

O'Neill out-wrote everyone in terms of page-count, breadth (and off-centeredness) of vision, and general offensiveness. His vehicles were two continuing stories. The first, "Silly Sympathies," a take-off on Disney's "Silly Symphonies" cartoons and comics, which were known for their "moral and ethical statement[s]," featured Bucky Bug, who is introduced "buggering" a pig. Run out of town, he immediately encounters June Bug with her "Crack of Doom." June blows Bucky. Bucky screws June. June takes off with Deadwood Dick ("the onliest man in the world with a left-handed prick"); and Bucky falls in with Lorna Jean, a centipede with fifty clitorises, each of which he is forced to satisfy. After he does, orally (she climaxes into a butterfly), Bucky wanders through a landscape riddled with demons, one of which is a skyscraper-tall, fanged and clawed, masturbating Mickey Mouse. Bucky then remonstrates with an assortment of planets and visions about the nature of Jesus's love. He rejects this love because you must be dead to receive it. He supports this belief by pointing out Jesus is against masturbation and "anybody who won't let a boy jackoff must have fatal intentions."

O'Neill's second story featured Mickey. His dilemma is earthier. "The whole world thinks I'm cute," he begins, "so why won't Minnie fuck me? Why won't Daisy fuck me? Why won't anybody fuck me?" The force of his lament is undercut four pages later when Minnie berates him for "that dose you and that dumb-fuck Daisy handed me! You dirty duckfucker!" Mickey and Minnie are kidnaped and held hostage in a dirigible controlled by his arch-enemies Sylvester Shyster, Black Pete, The Big Bad Wolf, and The Phantom Blot — the Air Pirates! After engaging in a mutually gratifying *soixante-neuf,* Mickey and Minnie are dumped overboard to be menaced in turn by a pterodactyl, King Kong, three crocodiles, a stampeding herd of elephants, and Don Jollio, The Latin Flash, who, at the second episode's end, has ordered them "to take these peels [from the cover's two bags] or die."

The Air Pirates had gone after Disney partly because of its reputation for striking back. But Disney had not obliged. So O'Neill gave copies of the books to a friend he had made at a dinner party given by the attorney Michael

[62] Disney's cartoon "The Three Little Pigs" not only won an Oscar in 1933 but its Depression-defying spirit, encapsulated in the tune "Who's Afraid of the Big Bad Wolf," made it so popular that it was billed over many features — and its run often outlasted theirs. It reportedly played in more theaters at the same time than any other film in history.

Kennedy for some clients at Narsai's restaurant in Kensington. (The guest list, as recalled by O'Neill, included Abbie Hoffman, Jerry Rubin, the Mitchell Brothers, and Paul Halvonik, a California appellate court judge busted for growing pot on his porch.)[63] The friend was "the gay son of the chairman of Disney's board of directors, [who was] kind of a remittance man running a book store in San Francisco." He smuggled the comics into a board meeting and laid them out around the table like notepads. "We called them out," O'Neill says, "I mean, why have a fight if no one comes."

[63] My recollection is that Halvonik's arrest didn't occur until years later. Insofar as he was an ACLU lawyer, I am sure it took Jerry Brown to put him on the bench, and Ronald Reagan was still governor in 1971. But O'Neill insists his account is accurate. "They got a big kick out of sitting me between this son of Disney and a judge."

Chapter Six:
For Every Little Head, a Cap of Mickey Mouse

For an outfit whose output couldn't keep it in mung weed, the Pirates' choice of opponents had it giving away significant weight. By 1970, Walt Disney Productions was grossing over $100,000,000 annually. Each year, 2,500,000 people saw one of its movies; over 100,000,000 watched its television shows; and close to 1,000,000,000 read its books and comics. It had won dozens of Oscars, several Emmies, and the French Legion of Honor. And in the United States alone, it had filed over 1700 lawsuits for infringements of its copyrights.

And by focusing on Mickey Mouse, the Air Pirates had attacked the company's symbolic heart and soul.

The story goes...

Walt Disney first dreamed of a cartoon mouse on a 1927 train ride back to Hollywood from New York, where his business partners had snookered him out of Oswald the Lucky Rabbit, his major creative and financial achievement to date. He chose a mouse, he later said, because he had made a pet of one that lived in his first studio.

"Mortimer Mouse," said Walt.

"Mickey," his wife Lillian replied.

Some skeptics, however, doubt the extent to which Disney sired Mickey out of thin air. Cultural archaeologists claim to have unearthed dolls whose date of origin is unknown but whose image is so similar to Mickey's that, it is argued, if they had appeared after he did, Disney would have sued the crap out of the manufacturer, which he didn't. Film historians believe Mickey's black face and white gloves were cribbed from Al Jolson in *The Jazz Singer*. Other folks say Mickey was the work of Ub Iwerks, Disney's brilliant chief animator, who filched the idea from a magazine cartoonist named Meeker. And still others say he was jointly created and was simply Oswald with shrunken ears and elongated tail.

Walt Disney, it should be noted, was Irish too.[64]

His father Elias's family had come to the United States from County Kilkenny. Elias grew up on a Kansas wheat and cattle farm and roamed the country as a machinist and carpenter before settling in Florida where, in 1888, he married Ella Call, a grammar school teacher. Elias ran a hotel (unsuccessfully) and grew oranges (also unsuccessfully). In 1899, with their first child, Herbert, they moved to Chicago, where Elias worked as a carpenter. They had three more sons, Raymond (1890), Roy (1893), Walt (1901), and a daughter, Ruth (1903). In April 1906, worried about the corrupting effects of big city life on their children, Elias and Ella moved to Marceline, Missouri, a town of 2500, one hundred miles from Kansas City.

They had a white, wood frame, one-story house, without electricity or plumbing but with forty-five acres. They farmed barley, corn, sorghum, wheat. They raised chickens, cows, pigs. The children had animals to play with, woods to romp in, a creek to swim. Marceline, in Walt's memory, was idyllic. He would never see a better America. He would not forget the one it formed within him. He made his first drawings there, some with coal on toilet paper, some in tar on the side of the house with sticks. But Elias did no better than he had with his hotel or oranges. He sold the farm and, in 1910, moved to Kansas City.

Though a convert to the universalist socialism of Eugene V. Debs, Elias Disney was a man who railed against the machinations of Hebraic bankers. A deacon of the fundamentalist Congregationalist Church (Ella was its organist), he also enjoyed playing the fiddle and saloons. He was so tight-fisted he would ban his family from buttering its bread, but his wallet could not resist a deck of cards. He forcefully impressed the importance of his not terribly consistent beliefs upon his children with a leather strap. And despite his own life's lack of material rewards, he swore by the virtues of hard work. In Kansas City, he purchased the right to deliver newspapers, morning and night, through rain and wind and several feet of snow, to a thousand subscribers. Herb and Ray had already left home because they could not tolerate their father's demands and beatings — and Roy would flee two years later — but Walt, from the age of eight, was up at 3:30, working routes without pay.

Walt was a mediocre student and not much of an athlete. But he was enthralled by the stories of Mark Twain, Horatio Alger, and Charles Dickens; and he continued to draw. While still in elementary school, he was swapping caricatures to his barber for haircuts. After Elias gave up the delivery business for the

[64] Ms. Disney's credit is also disputed. Some reporters state a distributor nixed the name Mortimer as non-commercial, and Bill Blackbeard has pointed out a Mickey and Minnie Mouse (mother and son) appeared in children's stories in *Good Housekeeping* in the early 1920s.

prospects of owning the O-Zell jelly factory — he would be unsuccessful — he moved the family back to Chicago, where Walt drew cartoons for his high school magazine. He had taken courses at the Kansas City Art Institute, and he took others through the mail. And he continued to work: delivery boy; janitor; candy butcher; handyman; security guard; mailman; clerk. Then, in 1918, not yet seventeen, he quit school and volunteered for World War I as an ambulance driver.

He arrived in Paris a month after the Armistice. He was there less than a year. He failed to meet Picasso, Stein or Joyce; but he drew posters for the canteen, decorated the canvas tops on ambulances, and picked up ten francs apiece for the Croix de Guerre he painted on the jackets of other servicemen and the camouflage coloration he added to German helmets, through which someone else had fired a strategically aimed bullet so they could be sold as coming from authentic (dead) snipers.

Walt returned to Kansas City. Unable to find work as a political cartoonist, he landed a job at an agency doing ads for farm equipment manufacturers and department stores. Let go because of a lack of work, he opened his own shop, then quit that to join a company that made one-minute, animated advertising films. The new medium fascinated him. He studied it on his own and soon began a new company, Laugh-O-Gram Films. He made cartoons based on fairy tales ("Puss 'n Boots," "Little Red Riding Hood"), filmed babies and newsreel segments, turned out a short on dental health, and began a series featuring a real six-year-old in a cartoon setting ("Alice in Wonderland"). But by 1923, while the '20s were roaring, with chickens about to roost in every pot, he was bankrupt. He sold his camera and, with two changes of underwear and socks and one clean shirt, set out for Hollywood.

Establishing a studio in his Uncle Robert's garage, Walt obtained an order for a series of "Alice" shorts from a distributor in New York. He convinced his brother Roy, who was recuperating from tuberculosis in a nearby VA hospital, to become his partner, inaugurating a relationship — Walt dreaming up projects and Roy figuring out how to pay for them — that would last forty years. Disney Brothers Studio borrowed $500 from Uncle Robert and moved into the back room of a real estate office for ten dollars a month. From there, they expanded into a small store and, in early 1926, onto their own lot. (At this point, Walt decided to change the company name to the Walt Disney Studio because, he explained, it sounded better.)[65] After several more "Alice" films, at the urging of a producer who wanted to compete with Felix the Cat, Walt came up with Oswald who, in such fare as "The Mechanical Cow" and "The Ol' Swimming 'Ole," became enough of a hit to make others plot to steal him. The brothers also found time to marry: Roy, in April 1925, to Edna Francis, whom he had known in Kansas City; and Walt, two months later, to Lillian Bounds,

[65] Other commentators believe the motivation to have been ambition, jealousy or the thirst for self-promotion.

who worked at the studio as an inker. Both marriages were for life and — particularly by movie-industry standards — trouble free.

Through all that being a struggling film maker entailed — unseemly hustling, shoestring budgets, banal work, meager profits, total failures — not even the most hostile Disney biographer suggests that he did not constantly work hard, that he did not continually seek to stretch his art's existing boundaries, that he ever doubted his inner worth or its eventual payoff. It was as if he had taken the readings of his childhood as manuals for success. As if he had seen in his small town roots, his childhood deprivations and abuses, his unflagging strivings precisely what he had read in Twain and Dickens and Alger, and believed he was guaranteed the same rewards as had been bestowed upon their heroes.

Mickey Mouse debuted May 15, 1928, in "Plane Crazy." The cartoon, an attempt to capitalize on the public's fascination with Charles Lindbergh's solo trans-Atlantic flight, introduced Mickey as a daredevil pilot who tried to frighten Minnie into kissing him with a series of aerial stunts. (She escaped by jumping, using her underwear as a risqué parachute.) "The Gallopin' Gaucho," which emphasized Mickey's swashbuckling side, followed. Then, November 18, "Steamboat Willie," the first animated cartoon with sound, opened at New York City's Colony Theater.

It was a smash. More Mickey cartoons followed — over one a month at their peak. Within ten years, in Disney biographer Bob Thomas's words, "Mickey Mouse was known in every civilized country in the world." His 1500 fan clubs in the United States enrolled over 1,000,000 members, more than the Boy and Girl Scouts combined — and England had another 400,000. (Members were expected to be fair, honest, helpful, obedient, morally upright, and law-abiding.) His comic strip was translated into twenty-seven languages. Mary Pickford proclaimed him her favorite actor. Charlie Chaplin and Douglas Fairbanks were photographed with him. (Mickey received 800,000 fan letters a year, more than anyone else in Hollywood.) Madame Tussaud installed his effigy in her Wax Museum. He merited entries in *Who's Who in America* and *The Encyclopedia Britannica*. His fans included Franklin Delano Roosevelt, the King of England (who wouldn't go to the movies unless Mickey was on the bill), and Mussolini. He was the second most popular figure in Japan after the Emperor. (Hitler banned Mickey, however, and Stalin condemned him as a capitalist and war-monger.) In Africa, his picture on a bar of soap was known to ward off evil spirits. In 1935, the League of Nations awarded him a gold medal as an International Symbol of Good Will. At the 1939 New York World's Fair, a Mickey Mouse cup was placed within the time capsule to be left for future civilizations as representative of what was noteworthy about our own.

"There was no character in the movies more American than Mickey Mouse," Richard Schickel wrote in *The Disney Version*. His carefully nurtured image was of a good-natured, humble, regular guy who, when trouble came, would prove himself loyal, brave, and heroic, sort of a peppier — and shorter

— Gary Cooper. He was a cowboy, fireman, frontiersman, football star, jockey, boxer, big game hunter, whaler, Secret Serviceman. Against great odds, he saved the girl; he saved the town; he thwarted the enemies of good. Disney so identified with his creation he was his voice in all his cartoons until the 1947 featurette, "Mickey and the Beanstalk." Thomas says, "Both Walt and Mickey had an adventurous spirit, a sense of rectitude, an admitted lack of sophistication, a boyish ambition to excel. Both were unashamedly devoted to the ideals of Horatio Alger... [and] clung to the old-fashioned notion of remaining steadfast to one's sweetheart."

Mickey also made his creator a lot of money. Oswald had had a chocolate-coated, marshmallow candy bar named after him; but the Disneys, happy for the publicity, did not even think to ask for a fee. Then, a manufacturer of school tablets offered $300 to put Mickey on his product. A few months later, the brothers signed a licensing agreement with a promoter who would line up products for Mickey to endorse — and pay them a royalty on every item he sold. Well, Mickey sold plenty. He sold over 10,000,000 ice cream cones. He sold 2,250,000 watches in one year. He sold 250,000 electric trains. *The Mickey Mouse Book,* sixteen pages long and written by an eleven-year-old girl, sold 100,000 copies its first year in print. Mickey sold balloons, baseball gloves, bibs, biscuits, blackboards, bottles, and briefcases. He sold everything from radiator caps to diamond bracelets to milk of magnesia. At some trade shows, forty percent of the merchandise was Mickey-related. He was licensed by seventy-five companies in the United States, forty-five in England, and twenty in Canada. By the mid-'30s, he was endorsing several hundred products and bringing in $20,000,000 a year.

Mickey's success did not go unnoticed. Shortly after he first demonstrated his popularity, a rival cartoon producer decided to develop his own mouse. The Disneys sued. They were not particularly interested in recovering monetary damages, but they wanted to establish their copyright's strength and scope. They possessed a valuable property; they hoped to possess others; and they knew that, all over the world, people would try to steal a piece of their action. They could not stop every thief, but they could make a head-busting, knee-capping defense of their creations a basic part of their company's creed. They especially welcomed cases that would generate publicity and make them look ferocious and cold-hearted, for those cases would scare others off from even thinking about taking them on.

The Disney company had followed Mickey's success with the "Silly Symphonies," a series of more experimental cartoons, some of which were original creations written around pre-existing musical scores ("The Skeleton Dance," "Monkey Melodies") and others which were adaptations of folk tales, myths, nursery rhymes, children's stories, and fables ("King Neptune," "Old King Cole," "The Ugly Duckling," "The Grasshopper and the Ant"). In 1932, one of these, "Flowers and Trees," the first all-color cartoon, won Disney its first Oscar.

(Mickey received a special Oscar the same year.) Over the next few years, Disney added Goofy, Pluto, and Donald Duck to its stable of stars, turning out dozens of cartoons a year.[66] Then, in 1937, with *Snow White,* the first animated feature-length film, it elevated its chosen art form to new levels of complexity and brilliance. By 1942, with *Pinocchio, Fantasia, Dumbo,* and *Bambi,* it had demonstrated a mastery of characterization, emotional depth, and technological virtuosity in animated works that was without equal.

Walt Disney had now established a unique place for himself within American society. His work was praised by Mark Van Doren, Sergei Eisenstein, Jerome Kern, Ernie Pyle, Gilbert Seldes, Arturo Toscanini. It was lauded in *American Scholar, Art Digest, Theatre Arts.* It was exhibited at the Los Angeles County Museum, the Metropolitan Museum of Modern Art, the Philadelphia Art Alliance, the Chicago Art Institute. It won thirteen Oscars in ten years. Disney, himself, won awards from *Parents* magazine for distinguished service to children and the Junior Chamber of Commerce for his valuable contribution to the country. He was on the cover of *Time* and profiled in *The New Yorker.* He received honorary degrees from Harvard, Yale and USC. He had a private meeting with the Pope. He was compared to Aesop, Homer, Hans Christian Andersen, Leonardo da Vinci, and Saint Francis — and simultaneously portrayed as a simple, hardworking, average guy, a good businessman and stellar representative of the American way of life.

Walt Disney also possessed strong personal and political beliefs, some of which were directly reflected in his work — and some inferentially. He loudly proclaimed a commitment to wholesome, family-oriented entertainment. The public should know, he believed, that it could see a Disney film without being offended or shocked.[67] He tried to make his employees representative of these values. He banned drinking on studio property and forbade the use of foul language around women. He tried to keep the men and women on his payroll from socializing together in order to prevent scandals that might sully the company name. He was even uncomfortable about having nude models pose for his artists' life drawing classes. And when some animators surprised him at his thirty-fifth birthday party with a specially made clip of Mickey and Minnie making the sign of the two-backed beast, he fired them.

---

[66] Mickey Mouse had become such a role model that parents complained if his behavior was less than perfect, and Walt Disney had realized he needed characters who could be foolish and clumsy and fly off the handle outrageously in order to create cartoons of interest. The decision was good for business, but Mickey's film career never recovered.

[67] When some of Disney's early cartoons were attacked by conservative religious groups for their bawdy, barnyard humor, he had quickly eliminated the objectionable chamber pots and outhouses from his future work — and covered Clarabelle Cow's udder with a skirt.

Disney possessed the gentleman's quota of anti-Semitic, homophobic, racist views common to WASP males of his era.[68] His politics, however, were more extreme than most. In 1934, he had forced his employees to contribute funds to defeat the Democrat-Socialist Upton Sinclair's gubernatorial campaign which had been built around the ominous slogan "End Poverty in California." When labor organizers tried to unionize his company, he resisted with strike breakers, alliances with racketeers, minor acts of violence, and wild charges of Communist influence. Marc Eliot, the nastiest of Disney's biographers, even tars him as an FBI informant, American Firster and attendee at American Nazi Party meetings and rallies.

Disney was also an ardent patriot. In August 1941, he made a State Department-sponsored tour of South America to strengthen those countries' political, economic and cultural ties to the United States. During World War II, he geared his company's output to support the war effort. He turned out military training films on chemical warfare and VD prevention. He admonished civilians to pay their taxes and save kitchen fats for use in explosives. He showed Donald, Goofy and Pluto at war with the Axis. His characters adorned warplanes and over 1200 pieces of military insignia. On his own initiative, he turned out the feature film *Victory through Air Power*, which argued for the long-range bombing of major population centers.

As the war came to an end, as vice-president of the Motion Picture Alliance for the Preservation of Ideals, Disney encouraged the House Un-American Activities Committee to investigate the influence of Communists in Hollywood. After the war, when HUAC held hearings, he testified as a "friendly" witness. He and Roy contributed generously to the political campaigns of Richard Nixon and other fervent anti-Communists and were consistent supporters of right-wing causes and conservative Republican political candidates like George Murphy and Ronald Reagan.

In the post-war years, Disney expanded the scope of his company's output — and increased its cultural influence. With *So Dear to My Heart*,[69] *Treasure Island*, *Robin Hood*, and *20,000 Leagues under the Sea*, it entered the realm of live-action feature films. With "Seal Island," "Beaver Valley," "The Living Desert," and "The Vanishing Prairie," it pioneered a series of remarkable "true-life" nature shorts. To its backlog of animated features, each of

[68] In fairness, it should be noted that few Jews and blacks were crazy about WASPs or, for that matter, each other; and absolutely no one was buddy-buddy with gays.

[69] This story — adapted from the novel *Midnight and Jeremiah* by that old comic book basher, Sterling North — of a turn-of-the-century, Kansas farm boy's love for his pet lamb, complete with Bible-reading grandmother and wild dog-infested swamp, was a major throat-lumper. I saw it four times. With *The Monty Stratton Story*, it topped my list of favorite movies of all time — the times being limited to the first ten years of my life.

which was re-released every seven years to appeal to a new generation of children, it added *Cinderella, Alice in Wonderland,* and *Peter Pan.*[70]

If you were a child growing up in these years, the Disney presence was formidable. The release of each new film was a major event. You rushed — or were rushed by your parents — to it. The Disney name conveyed a set of qualities that compelled attendance. Its pictures would be well-crafted, morally instructive, non-nightmare producing fare, unlike attractions you might gravitate toward if left to your own devices. Disney afforded mothers and fathers a way to demonstrate their certifiable "good parenting" qualities, sometimes at the cost of other values. (I still remember, for instance, my mother dragging me across Chestnut Street, in downtown Philadelphia, through three lanes of mid-block traffic, so that we would not miss the start of some Disney picture, just after my first-grade teacher had instructed us to cross only at corners on the green. I do not remember which picture, but I do that passage.)

By 1954, Disney films had been dubbed into fourteen languages and seen by a billion people. It had sold 30,000,000 comic books and $750,000,000 worth of merchandise — nearly 3000 items, manufactured by over 700 companies — worldwide.

And its influence was about to expand geometrically.

Disney had ventured into television with Christmas specials in 1950 and 1951. Then, on Wednesday, October 27, 1954, *Disneyland,* a one-hour, weekly show premiered on ABC. (Retitled *Walt Disney Presents,* it switched to Friday nights in 1958 and, in 1961, as *Walt Disney's Wonderful World of Color,* moved to NBC, whose Sunday evening line-up it anchored for nearly twenty years.) In every incarnation, it showed Disney cartoons, Disney nature films, portions of Disney features, and publicized future Disney productions.

Other motion picture studios had shunned television because of its threat as a competitor, but Disney recognized its ability to revive interest in his company's past creations and spark interest in its new ones. That this spark could be fanned into a conflagration was demonstrated by a series the show ran its initial season about the Tennessee frontiersman, congressman, and Alamo fatality, Davy Crockett. This squeakily-cleaned version of his life story made a star of its previously unknown lead, Fess Parker. It sold 7,000,000 copies of its theme song, "The Ballad of Davy Crockett," which, recorded by Bill Hayes, Burl Ives, Tennessee Ernie Ford, and Mitch Miller, among others, topped the Hit Parade for thirteen weeks. And it sold 10,000,000 replicas of

---

[70] During this period Disney also released the animated-live action hybrid *Song of the South,* an adaptation of Joel Chandler Harris's Uncle Remus stories. It won an Oscar for the song "Zip-a-dee-doo-dah" but was criticized for its "happy-colored-folks-on-the-plantation" attitude. Criticism intensified each time the film was re-released, so Disney agreed to stop showing it. It did — in the United States — but continued distribution abroad.

Crockett's coonskin cap. (The cap was so profitable that Disney threatened to sue manufacturers who produced similar ones without its permission.) Then, re-cut and released the following year as a feature film, it made another $2,500,000. (Davy had demonstrated such legs, Disney brought him back from the dead the year after that, teamed with the entirely fictitious Mike Fink, in the feature *Davy Crockett and the River Pirates*.)

Disney hosted *Disneyland* in his most genial, most comforting, most trustworthy, "Uncle Walt" manner. The show was so popular, so highly regarded, and so warmly received that corporate America lined up to sponsor it. Through it, the Disney name was quickly — and profitably — linked with American Motors, Coca-Cola, DuPont, Eastman Kodak, Portland Cement, RCA, Sears... (Because of Disney's concern for his company's image, however, he refused to accept advertisements for cigarettes or beer.)

Disney's other significant television presence, *The Mickey Mouse Club*, debuted October 3, 1956. It ran every weekday, from 5:00 to 6:00 p.m., for four years, before going into a syndicated half-hour version for another three. The host was Jimmy Dodd, an ex-B movie performer, who was president of The Hollywood Christian Group. His sidekick, Roy Williams, was a jovial, overweight cartoonist plucked from Disney's animation department. But the real stars were the Mouseketeers, two dozen bubbly, straight-arrow (they could be fired for saying "Hell" or "Damn"),[71] teen and pre-teen boys and girls, representatives of all to which Disney believed American youth should aspire.

The show mixed songs, dances, comic skits, Disney cartoons, Disney serials (*Spin and Marty*, *The Hardy Boys*), reports on children around the world, and instruction on safety, hygiene, and good citizenship. Viewers were taught to be well-groomed, well-mannered, and respectful of parents and other representatives of authority. They were taught the F.B.I. was our friend and rock'n'roll an evil to be shunned. At its peak, it had an audience of 12,000,000 children and 7,000,000 adults. It commanded seventy-five percent of its time period's viewing audience — and it sold 25,000,000 sixty-nine-cent Mickey Mouse-eared Mouseketeer caps.

For Disney's third major cultural contribution of this period, he converted 160 acres of Anaheim orange groves into Disneyland.

Its opening, July 17, 1955, was televised live in a two-hour special. Robert Cummings, Art Linkletter (who received a ten-year concession to sell film and cameras on the grounds as his fee), and Ronald Reagan hosted. Frank Sinatra, Sammy Davis, Jr., Lana Turner, Roy Rogers and Dale Evans,

---

[71] When Annette Funicello — the Mouseketeer with breasts — co-starred with Frankie Avalon in the *Beach Party* pictures of the mid-1960s, her still-binding contract with Disney forbade her to appear in anything racier than a one-piece bathing suit.

and Eddie Fisher and Debbie Reynolds attended. The Pledge of Allegiance was recited, "The Star-Spangled Banner" sung, a Protestant prayer delivered. Air Force jets soared overhead. United States Marines led a parade down Main Street, the five-eighths scale recreation of the heart of a turn-of-the-century town which marked the entrance to the park.[72]

Within two months, Disneyland, with its component parts, Adventureland, Fantasyland, Frontierland, and Tomorrowland, had drawn 1,000,000 visitors. By 1960, its attendance exceeded 5,000,000 a year. It was the most popular tourist attraction in the western United States. Former President Truman, the King of Belgium, the King of Morocco, King Hussein of Jordan, the Kings and Queens of Thailand and Nepal, Prime Ministers Smuts of South Africa, Nehru of India, King of Canada, and Nkrumah of Ghana, and the Nizram of Hyderabad visited. Henry Kissinger used to come to escape the stresses of being National Security advisor at the Nixon White House. (Wearing a Disneyland coat, he would answer the questions of tourists and sometimes sell popcorn.) Nikita Khruschev had a tantrum when told, because of security reasons, he could not attend.[73]

The predominant feature of Disneyland was how unlike a traditional amusement park it was. (Disney, who had been planning something like this for twenty years, had visited amusement parks, carnivals, circuses, and fairs throughout the United States and Europe, teasing out what he wanted from what he did not.) It was immaculate. Alcohol was banned. A hefty admission fee discouraged undesirable elements. The park's employees, disproportionately blue-eyed, blonde, Southern California cheerleader/athlete types[74] labored under a strict dress code: no beards, mustaches, or collar-length hair for men; no bouffant hairdos, nail polish, heavy makeup or perfume for the women; shined shoes for all. (During the '60s, some boys hid their true coiffures with

[72] One anti-Disney slur, reported to me by a fellow in the locker room at my health club, that he barred Charlie Chaplin's films from the Main Street Cinema because he deplored his politics, is denied by Mark Koenig, Disneyland expert, whose *Mouse Tales* informs much of this section. "Chaplin shorts," he says, "ran until the theater went to all Mickey Mouse cartoons about fifteen years ago."

[73] In August 1955, the Herbert Levins of West Philadelphia also arrived. Coming out of a simulated rocket ship flight, they were confronted by a free-ranging Richard Nixon. Before their terrified Stevensonian-Democrat parents could snatch them to safety, their two young sons had their programs blatantly autographed.

[74] Through the late '60s, Disneyland restricted its racial minority-employees to positions which had minimal public contact. It only hired its first black craftsworker (out of 400) in 1966. He was then subjected to racially offensive remarks and discriminated against in job assignments and promotions. When he filed a discrimination complaint, he was fired, eventually winning reinstatement and a $100,000 award in federal court.

short-hair wigs; and the girls were subject to investigative pats-on-the-back to make sure they wore brassieres.)

Once again, corporate America rushed to associate itself. Sixty-five major companies, including Kaiser Aluminum, Monsanto, Richfield Oil, TWA, and the Bank of America, signed on to sponsor exhibits, concessions and restaurants.

Walt Disney now occupied a place in American society like no filmmaker before or since. Within one three-year period, he was on the covers of *Look, Newsweek, The Saturday Evening Post, TV Guide, National Geographic*. He made guest appearances on *Talk of the Town* and *The Jack Benny Show*. He oversaw the increase of his company's gross income from $6,000,000 in 1950 to $70,000,000 in 1960 — and its amassing of $80,000,000 in assets. That year, the Beverly Hills B'nai Brith named him Man of the Year. In 1963, former President Eisenhower presented him with the Freedom Foundation's George Washington Award for his promotion of the American way of life. In 1964, the same year that Disney released *Mary Poppins*, which received thirteen Oscar nominations and won five, making it the studio's most honored film, President Johnson gave him the Medal of Freedom, the country's highest non-military honor. (Disney accepted while wearing a Goldwater button.) He had become, Steven Watts wrote, "a revered national monument, an example of American achievement, a trusted guardian of the nation's children, and a representative of average citizens and their values, beliefs, and desires."

The Disney company continued to churn out feature-length movies, almost all of them profitable and almost all of them insignificant. I have before me an incomplete list of over twenty released between 1956 and 1964: historical dramas; tales of the American past; adaptations of children's classics; situation comedies; some my memory can not classify. *Westward Ho the Wagons, Johnny Tremaine, Old Yeller, The Shaggy Dog, Son of Flubber, Greyfriars Bobby, Savage Sam, That Darned Cat, Moonspinners, Those Callaways,* and *The Parent Trap*, starring Hayley Mills. (She wasn't allowed to smoke or drink while under contract to Disney.) As a child, I had been as much a Disney fan as anyone. I had rushed to new releases, planted before the television, stocked up on comic books and ephemera — I mean, I had defied traffic on Chestnut Street — but in all those years, of all those movies, I saw none — and no one I knew ever mentioned they saw any either.

At some point, every kid, if you were a kid like the kids I knew — despite Disney's repeated claim that he made movies for families, not children — left Disney behind. Around the age of twelve or thirteen, you relegated him to younger brothers and younger sisters and the little kids on the block. As you whittled away what you felt you would not need from the safe, the tidy, the layers of the family-approved in order to formulate the identity you would carry into the world, you stuck it to Disney hard.[75] We might have left it at that — and welcomed him back when it became time to acculturate our own children — had not the hugeness of his presence intermingled him irrevocably — and passionately — with the upheavals that were soon upon us.

There was already a body of anti-Disney thought. In the 1940s, James Agee had attacked his corruption of the American folk legacy in *The Nation*, and Manny Farber had called him shallow and saccharine in *The New Republic*. When Max Rafferty, California's reactionary Superintendent of Public Instruction (and future Republican Senatorial candidate), championed Disney as the greatest educator of the century for his "decency" in the face of a beatnik-pornographer-degenerate cabal that would otherwise run roughshod over *die Kinder,* Frances Clark Sayers, a former director of children's services for the New York Public Library, spoke up for the minority by responding that Disney's mutilation of literature had, in fact, cost children a great deal.[76]

The anti-Disney line essentially ran that his fairy tales presented a falsely neat, dishonestly orderly, over-sentimentalized view of life. His domestic history omitted slavery, Jim Crow, child labor, women being denied the vote, and, God knows, what we did to the Indians. The morally complex, the socially disturbing was as absent from his work as hot dog wrappers and beer bottles from his park. His Pinocchio did not crush Jiminy Cricket, as did Carlo Collodi's original.[77] Cinderella's stepmother was not forced to dance herself to death in red-hot iron boots, as she was by the Brothers Grimm. "Sex and death," one writer put it, "longing and sorrow, ecstasy and grief, time and change held no sway in the world of Disney."

The art historian David Kunzle called Disney, not admiringly, "the century's most important figure in bourgeois popular culture. He has done more than any single person to disseminate around the world certain myths upon which that culture has thrived." Richard Schickel noted that, by focusing on children, Disney "placed a Mickey Mouse hat on every little developing personality... (forcing them) to share the same formative dreams." And those myths and dreams, which promoted the early twentieth

---

[75] While researching this book, I was more than a trifle embarrassed to learn that "Davy Crockett" had not come along in 1952 where my memory had placed it. His actual dates of screening meant I was already in the seventh grade while craving one of his stupid hats. Only a few months later, having digested *Blackboard Jungle* and *The Wild One*, I was wheedling, instead, for a motorcycle jacket.

[76] Sayers had also weighed in on the earlier debate about comic books, which, she said, "reduce everything to the lowest common denominator of violence, vulgarity and commonplace expression."

[77] Collodi's heirs were so upset with Disney's changes in the story they sued — unsuccessfully.

century, small town, Midwestern values that had formed Disney, were implicated in everything the now burgeoning counterculture was fighting.[78]

By the mid-'60s, Disney had been drawn fully into the struggle. "A growing oppositional culture of leftist intellectuals and students," Steven Watts wrote, "held up Disney's work as illustrative of the barriers that impeded the wholesale reform of American values — unquestioning patriotism, bourgeois moral nostrums, gauche middle-class taste, racist elitism, corporate profit-mongering, bland standards of social conformity. A silent majority of more conservative citizens, however, closed ranks around the Disney legacy as part of a defense of traditional American opportunity, entrepreneurialism, patriotism, middle-class decency and moral uplift."

The counterculture's first strike against Disney occurred shortly after Walt Disney's death in 1966, when Paul Krassner, who would become one of the founders of the Youth International Party, better known as the Yippies, but was then a one-man assault unit as editor of the savagely satirical, virulently anti-establishment *Realist* (I mean, there was nothing fucking like it), decided to "demystify" the entire Disney *oeuvre* and "signify the crumbling of an empire."[79] "Disney's characters were taken so seriously," he says. "They were spokesfigures for this entire system of stifling, arbitrary rules. I thought that, with Disney, the creator of these repressed characters, dead, it was time they went on a binge."

Krassner solicited the help of Wally Wood, the ex-E.C. great, whom he had met when he had sold a story idea to *MAD*, and Wood delivered "a magnificently degenerate montage." His "Walt Disney Memorial Orgy" showed Mickey shooting up, Goofy screwing Minnie, the Seven Dwarfs having their way with Snow White. Krassner ran it as a centerfold spread in his May 1967 issue, where it finished second in notoriety to Jacqueline Kennedy's alleged account of Lyndon Johnson fucking her husband's corpse through the throat on Air Force One's flight back from Dallas.

Krassner also released "Orgy" in poster form. The Disney organization ignored these defamations because, he says, it knew he was judgment-proof and didn't want to give him free publicity. But when the poster didn't disappear but

---

[78] Even Mickey Mouse had his critics. Ariel Dorfman and Armand Mattelhart, in *How to Read Donald Duck*, first published in Chile in mid-1971, about the time the Air Pirates were issuing their *Funnies*, wrote of him: "He is at once law and big stick, church lottery and intelligence agent... Through [him]... the power of repression dissolves into a daily fact of life."

[79] O'Neill says he and Krassner also started the rumor that Disney had been frozen through cryonic suspension, though they knew this was untrue because an actor friend had been working at Forest Lawn Cemetery when the corpse arrived. "So the ambulance leaves our buddy with this dead Walt Disney, and he figures, 'What the hell.' He sits him up, does his act; and then he puts on his resume 'Auditioned for Walt Disney' and gets the next part he's up for." Krassner admits to publishing the canard but doesn't think he did more than pass it along.

began appearing on dorm room and crash pad walls in a colorized, bootleg edition, Disney sued its publisher, a San Franciscan named Sam Ridge, and forced him out of business. (Ridge had graciously copyrighted the poster in Krassner's name — spelled incorrectly — but passed along no royalties to him.)[80]

Three years later, the counterculture stormed the Magic Kingdom itself.

Situated in Orange County, where, as my friend, the Kabbalist scholar-retired librarian Menchy Kauffman, who was in school nearby at the time, puts it, "The biggest ethnic group was Merle Haggard and his friends," Disneyland had never been particularly deviance-friendly. Blacks and Hispanics kept away. Anyone with long hair and smelling of patchouli oil was hassled going in, coming out, and passing through.[81] The park's dress and grooming policies had already been the target of picketing. ("Disney is Mickey Mouse About Haircuts" and "Jesus Isn't Allowed into Disneyland," placards protested.) Then, after a night of drugged brainstorming in the summer of 1970, Yippie leaders decided it would be an ideal site to commemorate the twenty-fifth anniversary of the bombing of Hiroshima.

One hundred thousand flyers went out. Posters sprang up on street corners and invitations in the underground press. They pictured Mickey Mouse with an AK-47 and promised "free love, free dope and free fun."[82] They offered the chance to strike back at corporate backers of the war. To liberate Minnie Mouse. To barbecue Porky Pig. (Wrong corporate, running-dog lackey there — he was with Warner Brothers.) And to have a "Black Panther Hot Breakfast at Aunt Jemima's Pancake House."

The Disney security staff, expecting 20,000 invaders, called in support from local police agencies and the National Guard. Anywhere from a few hundred to several thousand — estimates vary — fun-love-and-dope-seekers showed. Scattering into small packs, they roamed the park. They marched down Main Street, chanting "Free Charles Manson." They interrupted the Disneyland band with chants of "Ho! Ho! Ho Chi Minh. N.L.F. is gonna win."[83] (More patriotic

[80] Unable to learn through normal investigative procedures who was behind the poster, Disney opened its own bogus head shop in the white bread suburb of Glendale, hoping to entice the culprit into revealing himself. The effort was successful — but not before local protectors of civic decency, outraged by the emporium's presence, fire-bombed it.

[81] Koenig denies that Disneyland banned men with long hair and beards, but I came across newspaper stories from the fall of 1970 that it had only recently "relaxed... [a] longstanding ban on long-hairs," granting admission to anyone so long as they were shod and shirted.

[82] The same year, an issue of the *Seed* with a full-color Mickey on the cover, wearing a Richard Nixon watch, sold a record 38,000 copies in two days.

[83] Koenig reports the chant as "Ho! Ho! Ho-Chi-Minh is gonna win." Since neither of us were there, I'm going with what I recall from demonstrations of my youth. I refuse to believe the Anaheim Few-Hundred-to-Several-Thousand were as rhythmically-challenged as he has them.

customers riposted with "God Bless America.") They scaled the mast of the Chicken of the Sea Pirate Ship. They flew the New Nations flag (a marijuana leaf and red star) from City Hall. They hung a Viet Cong flag on Wilderness Fort. They took rafts to Tom Sawyer's Island, "liberated" it, and smoked dope in Indian Village.

The Park was ordered evacuated. Parents grabbed their children and fled. One hundred fifty policemen in full riot gear — helmets, visors, flak jackets, and batons, with a helicopter providing aerial support and another 150 police in reserve — moved in. Fights broke out. Fires were set; cherry bombs exploded; flower beds destroyed. No one was seriously injured; but twenty-three people were arrested on charges of assault and battery, possession of marijuana, disturbing the peace, malicious mischief, inciting to riot. The park was closed early for only the second time in its history — the first being the day John Kennedy was assassinated. Thirty thousand patrons received free passes for a future visit.

And Disneyland adopted new admission standards. No specific hair length was required of visitors, though words were uttered to the effect that not much more than crew cuts would be tolerated. Each individual was to be judged by his own "attire and attitude" and nothing "unorthodox" permitted. As a Disneyland representative put it, channeling homeroom teachers everywhere, "We went out of our way to show that two widely differing groups could have fun together, and a couple hundred spoiled it for everyone."

A final Disney-counterculture clash centered around the California Institute for the Arts. Cal Arts — or CIA — was a dream of Walt Disney's, which Roy Disney strove to bring to fruition after his brother's death. It opened in September 1970 on thirty-eight acres Walt had donated from land he owned north of the San Fernando Valley and funded with $25,000,000 — or $40,000,000, accounts vary — from his estate. The school acquired two financially troubled institutions, the Chouinard Art Institute (where Disney had sent its artists for training) and the Los Angeles Conservatory of Music, added other disciplines, and sought to provide practical, hands-on, non-egghead-tainted, interdisciplinary education for students of the creative arts. But creative students in California in 1970 behaved differently than their grandparents had in Marceline and Kansas City and Chicago.

Political protests rocked the campus. Dope smoking was rampant. Bandana-sporting hippie-dogs roamed the grounds. Students showed their rejection of the concept of private property by "liberating" cameras, electronic equipment, tape recorders, and pianos. Things came to a head when the school pool became a center for co-ed, nude swimming. At a board of directors meeting to address the issue, a photography professor punctuated his argument on behalf of the beauty of the human body by disrobing. Roy Disney became so irate he canceled his own planned bequest. According to Bob Thomas, the visual aid had cost the campus, one wit quipped, "about $30 million-an-inch."

Roy later tried to get Pepperdine University or the University of Southern California to take the school off his hands — and offered $15,000,000 as an inducement. Pepperdine refused and USC demanded an additional six. CIA was, Edna Disney later said, "the place that killed my husband."

Chapter Seven:
Stamp Out the Seditious and Heretical; Encourage Literature and Genius

When I entered law school in September 1964, the idea was to finish as high in your class as you could, so that you would be hired by the biggest firm, which would pay you the most money. The courses that were offered were those of most interest to those firms: Securities Transactions; Creditors' Rights; Advanced Tax. We learned how to draft contracts and establish trusts but not how to try a DUI or collect child support. Competition was fierce.

Every large city had several of these rainbow's-end firms. Their partners represented major corporations, stock brokerage houses, banks. They counseled political strategies, guided civic committees, chaired governmental commissions, filled appellate courts. These firms restricted the number of Jews and blacks and women they would employ — or ruled them out entirely. Homosexuals did not even consider cracking their closets.

By the time I came to California, the picture was different. At least in the Bay Area, it was as hard to find work as an assistant public defender or legal aid attorney as with a blue-chip firm. Now law students were regarding the law as an instrument for achieving social change and viewing these firms as enemies of progress and agents of oppression. I grabbed an offer from a guy who rented space from a labor lawyer. One afternoon, I went into the Garrett McEnerney Memorial Library at Boalt, and the portrait of the honoree that hung on the east wall had been covered by one of Che Guevera.

Cooley, Crowley, Gaither, Godward, Castro & Huddleson was one of San Francisco's grandee firms. The mere timbre of its name made it seem to have been constructed to shake the ground like a tyrannosaur's tread, causing opposition counsel to shudder that their positions must be untenable, their arguments sophomoric, their shoes insufficiently shined, their ties improperly knotted. In thirty years, it had grown from six men specializing in commercial litigation and the defense of negligence actions to an office whose thirty-five attorneys made it one of the city's largest — and whose roster of Wall Street-worthy clients made it one of the most prestigious. On October 21, 1971, Cooley, Crowley filed a near-half-pound of legal documents in the United States District Court for the Northern District of California, on behalf of Walt Disney Productions, against the Air Pirates, Hell Comics, Dan O'Neill, Ted Richards, Gary Hallgren, Bobby London, and Does One to Fifty, leaving ample room to add any additional defendants it discovered later. (Flenniken was not included because neither her name nor her work appeared in either issue of *Funnies*.)

The heaviest weapon in this paper arsenal was an eighteen-page, ten cause-of-action complaint. It accused the Pirates of copyright infringement, trademark infringement, unfair competition, intentional interference with business, and trade disparagement through the wrongful use of the characters Mickey Mouse, Minnie Mouse, Pegleg Pete, Bucky Bug, June Bug, The Three Little Pigs, The Big Bad Wolf, Li'l Bad Wolf, Goofy, Chief O'Hara, The Phantom Blot, Donald Duck, Horace Horsecollar, and Huey, Dewie, and Lewie, and the title "Silly Symphonies." It stated that Disney, through "great effort and… large sums of money," had created characters whose "image of innocent delightfulness… are known and loved by people all over the world, particularly children" and that the defendants' efforts to "disparage and ridicule" these characters threatened to destroy Disney's business.

The complaint prayed for preliminary and permanent injunctions against further "printing, making, manufacturing, publishing, selling, marketing, [or] displaying" of the offending publications or any future publications portraying any of the specified characters. It requested that Disney be awarded all of the Pirates' profits, $5000 for each copyright infringement, treble damages for the trademark infringement, punitive damages of $100,000 from each defendant, surrender of the offending books, and reimbursement of its attorneys' fees and costs.

Two weeks later, based upon declarations by Disney's attorneys that allowing the Pirates to continue to disparage Disney's work would cause it "irreparable" harm through the destruction of "business, goodwill and public image" whose monetary equivalent would be "difficult or impossible to ascertain" but which it was doubtful the Pirates would be able to pay, the court granted a temporary restraining order barring them from any further production or dissemination of their comics. The T.R.O. would remain in effect until a hearing on Disney's motion for a preliminary injunction. That proceeding would allow both sides to present written and oral arguments. If granted, that injunction would stand until a full trial of the case could be conducted.

The Disney lawyers expected to wrap things up within a few days.

Copyright infringement was the claim with which they had begun their complaint. It formed the basis for seven of their ten causes of action. And it would prove the most significant.

American copyright law derives primarily from the English which, in turn, is rooted in the sixteenth century, when the invention of the printing press made books widely and cheaply available for the first time since the Romans had reduced overhead by flogging slaves into reproducing manuscripts by hand. Enough of these new releases had pestiferous things to say about the royal and the rich that, in 1556, Queen Mary incorporated the Stationers Company, a claque of London-based booksellers and printers with the power to determine which tracts were worthy of publication. The Stationers enforced their power through the Star Chamber which was deputized to search out, seize and jail the publisher of any tome they had not vetted.

The first actual legislation in the field, The Licensing Act of 1662, memorialized the Crown's position by forbidding the publishing of any "heretical, seditious, libelous, or other improper political works." It granted publishers perpetual rights to those books tabby enough to gain release but did nothing for authors, who were presumably left to derive satisfaction from the joys of creation and the chance their efforts afforded for a lottery ticket on eternal fame. Writers who weren't happy with these incentives — and what additional remuneration they could squeeze out of the monopoly-holding publishers — were free to circulate their work without having it printed; but this left them ill-equipped to pursue a volume-business approach to financial security, as well as vulnerable to scoundrels who would obtain a copy and sell it to a printer for publication without their consent.

In 1710, Parliament, reacting to this state of affairs, passed the world's first copyright law: The Statute of Anne. Designed to encourage the creation of "useful works," it gave authors ownership of their writings for fourteen years, with the right to extend this another fourteen if still living at the expiration of the first term. Authors were allowed to print their own books, but they had to register them with the Stationers Company. And if an author contracted with a private printer, he could still be required to sign over his rights to his work.

The first American copyright statute was enacted by the state of Connecticut — "for the Encouragement of Literature and Genius" — after lobbying by Noah Webster, who wanted to protect his interest in his spelling book, *Grammatical Institute of the English Language*. (Wise man; it eventually sold 70,000,000 copies.) Soon every state, except Delaware, had its own copyright law, similar to the Statute of Anne but different from one another. To achieve uniformity, the United States Constitution, through Article I, Section 8, empowered Congress to grant "Authors and Inventors the exclusive Right to their respective Writings and Discourses... [in order] to promote the Progress of Science and useful Arts." On May 17, 1790, Congress passed our first national copyright law. It gave creators of books, maps and charts the right to publish or sell them for twenty-eight years and authorized them to sue anyone who reproduced their work without permission to compel them to stop and to recover any monetary damages caused by the unauthorized reproductions. Two weeks later, President Washington signed this bill into law.

By 1971, revisions had extended copyright protection to paintings, etchings, drawings, prints, sculpture, sheet music, musical works, photographs, dramas, movies, and — significantly for our story — "all copyrightable component parts of the thing copyrighted." (Later revisions added computer programs, records, tapes, architectural works, and boat hull designs.) The length of a copyright's existence had been extended, first, to forty-two and, then, fifty-six years. (In 1998, with Mickey Mouse about to fall into the public domain, after heavy lobbying from — and lavish cash-slinging by — Disney, Congress passed the Sonny Bono Copyright Extension Act, stretching it to the life of the author, plus seventy years. "A nifty legal heist," the business columnist James Surowiecki summed up. "A naked giveaway to the heirs of Walt Disney," legal affairs reporter Jeffrey Rosen said.[84])

The theory behind copyright law is that guaranteeing creators the economic rewards of their achievements will result in work that will benefit society. But the law also recognizes that since all knowledge derives from prior knowledge, society can benefit as well from a widespread dissemination of facts, ideas and theories; and this is best achieved if all material is equally available to everyone. These competing claims have led to two extreme positions being taken by commentators in the field: (1) the subject of a copyright should be treated no differently than any other piece of property — a latex factory, an Etruscan vase, a better mousetrap — and should remain the exclusive possession of its owner, permitting him to squeeze every last nickel from it; and (2) once a creator has cashed enough certificates of deposit to have induced him to set pen to paper in the first place, his creation should be open to unrestricted use by any Tom, Dick or Harriet. Within these two poles, for more than two centuries, courts and legislatures have bounced about trying to decide under what circumstances unauthorized use of what copyrighted material is okay by whom.

This country first judicially sanctioned what became known as the "fair use" doctrine in the 1841 case of *Folsom v. March*. The Rev. Charles W. Upham, a "learned" gentleman of "known taste and ability" — descriptives of a tenor that would prove notably absent from the Pirates litigation — had authored an 866-page "biography" of George Washington, 353 of which had been culled verbatim from a twelve-volume collection of Washington's correspondence previously compiled by Jared Sparks. While perturbedly referring to copyright as a

[84] In January 2003, the United States Supreme Court upheld the Bono Act's constitutionality. A majority of the Court, which had previously ruled Congress's attempts to regulate firearms and stamp out violence against women exceeded its authority, believed the protection of the economic interests of a wealthy few were an appropriate legislative exercise.

"subtle," "refined," and "evanescent" area of the law, bordering on "meta-physics," Mr. Justice Story of the Circuit Court of Massachusetts, one of the great men of early American jurisprudence, ruled this constituted an infringement. However, Story went on to say, even a lawfully granted copyright would not bar a "fair and bona fide abridgment." He then set forth factors to be considered in order to determine when such a permissible "abridgment" was at hand: "the nature and objects of the selections made, the quantity and value of the materials used, and the degree to which the use may prejudice the sale, or diminish the profits, or supersede the objects of the original work."[85]

By the time the Air Pirates came to poach upon Disney's preserve, Story's standard had been little sharpened by 130 years of courts jousting with cigarette ads boosting material from scientific journals, telephone directories rearranged in numerical order, schools for models advertised through brochures flaunting fashion magazines covers with similar names, portions of magazine articles that popped up between hard covers, opera librettos converted into plot summaries, and stroke books reproducing psychological studies. Cases that seemed peas-in-a-pod identical were decided in a could-not-create-more-of-a-rat's-nest fashion. One judge's confident conclusions would be reversed by an equally resolute appellate court, often in the teeth of a just-as-cocksure and strident dissent. These decisions had, one temperate commentator put it, "failed to define the bounds of fair use." Other assessments were more biting. The decisions were "inconsistent, unpredictable and incoherent." They were "incoherent, confusing, and uneasily reconcilable." Fair use had become "the most troublesome [question] in the whole law of copyright." It was "virtually undefinable," "except broadly, generally, and... vaguely," and it left courts "with almost complete discretion" how to decide cases. When the alleged infringing work was a parody, the problem was headache-inducingly vexatious.

Parodies mock well-known, well-regarded people or cultural icons in order to cause audiences to re-evaluate them and reconsider the messages they propound. For some of us who had grown up in the 1950s, parodists like the *MAD* artists, like Bob and Ray, Stan Freberg, Tom Lehrer, like Reuben Ship, author of "The Investigator," a Canadian radio play that garrotted McCarthy (my father practically smuggled a bootlegged recording of it into the house under his coat; we all but listened with the lights out and blankets on the doors to muffle the sound) had planted planks by which we could cross a spirit-stifling sink-hole of an era to reach an alternate way of being. Parodists cut down the powerful, deflated the pompous, swept away the stuffy. They let us laugh at all that threats of after-school detentions and withheld allowances sought to strap around our impulses like wool suits. They were about the only people out there — Marlon Brando,

---

[85] Story had arrived at his decision by following English case law; the English so admired his restatement, they adopted it for their own use.

James Dean, Jack Kerouac, Lenny Bruce would reach us later — saying, "Yo, kid, there's a different way to go." And what they were saying clicked a switch that lit us up inside more than anything else we were being asked to swallow.

But "the very nature of [this] art...," Kevin M. Wheelwright has pointed out, "requires exactly what is forbidden..." For a parody to succeed, the audience must recognize what is being mocked, "but the copying necessary to accomplish this identification is arguably an infringement of the original work's copyright protection." And while a copyright owner might license certain uses of his work, only the thickest-skinned would be apt to grant permission to the parodist who came politely seeking permission to proceed with his mockery. If the parodist was to work, he had to expect opposition; and he had to recognize that Congress had handed his opponent a gun which no court had effectively muzzled.

The federal court system, which has exclusive jurisdiction over copyright infringement cases, is three-tiered. The District Courts comprise the trial level. (The Northern District of California has branches in San Francisco, San Jose, and Oakland.) Their decisions may be appealed to one of nine Circuit Courts of Appeal, which divide the country geographically and whose decisions on questions of law bind all District Courts within their area. (California, nine other western states, Guam, and the Northern Marianas lie within the Ninth Circuit. At present, it has twenty-eight judges, and a case may be heard by a panel of any three.) Any party aggrieved by a Court of Appeal ruling may petition the United States Supreme Court for a hearing; but a majority of its nine justices must vote to grant one, and less than five percent of all cases seeking review gain it.

Three cases decided within a decade of one another had attempted to reconcile the rights of parodists with those of copyright holders. The Ninth Circuit decided the first of these, *Benny v. Loew's, Inc.,* in 1956. Eleven years earlier, Loew's, which had acquired the rights to make a film from the novel-turned-play, *Gaslight,* had given permission to the comedian Jack Benny to parody it in a fifteen minute radio skit. In 1952, without Loew's consent, Benny expanded his skit into a half-hour parody, "Auto Light," on his Sunday night television show. Loew's sued Benny.

In a decision that has been called "more outstanding for its ambiguities than for its articulated rules," the Ninth Circuit affirmed a District Court finding that Benny had infringed Loew's copyright.[86] The court found the skit's locale, period, primary setting, characters, plot points, development, and much of its dialogue identical to much of the film's; and, it said, merely replaying an existing work in "clownish garb, or movement, or [with] farcial distortion of the

[86] Victor S. Netterville has suggested that the decision can best be explained by a California court's wish to protect its home state's beleaguered motion picture studios from taking further hits from the then-New York City-centered television industry.

actors" did not constitute a fair use. If you copied "a substantial part" of the prior work, that defense would fail.

Benny petitioned the Supreme Court for review; but Justice Douglas, normally a First Amendment "absolutist" who would have been expected to favor his appeal, disqualified himself from voting without stating a reason. The petition failed four-to-four, and the lower court's decision remained law. (Benny, then, reportedly paid Loew's $100,000 for the right to re-run his show; but television remained a virtual "parody-free" zone for over a decade.)

The second significant parody case, *Columbia Pictures Corp. v. National Broadcasting Co.*, resolved at the District Court level in Los Angeles. On September 22, 1953, eleven days after Columbia's release of its film of James Jones's novel, *From Here to Eternity*, Sid Caesar had parodied it in a twenty-minute skit, "From Here to Obscurity," on his television show, *Your Show of Shows*. The judge, James M. Carter, was the same one whose decision in *Benny* the Ninth Circuit had upheld. But this time he reached a different conclusion.

While reiterating that "substantial" copying was forbidden, Carter now said that a parodist may take as much he needs to "conjure up" the original — including portions of its locale, theme, situation, characters, setting, title, dialogue, and plot — in the minds of his audience. Without enumerating what specifics made it so, he found Caesar's skit to be "new, original and different [in its] development, treatment and expression" than the movie. It was a question of the *quality* of the taking, he said, not the *quantity*. And unlike his decision in *Benny*, he made the purpose of the taking a major consideration. A creator of a burlesque or parody would be allowed greater freedom than someone simply trying to pass his work off as the original.

Finally, in 1964, the Second Circuit Court of Appeals, which is based in New York, decided *Berlin v. E.C. Publications*. That case had been brought by a number of prominent songwriters after *MAD* had parodied a couple dozen of their songs — converting, for example, "A Pretty Girl is Like a Melody" into "Louella Schwartz Describes Her Malady." While remarking gratuitously that "the social interest" in *MAD*'s parodies was "not readily apparent," the court found they constituted a fair use anyway.

The Second Circuit stated that both the *Benny* and *Columbia Pictures* decisions rested on whether or not the takings had been "substantial" — (a gross over-simplification as to the latter); and it felt that *MAD*'s use of copyrighted material — "a familiar line... interposed in a totally incongruous setting" — was not. "The disparities in theme, content and style...," it said, "could hardly be greater." The court then said that if the taking "has neither the intent nor the effect of fulfilling the demand for the original and where the parodist does not appropriate a greater amount of the original than is necessary to 'recall or conjure up' the object of his satire, a finding of infringement would be improper."

To sum up, then, "clownish" or "farcial" distortions do not establish a "fair use," but differences in "expression" and "style" do. "Substantial" takings are always improper unless, perhaps, the public is not confused as to the origin of the work. Parodists can always take enough to "conjure up" the original in the public's mind unless they fulfill its demand for the original. And they apparently can't copy *more* than a "conjure"-sufficient quantum, even if this is *less* than "substantial," and even if they don't fool or fulfill any of the populace. Finally, how one measures "substantial"-ness and "conjure"-sufficiency is anybody's guess.

These decisions brought the phrase "Solomon-like" to few lips. No significant number of litigants, lawyers or law review limners leapt from their baths, exclaiming, "Eureka!" More often, they scratched their heads, rolled their eyes, and awaited, with dread and apprehension, their next chance to bite this apple.

Chapter Eight:
Enter the Big, Fucking, Sick Machine

Now may be a good time for a note on methodology.

Any lawyer knows it is unlikely any group of people will agree on what they witnessed just before they left the room, let alone thirty years ago. This difficulty is compounded if those memories are recalled through a veil of resentments, jealousies, angers, unpaid bills, divorce. When those remembering are recounting days they experienced while drugged to the proboscis, when they are persons drawn by temperament and training to the creative arts, the chances for concurrence lessen geometrically. The hope of the innocent reporter is that five persons interviewed will recall five facts apiece, which will yield a solid twenty-five from which to build sturdy paragraphs. But when, as is more often the case, each recalls the same two or three — and recalls them differently — construction difficulties arise. Some disputes I have resolved by majority vote. Some by including dissenting opinions. Some by force of corroborative externals. And one or two, wickedly, by what served my own sense of story best.

One of Dan O'Neill's most repeated tales is that, despite a San Francisco phone book listing for "Air Pirates Secret Hideout," it took Disney four months to serve its complaint. Then, one day, Pinkertons were at the door.[87] One could wonder how the Pirates, who didn't move into the Coppola warehouse until August, could already have a phone book listing in October. (It takes three times that long now.) One could note that, by November, they had already scattered. Flenniken remembers a "commotion" when a process server arrived.

---

[87] A Junior Crime-Stoppers Tip from O'Neill: "You can tell Pinkertons from FBI because Pinkertons are tiny. FBI are Detroit Lions who can't play any more. With FBI, the best thing to do is answer the door naked. They hate that. Then every question they ask... 'Well, search me.'"

Richards recalls someone tossing papers on the floor, yelling "You're served," and splitting. Turner, the only person deposed during the course of the suit when memories were fresher, said he was speaking by phone to London when he began shouting semi-coherently because "some Muni-man had come to the door... [and they] had just got popped." London says this never happened. ("Why would Turner be talking to me?") He says the process servers arrived three days after O'Neill's last fight with Richards, and only Hallgren was there. They asked him "Is Dan O'Neill here?" "No." "Is Gary Hallgren here?" "No." "Who are you?" "I'm Harry, his brother." Hallgren, who believes they all learned of the service after the fact from O'Neill, says, "That's a great story. It could even be true. I was smoking a lot during this period, and it takes some deep relaxation and memory-jogging to recall." Which returns us to O'Neill, who says that when the Pinkertons arrived, the dialogue ran in Bizarro-*Spartacus* fashion, "Are you Dan O'Neill?" "No, he's Dan O'Neill." "No, he's Dan O'Neill." "No, he's..."

Disney's lawyers recall no problems effecting service. Court records show they first mailed notice of the suit to O'Neill in Jenner. The Post Office told them he had changed his address to General Delivery, Sausalito. They sent notice there October 28; but he never responded, so they hired a process server — neither Pinkertons nor the FBI that I can tell. Service of something on someone had to have been accomplished by January 14, 1972, because on that date a stipulation postponing the hearing on Disney's preliminary injunction motion was filed, signed by an attorney for each Pirate.

And service had to have occurred before that. Something made the Pirates stop publishing *Funnies* after August. And when that happened, O'Neill needed time to get lawyers.[88] Utilizing the same persuasive skills that had formed the Pirates, he now assembled a defense team that matched Cooley, Crowley's stature among deep carpet firms with its own within the counterculture Bar.

O'Neill first approached Kennedy & Rhine, which operated out of a fire-engine red Victorian decorated with gum-ball machines and tiger-print wallpaper and boasted a garden patio patrolled by a shaggy dog named Clarence. The building had been purchased from the Catholic church across the street which, having heard "Rhine" as "Ryan," believed it was getting two nice Irish boys as neighbors. It was located in what the firm's senior partner, Michael Kennedy, a sophisticated, stylish, ex-New Yorker with shoulder-length blonde hair, granny glasses, and an Edwardian suit-centered wardrobe, termed "the DMZ between Pacific Heights and the Fillmore." Kennedy had made his reputation as a take-

[88] London thinks Don Donahue arranged for the lawyers. "It's just hard for me to believe that Dan was able to find any lawyers," he says. "There were mornings when he couldn't find his shoes." Donahue denies involvement; and it should be noted that, unlike Hallgren ("I wouldn't've missed it for the world"), Richards ("A great experience. I wouldn't trade it for anything"), and Flenniken ("I expected to be in a revolution and die. Anything more than that was just fine"), London's feelings for the Air Pirates... Well, John McCain retains a warmer glow for the North Vietnamese.

no-prisoners defender of draft resisters, Timothy Leary, and one of the alleged cop-killers in Los Sieta de la Raza, a group of young Mission District Hispanics. Kennedy's operating principle, as expressed to an inquiring *Berkely Barb* reporter in the heat of the times, was: "The legal system is a big, fucking, sick machine. It's rotten, it's decayed, it doesn't work. But the more you fight and the more aggressive a fighter you are, the better deals you get your clients." The firm was dedicated to defending the political left; but pornographers, particularly the Mitchells, at whose theater Kennedy's brother, Biff, was employed, paid most of its bills.

Kennedy, who had represented O'Neill in some minor matters, gave his latest set of papers to the office's junior member, David F. Phillips, a June Penn Law School graduate and anti-war activist, to review. "I told Michael we should get involved," Phillips says. "It raised important First Amendment issues, and I didn't like this large corporation sitting on these four little cartoonists." Kennedy became O'Neill's lawyer and Phillips London's.

Next on board — with roots in the legal arm of the Freak-the-Fuck-Out Movement dating back to Ken Kesey's Acid Tests — was Rohan and Stepanian. Phillips thinks Kennedy brought them in to share the work and avoid any appearance of a conflict of interest. Kennedy believes they had represented Hallgren or Richards before. (Hallgren and Richards say no.) O'Neill says he knew — there weren't that many hip lawyers to choose from — and got them. In any event, Michael Stepanian became Richards's attorney. Stepanian, one of the city's top "dope" lawyers, was a thirty-one-year-old, black-curly-haired, Avery Schreiber-mustached, rugby-playing, ex-hungry i waiter, ex-Enrico's host, and the Committee's first bartender, who possessed a fondness for burgundy silk bow ties and fine cigars.[89] His associate — and former Boston University Law School classmate — the portly, Rutherford B. Hayes-bearded Albert Morse, signed on for Hallgren. Morse was a "bon vivant," drawn to black derbies and black three-piece suits, with a Robber Baron's gold watch chain strung across his equator. A photographer, a collector of exotic pipes and circus cards, he was also the defense team

[89] Stepanian had previous experience defending UG art in obscenity trials. The most notable arose from the prosecution of an Erotic Art Show held within the Cannery, a collection of tourist-courting shops and restaurants near Fishermen's Wharf. It didn't bother the natives; but, he says, "People from Iowa with four kids seeing this shit went out of their fucking minds."

Stepanian's strategy was to insist that the prosecution's ten-foot-tall Mylar reproductions of the most offensive work seized — Wilson's dykes chopping off pirates' cocks, for example — be displayed before the jury the entire three months of trial. "Then, cross-examining the City and County's chief expert, some putz from New York, I said, 'Are you saying, doctor, that a person's prolonged exposure to these pictures would inevitably result in their being led to inflict physical pain on another during sexual relations?' 'Absolutely.' Well, at that, juror Number Ten, a lovely woman — a sixty-seven-year-old librarian — starts laughing. The judge has to say, 'Madam, please control yourself,' which gets the other jurors laughing too. They come back, after three days, ten-two for acquittal, and the case is dismissed."

member with the most experience in copyright law, having represented a number of UG cartoonists, most notably Robert Crumb in *his* infringement claims against people who had ripped off his "Keep on Truckin'" logo.[90]

The attorneys agreed to donate their services, but the Pirates promised to pay costs.

Disney's preliminary injunction motion, after several more postponements, was scheduled to be heard by Judge Wollenberg on March 10, 1972. The only change among the litigants was that Phillips had left Kennedy & Rhine and now represented London on his own.

The day before the hearing, the Pirates held a press conference at Rohan and Stepanian's converted Victorian on Eddy Street, above Van Ness. (In the '70s, you practically couldn't *be* an anti-establishment lawyer in San Francisco without a converted Victorian.) Its high ceilings, narrow halls, dark woods and red-flocked wallpaper provided a sportive, bordello-ish air to the proceedings. The purpose of the conference, Kennedy says, was to rally public support for the Pirates' position: "The line belongs to us. If it ends up a mouse, it's still a line. We have absolute freedom to copy anything as long as we add to it." The Pirates handed out hastily cobbled-together press kits, which contained copies of the lawsuit and statements of support for their work, and answered questions from the media.

Newspaper pictures of the event show O'Neill in cowboy hat, wire-rimmed glasses, and gunslinger mustache. Hallgren is smiling, moderately 'stached, a Mr. Zig Zag patch sewn onto his jacket sleeve. Richards has shoulder-length hair, a cowboy hat and rakishly angled cigar. London's hair flops over one eye. At one point, with television cameras rolling, he recalls yelling, "We're guilty! We're guilty!" while the lawyers yelled "Cut! Cut!" O'Neill is quoted as saying "Thank you very, very, very, very, very much" to process servers in attendance.[91] He tells the reporters "Mickey Mouse wasn't a successful cartoon character. He had no personality. But he was a success as a trade-

---

[90] Stepanian's view of the defense team is, "Kennedy was a revolutionary; O'Neill was a revolutionary, both of them Irishing around. Kennedy was an expert; Morse was an expert; I was no expert. My thing was, 'You get arrested; you call Mike.' To me, that's what it was about. It was a *case*. It was about a client who was accused of doing something wrong. Richards was talented, and he was smart, and I liked the Wolf; and I was going to be there for the kid until the fucking end so nobody rolled over him. Plus, Richards was *right*."

[91] Just what was being served on whom is puzzling, since something had to have been served on everyone already or none of this would have been happening. Normally, to start a lawsuit, a complaint is served on a defendant who files an answer. (If it doesn't, it can lose by default.) On February 3, Hallgren's and Richards's attorneys had filed a memorandum opposing Disney's request for an injunction but no answer. The next day, O'Neill's and London's lawyers filed both an answer and a memorandum in opposition. It wasn't until two weeks after the press conference that

mark for Disney's junk. I can put character into that mouse. As an artist, I am concerned with the image of that mouse that stuck in my head as a kid. You might say I'm a mouse junkie."

Richards recalls the conference as less than a public relations triumph. "We had," he says, "a lot of '70s' acid energy but no talking points." Hallgren says, "You have to remember, we were all high as kites. This was a time you would light a joint first thing in the morning and not stop until you went to sleep." Flenniken says, "The guys were loving it, thinking they were taking on this huge battle, feeling very self-important. I spent the whole time lying on the floor with a stomachache, thinking I was getting an ulcer."

The Pirates in these pictures are young, rebellious and hanging loose. They are thriving in their rebelliousness. They radiate confidence. They have engaged with the beast, and they will conquer it because they are right. They will win the battle, and they will win the war. Or they will lose the battle, and they will win the war. But they will win the war. We were going to win all the wars then. What was the point of being young if you were not going to win the wars?

I think now, distanced by decades, modulated by irony, insight, and all the instruct cosmic humor can allow, that at the same time the Pirates set forth with pen and ink to abolish the Disney world-view — as so many of us set forth on so many quixotic, unfathomable-to-our-elders missions of our own — if it were not for what we owed to that view, we might never have dared our challenges. For what had Mickey demonstrated but that little guys could topple giants? Had not Dumbo made it clear that the most scorned outsider, if his heart was pure, would triumph? "Be sure you're right," Davy Crockett had instructed us, "then go ahead."[92]

San Francisco's federal District Courts are in a block-long, block-wide, smokey-glassed, twenty-story, grey-stoned slab of a building, on the western

---

Richards's and Hallgren's answer was filed so, maybe, to guarantee they were in the suit, Disney served them then.

Adding to the mystery are declarations in the court file, dated April 25, 1972, by Robert McKeen, that he served the summons and complaint on O'Neill, Hallgren, London, and Richards at the press conference. That explains Hallgren's and Richards's answer but not why London and O'Neill had responded five weeks earlier.

[92] Robert Heide and John Gilman, in their recently published — and Disney-ratified — *Mickey Mouse: The Evolution, The Legend, The Phenomenon,* make my view look niggardly by all but claiming the entire counterculture as Disney's creation. "'Do your own thing,'" they write, "the message of the sixties' hippies and outcasts, exactly sums up what Mickey always did.... [R]evolutionary youth saw something in Mickey with which they could identify: a rebellious nature combined with a sweetly confident naivete."

The word co-option comes to mind.

edge of the Tenderloin. Proceedings are conducted in rooms whose opulence suggests materialization from the Nieman-Marcus catalogue.[93] Fifty feet long, thirty feet wide, another thirty high, they are accessorized with wall-to-wall carpeting, wood paneling, rows of well-polished, pew-like benches, recessed lighting in delicately arced ceilings. The attorneys sit at glossy tables in leather, rock-and-swivel arm chairs. The judge presides from an elevated, shielded desk, flanked by the American flag. On a marble-like section of the wall hangs a gold United States seal: a bald eagle clutching arrows and an olive branch.[94]

O'Neill entered in his "Jack Palance-*Shane* outfit": black hat; buckskin jacket; gun belt with holster. He carried a paper bag which, when checked by security officers on the ground floor, revealed his lunch. "On the elevator, I tie down the holster so they can see it sticking out under my jacket and step out on the eighteenth floor like I'm gonna draw. The U.S. marshal leaps over his desk, grabs me by the throat, and hoists me in the sky. I'm strangling; and he whips open my coat, and in the holster is a banana. All night I was trying out fruit in the refrigerator, and the banana won. It looked more like a gun than a turnip. He's yelling, 'There's a guy with a banana!' And I'm going, 'It's a Chiquita!'"[95]

To obtain its injunction, Disney had to convince Judge Wollenberg it was likely to win the eventual trial and that it would be severely damaged if the Pirates were allowed to publish their comics in the interim. Its attorneys' moving papers were cursory, conclusionary — but to the point. They filed certificates which documented Disney's copyrights on books and comics — attached as exhibits — that contained cartoon characters copied by the Pirates in their comics — also attached. The "striking and unmistakable" visual similarities between the two sets of characters, they argued, proved infringements had occurred; and the behavior engaged in by the Pirates' characters so drastically departed from that normally associated with Disney's that it must, if not

[93] To extend this analogy, state courts manifest assemblage from J.C. Penney's or Land's End and workers' compensation hearing rooms, where I practice, from those flyers stuck under your windshield by distress-outlets. When I was most recently in federal court, witnessing a libel trial involving two noted authors, having taken in the burial mounds of exhibit boxes, the hordes of scurrying para-legals, the electronically enhanced demonstrative evidence, the professional actors hired to read the deposition testimony of unavailable witnesses, I remarked to a friend, "They must be spending $200,000 in costs apiece! We spend $100." "Yes," he said, "and you have just as much chance of getting the right verdict."

[94] Assuming the point of these expenditures is the fostering of awe and respect, one wonders what it is costing them these days in Washington to offset the chicken droppings seeping out of the Scalia-Thomas wing of the Supreme Court.

[95] Others' memories omit the *mano a mano* portion of the exchange. "They made him take the banana out and check it," is all Flenniken says. "They also made me check my sketch pad," adds Hallgren.

stopped, immeasurably harm their public image and reduce their commercial value. The Pirates should, therefore, be enjoined from publishing any further Disney-related books, and all copies of their existing ones should be impounded until the court could decide whether to destroy them.

The Air Pirates' attorneys had crafted a defense which began by interpreting the very stories which Disney vilified in terms so positive and respectful that any reader who had not been immediately awe-struck gazing upon them — me, for instance — felt like a Philistine deserving David's stone. Hallgren's "Keyhole Komix" was placed in the grand tradition of exaggerated burlesques dating back to sixteenth century Italian opera. Richards's "Zeke Wolf" turned out to be a response to Disney's repeated portrayal of poor Southern whites as "vicious and ignorant simpleton[s] with nothing to do but commit crimes," a slander which had kept North and South from uniting against "the true cause of Southern problems... ruthless exploitation... by a cabal of powerful interests... the banks, the media, and the military [The Three Pigs]." O'Neill's "Silly Sympathies" was revealed as a parody of the "very conventional and very trite" lessons which Disney drummed into children, addressing deeper issues of morality and theology: sexual greed and masturbation. (They also noted that this story abstractly paralleled "defendant O'Neill's own maturing." How this aside was expected to win over Judge Wollenberg is unclear.)

"The Mouse Story," characterized as a tale of "the awakening within Mickey... of an awareness of his sins and his subsequent transformation and redemption," received the most impressive revisiting. Mickey, it noted, is initially presented as "depressed." (The Pirates' attorneys voiced regret at having to quote the exact language of his discontent — "Why won't anybody fuck me?" — but puckishly cited precedents for forcing courts to confront such unseemliness.) He is, then, set upon by an alliance of old foes, whom Disney had derived from various offensive stereotypes: the Jew-lawyer (Sylvester Shyster); the French-Canuck (Pegleg Pete);[96] the trashy Southerner (The Big Bad Wolf).[97] Having been "wrongfully persecuted" by Mickey for years and unable to best him physically, they decide to "work on his head" through the "peel" thrust upon Mickey at the end of *Funnies* #2: LSD.

As recounted in the brief, the never-completed third segment would have provided a powerful, inventive conclusion which, if allowed to appear, might have led to the story's being viewed with more respect than the first two chap-

[96] Pete and the Phantom Blot — both big, black and menacing — have also been cited as racially offensive.

[97] And when "The Three Little Pigs" was originally released, the Wolf was attacked as an anti-Semitic representation of a Jewish peddler. Disney defended his characterization on the grounds that (a) many of his friends were Jewish; (b) he only intended to entertain; and (c) the Wolf merely mimicked many Jewish comedians. Then he had the scenes in question redone.

ters standing alone. Mickey escapes Don Jollio; but a series of hallucinations reveal to him the violence, rage and evil within him. He meets his "nephews," Mortie and Ferdie (actually his and Minnie's illegitimate children). He meets Oswald Rabbit, now a drunken has-been, and Sylvester, his former attorney — and Minnie's ex-husband. (When she and Mickey began their affair, he had Chief O'Hara frame Sylvester on drug charges; and she divorced him.) Mickey is placed on trial before The Phantom Blot in front of an audience of famous cartoon characters. Everyone he has wronged testifies against him. He is convicted and sentenced to pass through the Doors of Doom. There, he finds Minnie. They marry and acknowledge their children. Mickey can't return to his old life; but, before embarking upon his new one, he glances back through the Doors to see Donald Duck musing, "The whole world thinks I'm cute..."

Having dressed the Pirates' work appropriately for court, the defense then legitimized their pedigree. It established them — not as nose-thumbing smut-peddlers — but as respected parodists, following in the footsteps of Cervantes, Shakespeare, Swift, Fielding, Bret Harte, Henry James, James Thurber, E.B.White, Poe, Whitman, Hemingway, and Faulkner. All humor, it philosophized, is based upon "conflict between the expected and the actual"; and parody juxtaposes a "known existing work" against "something else." To succeed, "the reference to the original must be made clear and kept clear." Here, it always looks like Mickey Mouse; but it never behaves like him. Parody, at its most base, may exaggerate without greater purpose; but the Pirates are engaged in "aesthetic and political criticism of a deeply serious nature."

The defense next examined the applicable law. With respect to the major issue of copyright infringement, it argued that while an entire work can be copyrighted, characters within it can not. Second, even if they can be, the Pirates were protected by the fair use doctrine. By restricting their copying to the visual representation of the characters, they took the minimum necessary for their parody to succeed. (Only one panel was copied from an actual Disney comic — a recollection by Don Jollio of a past event — and it was drawn from a different perspective than its source.) They had, then, created an original work, distinct in plot, dialogue, setting, themes, and character personalities from anything Disney had ever done. Moreover, the Pirates were not trying to pass their comics off as a Disney product. They aimed at a different market: adult hippies, not children. They sold through different outlets: head shops, not newsstands. They were not competing with any past, current — or probable — future Disney creation. The Disney-buying public was unlikely to have its craving for Mickey Mouse satisfied by an issue of *Air Pirates Funnies*. Disney would not lose a dime.

The Pirates also claimed protection for their work from the First Amendment. Mickey, they argued, had become "part of our national collective unconscious," as well as an internationally known symbol of American culture and power. While he may once have been accurately perceived as "innocent and delightful," he now could be viewed as "a reactionary force... [devoted to]

Establishment values," "an enthusiastic promoter of... capitalism... vigilante justice, the automobile, unrestrained violence, and willful adoration of movie stars," "a partisan of elements and values in American government and society which the Air Pirates oppose." Disney's worldwide success and importance should make it more, rather than less, available for criticism. A copyright holder should not be allowed to immunize itself from parody simply by the fact of that holding. It should not be permitted to stifle the creativity of others when its property rights weren't being interfered with. Its proprietary interest in its creations should be "subordinate to the greater public interest in this free-spirited debate," for "[w]here the country went wrong, the Mouse went wrong." "Two generations of the American public," the Pirates' lawyers concluded, "have been bottle-fed from infancy upon the insipid, bloodless, vanilla ice cream image propagated so lucratively by the Disney empire. It ill behooves Disney to complain that this myth is now being parodied in a manner which we must assume to be effective from their protestation."

The Pirates dismissed Disney's other causes of actions. The trademark infringement claim, which was based on the similarity between their "Silly Sympathies" story and Disney's "Silly Symphonies" cartoon series, was frivolous because the public could not be confused into thinking one had anything to do with the other. The titles were different on their face. The Pirates' title did not identify the source of a product but one piece within a book; and by the time a reader encountered it, he had to know he was not reading Walt Disney. Similarly, the trade disparagement and destruction of business claims lacked merit. Since the public could not confuse the Pirates' books with Disney's, Disney could not be damaged by being mistakenly associated with their content. Disney might not like how its characters were being portrayed, but that did not give it the right to stop the portrayal.

The Pirates' bolstered their case with affidavits from Arlington; Blackbeard; Hoppe; Krassner; McCabe; Jon Carroll, the editor of *West Magazine*; William Loughborough, director of The Committee; John Putnam, *MAD*'s art director; and the popular arts critic Grover Sales. The affiants presented themselves as students of comic art and satire, who were familiar with the works of Disney and the Air Pirates. They concluded the Pirates were serious artists who had created significant, unique work that could not be mistaken for Disney's or harm Disney financially. "It is the highest tradition of a free society," Krassner wrote, "to encourage the testing of ideas in the open marketplace... [The Pirates'] comic books... are classic examples of artistic responsibility in action." And Sales declared, "It is vital to the public interest and to the free play of artistic and comedic expression that the time-honored prerogative of the parodist be kept intact, particularly when the parodist is as creative, laugh-provoking and socially incisive as Dan O'Neill."

Each Pirate also filed a sworn statement of purpose. Hallgren wrote: "As a bread-and-butter American youth, I believed in the myth of Mickey Mouse. I became an adult when I discovered the Mouse was oleomargarine. As a cartoonist and member of a socially critical generation, I must use whatever faculties I command to reflect upon this change of status. The faculty of draftsmanship enables me to reply to cartoon media myth in kind. I see this as the only method by which I might approach parity of impact in the American consciousness. I have no wish to replace Walt Disney. I merely wish to have the right to offer my views to the public for its examination."

London said, "Throughout my childhood, Mickey Mouse was used as a placebo to lull me into thinking everything was all right. But I found the happy-ever-after-world of Walt and Mickey Mouse to be a poor half-truth. *Air Pirates Funnies* shows that Mickey Mouse doesn't always win. I am an artist. I speak best to my world in symbols, in pictures. Any attempt on my part at over throwing the Disney enterprise is absurd. How can our messed-up, unhappy, paranoid, little mouse be mistaken for the always victorious hero of American mythology?"

Richards said, "'The Wolf and the Pig' has existed within folk literature for well over five hundred years. Walt Disney studios cannot claim exclusive ownership of an old folk tale. My parody not only speaks for the American war baby generation but spans the ages. It is only in the Disney studio version that a pig is a heroic character. This breaks from a long-established folk tradition of swine as the dirtiest, most repulsive of people. This argument also justifies my involvement with Mickey Mouse. Traditionally, mice are filthy, disgusting, little rodents. I only helped to portray Mickey Mouse in an authentic mouse role, and I merely wish to have the right to offer my view to the public for its examination."

O'Neill's affidavit was the lengthiest, the most interesting — and, ultimately, the most damaging: "I draw a cartoon... and the cartoon draws a response from those who read it, sometimes positive — laughter; sometimes negative — indignation. Still there has to be a response for the cartoon to be successful. If the cartoon receives no response it is merely a drawing.

"Disney presented Mickey Mouse to us when we were children. As cartoonists and adults, we approach Mickey Mouse as our major American mythology. We work in the failure of this myth and construct in these visual forms because it expands our impact on the American consciousness. I chose to parody *exactly* the style of drawing and the characters to evoke the response created by Disney. My purpose in using the Mouse as a character is not to destroy the Disney product, but to deal with the image in the American consciousness that the Disney image *implanted*." (Emphases in the original.)

O'Neill did not dispute Disney's right to develop a mouse or duck or paramecium and market the hell out of it. He was not trying to capitalize on Disney's accomplishments. He did not intend to fool anyone into thinking they were buying Disney comic books and siphon off its royalties. "That's piracy," he told Groth. "Parody is taking them apart seam-by-seam, philosophically, sexually, every-which-way. And it had to be comics. It couldn't be that deep, that heavy, but it couldn't be cheap. It had to be more than potty jokes, and it had to make you laugh. What good is it, if it doesn't make you laugh? How can you pass as a comic and not be funny?"

O'Neill rejected any restraint on his grappling as closely as he wished with this symbol of the corporate culture he resented. He would not settle, he said, alluding to the Harvey Kurtzman/Bill Elder classic satire "Mickey Rodent" in *MAD* #19, for some "watered-down version that needed a shave and wasn't the real critter." "This here is a free republic; and if I don't like what this guy is saying, and I happen to have the same language gift he has — the same ability to speak with words and pictures — I can reply in his language. The characters might look like Disney, but the soul is 180 degrees turned away. The original work is conjured up to the reader's eye as closely as possible, but the behavior is exactly opposite. The closer you draw the parody, the greater the shock, the greater the criticism. The less you look like the original, the weaker the parody; and, no matter how weak it is, there's always the possibility of a lawsuit, so publishers will fear to print all but the very weakest. You try to explain that to lawyers and judges, they just go 'What?' The trouble with evolution is it's not happening for some people."

Disney's case was presented by Frank Donovan ("Sandy") Tatum, Jr., a partner at Cooley, Crowley who specialized in commercial law. He was a solidly built six-foot-one, with a square jaw and thick thatch of well-brushed, graying hair. His courtroom presence was inevitably stamped for propriety and seriousness of purpose by his dark, single-breasted Brooks Brothers suits. Tatum had graduated Phi Beta Kappa, with a B.A. in Engineering, from Stanford in 1942. After serving in the Navy and studying at Oxford as a Rhodes Scholar, he had returned to Palo Alto for law school, graduating Order of the Coif in 1950. Admitted to the Bar that same year, he had been a practicing attorney for about as long as the Pirates' four lawyers combined — and his brother was chairman of Disney's board of directors.[98] (Tatum was also a top flight amateur golfer, an NCAA and Danish Amateur champion, who would become president of the United States Golf Association.) While Flenniken has said that Disney would have ignored the Pirates if Dell, its comic book publisher, had not felt threatened, Tatum says this is untrue. "The *Funnies* had received a fair amount of exposure, and Disney regarded it as a very serious problem." Since Disney had no way of knowing how long the Pirates intended to continue their affronts or what further outrages they would attempt if not quashed, this fear seems likely.

Tatum began his argument by pointing out that Disney had created and properly copyrighted its books and comics. For the protection this copyrighting afforded to be meaningful, the characters within these works had to be regarded as "copyrightable component parts," for they had "achieved identification inde-

[98] Donald B. ("Donn") Tatum had joined Disney in 1955 as a vice-president and business manager. Also an attorney, with degrees from Stanford and Oxford, he had headed the West Coast division of ABC. After Walt Disney's death, he had become vice-chairman of the board of directors. When Roy Disney died, in December 1971, he took over as chairman.

pendent of the cartoon strips, books and pictures in which they have appeared." Disney had spent "millions of dollars and years of effort" developing these characters. They had become known worldwide and were "vitally important" to Disney, having earned even more millions for it. Now the Pirates' venomous portrayals threatened to destroy them. Never has "misuse [been] so blatant," Tatum said. Never has it been "more calculated to damage the copyright owner..."

Tatum dismissed fair use "a potpourri of so-called principles... most of which are virtually meaningless." Whatever it meant, by no stretch of the imagination could it embrace the "perverted," "obscene nonsense" the Pirates had authored. The term "fair" simply could not append to a "use" whose purpose was "to defame," "to destroy," "to degrade and disparage all that Disney has done..." It could not apply to a taking so substantial: "the essence of [Disney's]... popular appeal and commercial success."

Since visual representations of cartoon characters must be regarded as copyrightable, the Pirates were not taking a small portion of a larger whole but "the entire subject of the copyright." Calling their work "parody" gave the Pirates no special rights. When "the copying is complete and exact," Tatum said, it is not parody but theft. He proposed the court adopt the following test: Would a reasonable copyright holder consent to the use in question? If it would not, the use was not fair.

Tatum termed the Pirates' First Amendment argument "nonsense." If followed, all copyright laws would be "utterly nullified..." The Pirates failed to recognize the distinction between ideas and means of expression. While they had every right to deliver whatever message they desired, they had no right "to use Mickey Mouse as the vehicle..."

Tatum argued that the "Symphony"-"Sympathies" trademark infringement claim was meritorious because from the Dell/Hell similarity to the "drawing, figures and attitudes" on both covers, the Pirates were trying to link their books "as closely as possible" to Disney's. Actual public confusion need not be shown, he said, when it was "patent" from such obvious similarities. The likelihood of harm to Disney if the flow of these books remained unchecked was equally obvious. Such "cancerous imagery" would "inevitably destroy the value of the Disney product image." It would "inject a peculiarly unwholesome association of ideas and connotations" into the public's perception of Disney and "damage the affirmative mental associations [it has] achieved." Mickey and his friends had established a hard-earned, secondary meaning to their names which would be irremediably "degraded and cheapened."

Tatum responded to the Pirates' "purported experts" by quoting the admonition of Learned Hand of the Second Circuit Court of Appeals — Hand is one of the few American jurists so well-regarded that attorneys will regularly drop his name whenever one of his opinions is cited — to exclude such testimony from infringement cases because it "encumbers the case and leads to confusion," distracting the court from its own "firmer, if more naive... considered impressions" of the only questions properly before it: Was the work copyrighted? Did the defendants copy it? But he provided Judge Wollenberg his own sworn statements. Not one came from a cartoonist, critic or historian. None discussed parody. Each came, instead, from a Disney corporate official or employee.

The Disney affidavits attested that the company had devoted forty-four years to creating, developing and promoting a stable of cartoon characters. They appeared in newspaper strips, comic books, and children's books, where their "distinctive design and personality traits are the essence of the publication." They had become "extraordinarily valuable component parts of the total Disney operation," appearing in movies and on television shows created by Disney, publicizing Disney in other forums, and bringing Disney licensing fees from over 130 products their likenesses helped sell, including ballpoint pens, bowling sets, building blocks, Christmas plaques, costume jewelry, curler bags, dolls, Easter baskets, frisbees, greeting cards, hair dryer hoods, handbags, ice cream scoopers, inflatable pools, jewelry boxes, leather goods, lunch pails, magnetic puzzles, masquerade costumes, night lights, novelty hats, pinball games, plastic straws, poly-urethane foam jigsaw puzzles, pre-seeded garden mats, punch balls, scatter rugs, sewing kits, skediddles, sunglasses, talking telephones, tape measures, tea sets, toiletries, toy luggage, transistor radios, tree skirts, umbrellas, wallets, wind-up vehicles, and yo-yos.

The characters whose reputations the Pirates had sullied had won Disney awards, certificates, diplomas, medals, plaques, scrolls, and statuettes from, among others, Argentina's National School of Decorative Arts, the Artists of Brazil, France's Committee for Literary and Artistic Advancement of the Cinema, El Radio in Ecuador, Italy's International Festival of Motion Picture Art, the Biennial Motion Picture Festival, and Internationale del Film d'Arte e Sull'Arte, the Havana Association of Cuban Artists, Mexico's Instituto de Cultura Cinematographica, and, domestically, the Academy of Motion Picture Arts and Sciences, the American Art Dealers' Association, the City of Los Angeles, NBC, the National Cartoonists Society, the Sister Kenny Foundation, and the U.S. Time Corporation.

The images the characters projected were "vital" to the public's "impression of the Disney organization and its products." If these images were "altered or affected in any negative way," Disney would be irreparably harmed. (The only specific figures Disney disclosed were that it had spent over $16,000,000 on movies and television shows featuring Mickey Mouse and that Mickey, who had not had a leading role in any of its productions for decades, had earned it over $6,000,000 within the last five years.)

Judge Wollenberg took the matter under submission. Phillips, who had written his firm's brief — and spent a great deal of lifestyle-enhancing time hanging with the Pirates in Osgood Alley — was pessimistic. "I was prepared to really argue the case," he says. "There was no possible confusion. The Pirates' Mickey was not Disney's Mickey. It was a comment on a values system. But the judge didn't want to hear it. His mind seemed made up. Later, I was scandalized by his opinion. He paid no attention to anything I said." Kennedy says, "If he wasn't a fan of Disney's at the start, he was by the end. We may've driven him there by being so obnoxious and the work so profane. Jonathan Swift, he did not think we were." Tatum agrees with this last point. "I was comfortable with Wollenburg as the judge. We had no personal relationship, and he was considered liberal; but he was effective and thoughtful and conducted his courtroom with humane decorum. I think the salaciousness of the use was an absolutely fundamental factor in the outcome. It was so far out of context as to be outrageous. I certainly felt confident."

Stepanian remembers only a lot of yelling. He had expected such a reception but had hoped for more. "Wollenberg was an old Jewish guy, a beautiful guy, a brilliant guy, an independent guy, a sophisticated guy, a tough guy. He wasn't a judge who played golf with Disney guys. He was a *mensch*. And parody is Jewish humor. The great humorists were the Jews: Mort Sahl; Lenny Bruce; Shelley Berman. I thought he'd get it. 'Ach, they're futzing around. What's the big deal?' But maybe he grew up on Mickey Mouse. Maybe that's what he showed his kids. 'Mickey is nice.' 'Mickey is good.' Now here he is *schtupping*. Then there was this whole thing of 'What're you doing in federal court?' People were going to prison. Gazillions of dollars were being spent. It was not a time to be satirizing when serious shit was going on."

The courtroom atmosphere also had its effect on the Pirates' morale. "Reality started setting in with the hearing," Hallgren says. "We were fucked." ("I thought they were fucked," Flenniken says, "way before that.")

Judge Wollenberg ordered each side to submit its own proposed findings of fact and conclusions of law for him to follow in the event he ruled in their favor. The Pirates took the opportunity to argue that the injunction should be denied because Disney had not proved it was likely to prevail at trial. It remained an "honestly debatable" question whether copying only the visual depiction of a cartoon character in a copyrighted book equated to infringing upon an "entire subject" of a copyright. The realities of public confusion and loss of business remained unproven. And courts should be particularly sensitive to making rulings that would curtail a free press.

Tatum confined his ancillary remarks to quoting Mark Twain's *Pudd'nhead Wilson*: "There is no character, howsoever good and fine but it can be destroyed by ridicule, however poor and witless."

CHAPTER NINE:
PART OF THE REASON WAS TO BE WISE ASSES

On April 7, 1972, before Judge Wollenberg's decision had issued, Disney moved to re-open the case for the admission and consideration of newly obtained "material evidence" that, Tatum alleged, would "establish the likelihood" that, unless enjoined, the Pirates would continue to violate Disney's copyrights.

Eight days earlier, David R. Smith, a thirty-one-year-old Disney archivist, had received G.B. Love's *The Rocket's Blast — Comicollector* #89. *RB-CC* was an ad-loaded fanzine. Though its circulation never topped 2,500, it provided comic book dealers and publishers a forum in which to announce available stock and new releases. Last Gasp's spring list had included *The Tortoise and the Hare* #1, provocatively featuring material "originally intended for *Mickey Mouse Meets the Air Pirates* #3," as well as *Air Pirates Funnies* #1, an eight-page, twenty-five cent, all-cartoon tabloid on newsprint stock. Smith had proceeded to Adam & Eve's Adult Books on Vine Street in Hollywood to investigate further. (When asked how he came to choose that particular outlet, whose name doesn't immediately stamp it as a place toward which a Disney archivist would normally gravitate, even for UGs, he said, "I have no recollection other than that someone told me they had seen the comic at that bookstore. You're right, I didn't usually frequent such establishments.")

Funnies, reminiscent of the comic page of a 1920s newspaper, had been mothered into existence by O'Neill's admiration for the work of Billy DeBeck and Sidney ("The Gumps") Smith, as well as the Pirates' pressing need for income. (It had even opened to the corrupting influence of advertisers, but the only corrupter it attracted was The Committee.) It contained work by all five Pirates, plus Murphy and Todd, but nothing to concern Disney.[99] *Tortoise,* however, trumpeting itself as the successor to work "now banned in Boston, Berkeley and the rest of continental Disneyland," was a thumb in the eye.

Tortoise had a little Dirty Duck and some Zeke Wolf. Flenniken debuted strikingly with "Trots and Bonnie," a story in the style of H. T. ("Casper Milquetoast") Webster, about a thirteen-year-old girl and her dog, which climaxes when he performs oral sex on her. O'Neill contributed a couple of pages reprinted from *The Realist* and a story about a murderous, coke-dealing rabbit named Roger, who became significant some years later when Disney released the film *Who Framed Roger Rabbit?* based on Gary K. Wolf's novel *Who Censored Roger Rabbit?* and O'Neill sued it for stealing *his* character.[100]

But the book was primarily Hallgren's. He did both covers. The front showed Toby Tortoise and Max Hare smoking a joint. The back had them marching with harmonica and drum, the Spirit of '72, proudly waving Old Glory, upon which was printed the caption of the Disney lawsuit, a recitation of its causes of action, and the $700,000 damages it was said to be seeking.[101] He did over half the pages, reprinting the Tortoise and Hare story from *Air Pirates* #2 and adding a lengthy conclusion in which the old rivals realize they have been exploited by race promoters to entertain others and "sell popcorn" and split for Nepal.[102]

The problem was that reprint. The TRO forbade the Pirates from further distribution of the enjoined material. And this story had one panel — out of

---

[99] Whatever hole in the market the Pirates expected *Funnies* to fill, their effort only confirmed the good reason for its existence. There was no #2. Hallgren explained why. "Damned if I know. I was willing to draw for it. In those days, whoever had the $100, that's the way you went."

[100] O'Neill based his claim on the following. Both Rogers were married, had big feet, and wore pants but no shoes or socks; Disney had undeniable access to his story, which made the theft possible; and Wolf was "a known comic store frequenter." "But," O'Neill says, "he died before he could testify. Let's start another rumor. 'Disney killed him.'" (I would gladly do my part; but, according to current sources — see p. 243 *supra* —Wolf is alive — and well enough to be suing Disney himself.)

The case's irony was deliciously attractive, but most Bay Area copyright lawyers had already represented Disney in some capacity and declined involvement because of a conflict of interest. Eventually David C. Phillips (no relation to David F., London's attorney), who would later represent Mountain Girl in her litigation with the estate of Jerry Garcia and three of the four Dead Kennedys (East Bay Ray, Klaus Fluoride, and D.H. Peligro) in theirs with Jello Biafra, agreed to handle it if O'Neill paid all costs. Artie Mitchell offered to put up $40,000, but Jim Mitchell refused to authorize the funding because of the amount of other litigation the brothers had on their hands, so the suit was dropped.

[101] The origin of this figure is a mystery. The only specific number in the complaint is the $100,000 per defendant in punitive damages. But it, like other numbers floated by O'Neill and others over the years that came to ground in various journalistic accounts of the case — an initial prayer for $750,000, later increased to $1,200,000; a prayer for $800,000; an *award* of $800,000, later reduced by the Supreme Court to $250,000 — has a close-enough-for-jazz appeal.

[102] London says O'Neill wrote the second installment. Hallgren admits receiving help with the first, "But the embarrassing puns and pointless dialogue prove the second is wholly mine."

forty-two — with an unambiguous Mickey and Minnie ("I figured," Hallgren says, "if anything would, that would be the one to draw fire") — and a probable Pluto elsewhere.[103] Kennedy summarized Disney's response: "The funnier things became, the madder Cooley, Crowley and Fartbreath got.[104] They saw this great manifestation of American culture being trashed. Unfortunately, truth was not a defense. Neither, it seems, was satire."

O'Neill says the publication of *Tortoise* was a deliberate, defiant act. *"Air Pirates #3* was only half done; but this was sitting there ready to go, so we put it out, telling them to take their injunction and put it where the sun doesn't shine." Hallgren, more or less, agrees. By some oversight, Disney's complaint had failed to list Toby and Max as characters to be protected from further unauthorized use, and he hoped to take advantage. "The story was done; someone was willing to print it; and Dan wanted it out. Part of the reason for doing the whole thing was to be wise asses, and this was my chance to be one of the big ones."

Ron Turner recalls that in late 1971 or early 1972 the Pirates approached him about publishing a new comic. They wanted to continue working together; and since Disney's restraining order had put the kibosh on *Funnies*, they had something else in mind. He said he would be interested in whatever they came up with. Some time later, Hallgren brought him *Tortoise* and said Stepanian and Morse had green-lighted its publication. (Kennedy says, "That sounds like advice Stepanian and Morse would have given. 'Ah, fuck 'em. Go ahead.'") He paid the Pirates $1000 and had 20,000 copies printed. After Disney moved to reopen the case, the Pirates, Stepanian and Morse called him to a meeting. The attorneys denied ever giving anyone any go-ahead. They were furious because Wollenberg would think the Pirates were defying him. ("Yelling and screaming sounds like me," Stepanian says, "because I didn't want to violate a court order.") Turner agreed to stop selling the book and asked the Pirates to refund the $1000. They didn't. *Tortoise* sold 10,000 copies, and he lost $2,500.

According to O'Neill, *Tortoise* had its silver lining. After it had incited Disney into increasing its claim for damages, he pointed out to the *Chronicle* it housed a potential $400,000 worth of litigation in a comic strip it owned. "In ten minutes, I had my copyright back."

---

[103] Disney also alleged that O'Neill's story about a shapeless character called the Phantom Roar-Shock constituted an improper use of the Phantom Blot; but, one blot/blob looking much like any other — unless they look like someone having sex with an oak tree (we've all seen that one, right?) — this seems a stretch.

[104] This comment further differentiates the two sides. When I asked Tatum if he had found litigating this case different than those where his opposition was other corporate attorneys, he measuredly replied, "I found them to be interesting characters. There was an element of our being representatives of the establishment and they the counterculture, so things were not entirely amicable, but I was interested on a personal level in how they functioned."

O'Neill refers to his mining of "Odd Bodkins" with Disney characters, followed by his formation of the Air Pirates, as a calculated "two-pronged movement" to carry off this coup. If things worked as he says, it speaks strongly for his shrewdness and persuasiveness and the *Chronicle*'s good heart, weak stomach and/or poor counsel. For if the statute of limitations had not already run on Disney's claim, the *Chronicle* could no more escape liability by transferring the copyright than I could avoid liability to you, after running over your foot, by transferring title of my Mustang to Aunt Maud.[105]

O'Neill also says that once his copyright was returned, other cartoonists thought, "'Gee, if O'Neill can get his back, I should get mine. His strip isn't going anywhere, and I'm making money for these people.' So 'Doonesbury' got his. They all got theirs. Within a year, the syndicates were stripped of their power."[106]

By mid-1972, to keep the context flowing, President Nixon had ordered the bombing of Hanoi and the mining of Haiphong harbor; George Wallace had been shot, and J. Edgar Hoover had died; the National Commission on Marijuana and Drug Abuse had called for the legalization of the private use of pot — the ink should be dry on the signature on that bill any minute; and six men had been arrested for burglarizing the Democratic Party National Committee Headquarters at the Watergate complex in Washington, D.C.

On July 7, Judge Wollenberg rendered his decision. It was patient, good-humored, thoughtful — and entirely predictable. Its tone was of a tolerant father reining in children whose antics had upset the adults in the neighborhood. It did not mention cunnilingus or Nepalese temple balls, but it had the sound of "I don't care what you do as long as you don't do it in the road and frighten the horses — and you have — and their bloodlines are pure — and the citizens they belong to are boss."

Wollenberg recognized Disney's valid copyrights on numerous books and comics that pictured various animal and insect characters. He acknowledged its devotion of "considerable effort and resources" to making these characters known and "exploiting [their] value..." He noted the Pirates had not only deliberately copied these characters' visual representation but had usurped their names. They had, however, delivered a "markedly" different message than Disney's. "The depths of that message aside, [it] could not fairly be called innocent."

[105] O'Neill's story has other problems. First, Disney didn't amend its complaint to include *The Tortoise and the Hare* until 1975. Second, Disney never increased its prayer for damages. And third, the reprinting of "Odd Bodkins" in *Comics and Stories,* as I've said, indicates he already had his copyrights.

[106] R.C.Harvey calls this claim "fairly outlandish." He cites Milton Caniff and Roy Crane as earlier cartoonists who owned their strips. He believes the breakthrough that allowed cartoonists to regain or retain the rights to their creations was "the founding of the Creators Syndicate which routinely gave cartoonists the rights to their own work, forcing other syndicates to follow."

Wollenberg believed that Disney would be irreparably damaged if the Pirates continued publishing their comics. And their conduct had convinced him they would publish them unless enjoined. But to receive its injunction, Disney had to show it was likely to win the case at trial; and that probability required analysis.

The most troublesome question for Wollenberg was whether Congress's protection of "all copyrightable component parts" within a copyrighted work extended to cartoon characters. In other words, did Disney's copyright of *Walt Disney's Comics and Stories,* Vol. 24, No. 10, prevent the Pirates from lifting an image or two from it and lasciviously entwining them upon a zeppelin's floor?

Disney had marshaled an impressive posse of funny paper support for its argument that it did. In 1914, in *Hill v. Whalen and Martell,* a federal District Court judge in New York had held that a "dramatic performance," "In Cartoonland," featuring the characters Nutt and Giff, infringed upon the copyright for the "Mutt and Jeff" comic strip.[107] In 1924, the Second Circuit Court of Appeals, in *King Features Syndicate v. Fleischer,* had held that Spark Plug, a horse in "Barney Google," could not be reproduced as a doll without permission. Ten years later, the same court, in *Fleischer Studios v. Ralph A. Freundlich,* stopped a toy manufacturer from turning out dolls based on the cartoon character Betty Boop. And in 1940, in *Detective Comics, Inc. v. Bruno Pub.,* it ended the career of Wonderman because he was too much like Superman. But this entire Man of Steel-anchored line-up seemed incapable of withstanding a judicial slap in the puss from Sam Spade or, more precisely, *Warner Brothers Pictures v. Columbia Broadcasting System.* That 1954 decision was not only more current — lawyers with contemporaneity on their side like to dismiss older, contrary authority as "outdated"; if you have seniority on your side, you go for "long-standing" — but, more importantly, it bore the imprimatur of the Ninth Circuit Court of Appeals.

The facts were these. In 1930, Dashiell Hammett had sold the story rights to *The Maltese Falcon* for $8,500 to Warner Brothers, which made three films from it. Sixteen years later, he sold the rights to that novel's characters to CBS for a radio series. After one of those episodes ("The Kandy Tooth") aired, Warners sued CBS, alleging it owned these characters. The Ninth Circuit held for the radio network. "The characters were vehicles for the story told," it said, portraying itself as looking out for authors who might only have one or two marketable characters within them, "and the vehicles did not go with the sale of the story." It did not specifically rule all fictional characters uncopyrightable

---

[107] Interestingly, in light of future developments, the judge said the key to the infringement was that the public could be fooled into thinking the play featured the original's characters and not pay to see them in another. But, he added, absent this likelihood, "criticism of the original, which lessened its money value by showing that it was not worth seeing or hearing, could not give any right of action for infringement of copyright."

and, therefore, available for free use by others, which would have been, as Wollenberg pointed out, "a strange sort of protection [for an] author... trying to make a living from a finite assortment of ideas," but the Pirates' argument that this was implied struck him with "considerable force."

While *Warner Brothers* had been criticized by most commentators, followed by no other courts, and ignored by the movie industry, which continued to insert clauses into contracts giving it control over characters in works it purchased, its seat of origin meant it bound Wollenberg. He found no authority to allow him to interpret it as Disney's lawyers urged and restrict its application to literary characters, exempting cartoon ones, but he discovered "a narrow gap" in its reasoning through which he could wiggle to Disney's advantage.

One of the law's charming lunacies allows it to posit standards — "due process," for instance, or "serious and willful misconduct" — which are essentially meaningless combinations of words but against which behavior is solemnly measured as if they are as definitive as twelve inches or sixteen ounces, thereby allowing courts to achieve any results they desire while claiming an impartial inevitability for them. Wollenberg found such a standard here. The Ninth Circuit had said a character could be copyrighted if it "really constitutes the story being told," as opposed to being "only the chessman in the game of telling [it]." So that became the test: "chessman" vs. "really the story." No case had ever held such chessmen existed. Only Judge Hand had ever suggested he'd located a work of literature — *Point Counter-Point,* a fine novel and a strange choice — that contained any. Disney had not even argued this approach should be applied. But Wollenberg found its plots "quite subordinated to its characters." The former were easily forgotten; the latter lingered in memory. They had "achieved a high degree of 'recognition' or 'identification.' To an extent much greater than a mere name, the distinctive style in which each character is drawn conjures up in a worldwide audience... associations with rather extensive groupings of traits, characteristics and qualities." Their postures and expressions, he said, often conveyed more of significance than their speech or accompanying text. "The principal appeal [of Disney's books]... to the primary audience of children for which they were intended lies with the characters and nothing else." The test he had devised had been met, though, of course, if he hadn't been planning to conclude it had, he would not have needed to formulate it. He could simply have followed *Warner Brothers.*

With characters copyrightable, the question now became: Had the Pirates taken too much for a fair use. Here, the controlling precedent within the Ninth Circuit remained *Benny.* The meaningless test *it* had established, in Wollenberg's words, was whether "the defendants had copied a substantial part of the protected work and... [if] the part so copied was a substantial part of the defendant's..." He easily found this test passed. While conceding that the Pirates' plots and dialogue could not have differed more from Disney's, he had already held characters to be the crux of Disney's work. And since O'Neill had admitted copying Mickey and his cohorts *"exactly,"* a "substantial" taking and a "substantial" contribution were self-evident. (It did not necessarily follow that even if character depiction was the end-all and be-all of Disney's work, it was equally so of the Pirates; but Wollenberg made no such distinction.) The literary value of the Pirates' books — whether brilliant satire or twisted grotesque — was irrelevant once it was shown they had copied the heart of someone else's work.

Which left the First Amendment. Wollenberg brushed it aside. To apply it would "obliterate copyright protection" anytime anyone asserted their infringement conveyed an idea. For copyrighted material, no greater right to expression existed than fair use. Besides, he let slip in an aside which may have tipped his true feelings about the entire matter, he had "some difficulty in discovering the significant content of the ideas which the defendants are expressing."

Having found that Disney was entitled to an injunction on the basis of a copyright infringement, Wollenberg found it unnecessary to address Disney's trademark infringement and unfair competition claims. He granted the injunction and ordered the Pirates to surrender all copies of the offending books and all material for making additional copies.

According to Stepanian, he and Morse wanted to appeal Wollenberg's order and try to gut Disney's case by having the law reinterpreted in the Pirates' favor, while Kennedy and Phillips wanted to leave the injunction in place, proceed to trial, and beat Disney's brains out there. Kennedy, confessing to a "recollection as dim as Disney is dull," believes a "two-track strategy" was implemented: appealing the injunction, since it kept the Pirates from doing their books, *and* pushing for trial, in order to expose "the fundamental absurdity" of Disney's position. The court file, however, shows that only Kennedy, on behalf of O'Neill, filed a notice of appeal, in which no one else joined, and that the case otherwise lay fallow.

Chapter Ten:
Kiss this Underground Stuff Good-Bye

Despite the studio's break-up and the six figures of damages hanging over their heads, the Air Pirates had been pursuing careers in their own fashions.

Gary Hallgren contributed stories to comic books — *Facts of Life Funnies, El Perfecto Comics, The San Francisco Comic Book* — while planning to diversify into the more lucrative field of caricaturing vacationers and tourists. He had intended to spend the summer of 1972 tapping the rich Cape Cod market; but Willy Murphy, who had worked there, convinced him he was not ready for that big a show. Instead, he sharpened his skills in a more minor league, hanging at an outdoor café in Sausalito with sketch pad exposed and pen cocked.

Ted Richards had achieved his goal of having his own comic book when Last Gasp published *Dopin' Dan* #1 in May. An all-military-themed anthology, it contained Murphy's "Harry Kirschner" (a pointy-headed goofus experiences basic training); Flenniken's "The General's Daughter" (Bonnie shoots marbles with a neighbor's glass eye amidst lamp shades of human skin and tables made from Viet Cong skulls); London's "All-American Hymie" (a druggie enlists in order to score "Grade A-plus boo from Nam"); Hallgren's "G.I. Blues" (a pin-up caliber spread of nipples, muffs and oral cop); and Scott Judge's "Sgt. Jock and Kilo Co." (A Sgt. Rock send-up fells a plane with a bayonet and K.O.s a tank with brass knuckles, while blithely wiping out half his men in the process.)

Dopin' Dan, himself, constituted Richards spinning Sad Sack and Beetle Bailey for his generation. This time, though, the protagonist's bumblings were less central than the stimulants that accompanied them and the nature of the conflict that had him in uniform. Dan is just back from Viet Nam, a "short-timer," finishing his tour at Fort Fragg, near Fatalsburg. His days are spent — with startling been-there, done-that authenticity — amidst joints, lids, STP, orange sunshine, and a cafeteria that stocks methadone beside the chocolate milk. His service, he fumes — ripping a jagged edge of contemporaneity through the comic book conventional — has been for the protection of "generals... congressmen, senators, sheriffs... corporations... fumes, pollution, poisen [sic], greed, hate, lust, destruction... Bob Hope, Billy Graham, Laird, Mitchell, Nixon, [and] Agnew..."[108]

Bobby London published three comics in 1972. The first, *The Dirty Duck Book*, carried forward his tales of Dirty, his servant/foil Weevil, and other residents of Gnatfucca Flats, which was near to — and closely resembled — Coconino County, Krazy Kat's home turf. The dialogue — "eighth-a-yistick," "hoss toids," "phillipsteins" — was creative and the visuals — shifting backgrounds, vanishing panel borders — anarchical in a Herriman mode. The humor involved falls from cliffs or through skylights, interspersed with insults, assaults, collisions, shootings, and swallowings by alligators. The book began with a Grateful Dead concert but soon abandoned all rootings to a particular time and place, mind-bendingly uniting all points of cartoon history from Krazy to the UGs.

London's anthologies, *Merton of the Movement* and *Left Field Funnies*, examined assorted aspects of the newly "greened" America. Richards had Dopin' Dan contending with bombs in the barracks and relying on longhair wigs to pick up hippie girls. Flenniken portrayed Bonnie padding her bosom to attract boys — and studying self-defense to repel horny men. Hallgren involved Bernie Bush — who bore an unsettling resemblance to Paw in Cliff Sterrett's "Polly and Her Pals" — with sex, dope, and frontal nudity; Murphy put the Beasley Boys to work selling UG papers to raise drug money; and Gary King tripped on sex, coke and STP.

Most of London's contributions examined the more fervid side of the counterculture's political wing through the adventures of Merton and some friends: the feminist Libbie; the revolutionary Fidel Goldstein; the drug dealer Hymie ("Hashish") Goldberg; and Yiddie Yippie (no explanation necessary). The experience was hardly a rallying call. All New Left activists were presented as clowns, clods, or publicity seeking egomaniacs. The UG press (exemplified by the *Berkeley Tripe*) was dismissed as "intellectual JHACKOFFH." Racial solidarity reduced to black studs screwing white chicks. Gay Liberation equated to bearded guys in dresses. Drugs didn't expand consciousness but caused zonked-out misadventures. Sexual freedom resulted, not in liberated bodies, but yeast infections.

The stories, while lapel-grabbing, scream-it-in-the-face, all-spittle-flying sincere, are uncomfortably over the top. This was not a package designed to ingra-

[108] *Dopin' Dan*'s three-issue run ended in October 1973, when the winding down of the war stripped it of its motor. In 1977, Richards revived it as a strip for the newly created, leftist military paper, *Enlisted Times;* but political radicalism had lost its appeal, and the focus shifted into a "how-to-cope-with-the-service" mode. That period was collected in *Dopin' Dan* #4 in 1979.

tiate its presenter with many in whose circles he ran. The sense of an outsider settling scores is palpable. The most interesting piece, in light of subsequent events — not only for its uncompelled-by-O'Neill depiction of London, at age two, suckling on Minnie Mouse's breast — is the autobiographical "Why Bobby Seale Is Not Black." Its narrative lurches back and forth in time, hip-hops between California and New York, heaping scorn upon family and collectives, suburbia and *Rolling Stone* en route. The main thrust is London's effort to justify himself against those who had criticized him for "mak[ing] movement men look like incompetents."

"Why Bobby..." is courageous, noble, worthy — and bleak. Essentially a call for artists to assert themselves unfettered, its conclusion leaves London imprisoned within a panel of his own creation, alone but for his shadow, realizing, when it came to opinions, "As usual... there were more of THEM and less of ME!!" By year's end, he and Flenniken would leave San Francisco and, as she put it, "Kiss this underground stuff 'Good-bye.'"

Dan O'Neill vanished. Shortly after the hearing on the preliminary injunction, using means more conventional than the Australian crawl, he had reached Ireland, "slipped through" British lines, and entered Belfast. On January 30, 1972, Bloody Sunday, British soldiers, firing on demonstrators against internment, had killed thirteen people in Derry. Bernadette Devlin's Northern Ireland Civil Rights Association had then invited O'Neill to observe the situation and report to Americans about it through his cartoons. He was the first member of his family to return, and it was a disappointment. "Belfast is the same latitude as Labrador. Nothing's green. It's just barbed wire, rocks and bombs. With a hometown like that, you wish you were Italian or Puerto Rican or French. I wouldn't've even minded being short if I could've been born on the Riviera."

O'Neill remained several terrifying months, seeking action where, those with knowledge of the situation say, the winged and haloed set would have feared to tread. He did a topical strip for the NICRA newspaper, which also ran in the *San Francisco Bay Guardian*, dean of the area's weekly giveaways. He also filed taped reports — later incorporated into a Peabody Award-nominated show — that were broadcast on KSAN-FM, the city's hippest rock-radio station. (Its stance on public affairs was best captured by the tag line of its anchorman, Wes "Scoop" Nisker: "That's today's news. If you didn't like it, go out and make some of your own.") He knew little about the situation when he arrived, but what he learned inflamed his work sufficiently that he claims to be "still wanted for anti-British propaganda." He had tipped Herb Caen as to his whereabouts, and the thought that 10,000,000 of the columnist's readers had an eye on him provided some comfort, though the trip had moments that made facing Disney look like a walk through Buena Vista Park.

One evening, while O'Neill was riding in a car with members of the Alliance Party, a group which tried to bring Protestants and Catholics together ("like Hubert Humphrey Democrats, kind of a hopeless position"), he was stopped at a British army checkpoint. "It was a UDR patrol, Saracens in gear, and the first thing through the window is a cocked .45 in my ear. 'Your papers!' They go, 'Oh, Hugh O'Neill, the arch traitor.' I go, 'I don't know nothing about 1604.'[109] The guy checks on the radio and comes back, pistol in his pocket now and something in his hand he puts through the window. 'Will you autograph this?' It's *O'Neill Comics and Stories* with The Big Bad Wolf on the cover. How the hell this Presbyterian killer had this in there...? It was a great place to run into a fan."

While O'Neill had been away, Richards and Murphy had set up a new studio. Fast Draw was in Sheridan Alley, south of Market, in a loft above Tea Lautrec Litho, which was run by Levon Mosgofian, an old Socialist who printed Fillmore and Avalon posters. Hallgren worked there. So did Gary King. London had been invited but declined. ("That was the last thing I wanted to do," he says.)

O'Neill joined on his return, but his stay was brief. Everyone was working individually, not in the cooperative fashion that had appealed to him about studio work. And he felt the others resented him because he had skipped out on them and because the press had billed the Disney suit as being against Dan O'Neill and the Air Pirates, as if they were his appendages, not equals. "They were kind of like don't-want-to-see-me-anymore. It was painful." Richards has said that, in part, the studio was an effort by the others to assert their independence from O'Neill; and Hallgren points out he had changed too. "He wasn't the same person. He'd moved beyond the Air Pirates. He'd been to a real war, not a cultural war, and that raised his level of confidence to dangerous levels."[110]

O'Neill found work making promotional cartoons for KSAN. He also self-published several issues of the politically-edged *Penny-Ante Republican*. People sent a penny and SASE and received a four-page comic: an eight-and-a-half by eleven-inch sheet of paper, doubled over. With the profit margin that allowed, his financial planner must have been delighted by the opportunities the uprising at Wounded Knee provided.

On February 27, 1973, at the request of Oglala Sioux elders outraged by their people's living conditions, 200 members of the American Indian Movement seized the village of Wounded Knee on the Pine Ridge Reservation in South Dakota, where, on December 29, 1890, the United States 7th Cavalry had massacred 300 unarmed Native Americans, mostly old men, women and children. Now authorities imposed a blockade to keep reinforcements and supplies from reaching the insurrectionists. Feelings were so intense, O'Neill says,

---

[109] According to historian R. F. Forster, Hugh O'Neill, Earl of Tyrone, led the "last great Gaelic counter-attack" to the Tudor reconquest.

[110] Fast Draw lasted about a year, until Richards, newly married and in college, moved out. Later – see below – it would be reborn.

"They were picking up Japanese guys in San Diego. If you had brown skin, you were frozen in place." He joined efforts to organize a relief mission.

By O'Neill's account, Metromedia, which owned KSAN, provided press passes for a ten-man news crew which were given to Indians. Lifters were added to a 1957 Chevrolet so it could hold 1000 pounds of freeze-dried food, 1000 pounds of battle dressing, and 1000 pounds of Winchesters — and still look like a Chevy with ten Indians in it. His personal IRA contacts convinced sheriffs (presumably Irish) throughout the west not to inspect the vehicle closely.

"It was the first armed revolution against the United States, and I had to show up. I flew in with my suit on and one of the girls from the O'Farrell. The night before, I'm watching this orgy scene — 150 people fucking; Big Daddy Eric Nord's face buried between some woman's legs; and someone giving it to him from behind, a regular daisy chain — and I said to Laughlin (Chandler "Travis T. Hipp" Laughlin, host of KSAN's *Rawhide Reality Review*), 'I'm tired of going to war with no help. Six months of celibacy in Ireland's enough. Pick out a pretty one, and see if she wants to go.' Her job was to look so beautiful those sexist bastards wouldn't look at me. In Denver, we had to hop a plane to Rapid City; and it's all cops and marshals, and they're all looking at her, except one Texas Ranger,[111] who could tell from my hat I'm from Oklahoma and something was up. He followed us from the airport; but when we turned into the Holiday Inn, where the Indians met us, he figured, 'Oh, he's okay.'"

O'Neill says he remained at Wounded Knee for forty-five of the sixty-five-day siege. He drew cartoons to educate children about the struggle. He put out *Penny-Ante Republicans*. He filed five radio reports a day. "That's when they caught me with the guns; but I knew my friends were screw-ups, and I'd checked the law. If you're an Indian who's registered on a reservation, you're entitled to have a weapon because you're allowed to hunt. The only Indians I smuggled back were Indians from that reservation. So when they caught us, they had to give the guns back and let them go. They were reporters until they got on the reservation; then they magically turned back into Indians. The FBI was really ticked off at me for that one."

---

[111] When I asked O'Neill by what authority a Texas Ranger could act in South Dakota, he explained, "They just like to kill Indians."

Chapter Eleven:
A Big, Hairy Freak on Acid

Disney's lawsuit had lain dormant since January 4, 1973, when Kennedy had withdrawn O'Neill's appeal of Judge Wollenberg's order granting the preliminary injunction. Tatum had assigned the file to Paul J. Laveroni, who had joined Cooley, Crowley less than two years before. Laveroni was a lanky, Jimmy Stewartish six-foot-four. He had graduated Catholic University in 1965, with a B.A. in Philosophy, and Georgetown Law School in 1968, where he had been on the law review. He had served four years in the Marines, prosecuting or defending over 500 court martials. On August 22, Laveroni initiated formal discovery proceedings by serving a set of interrogatories — twenty-one written questions, some with over a dozen sub-sections — to which each Pirate was to provide written answers within thirty days.

Discovery is permitted because courts favor settlements over trials and believe settlements will occur more frequently if parties can be compelled to lay their cards on the table, rather than keep them up their sleeves. The significance of Laveroni's interrogatories seemed to hover somewhere between an *ad hoc* litigatory reflex action and a serious intent to shake all available change from every Pirate's pocket. What was, he asked, the legal business status of The Air Pirates? Of Hell Comics? Who were the principals? The employees? Where could they be found? Where had they carried out their activities? Who did what with respect to each issue of *Air Pirates Funnies*? Where was it sold? What did it earn? Who published? Printed? Promoted? Distributed it? To what other uses had O'Neill put Mickey Mouse? What profit did he make? On what evidence did the Pirates rely in denying the truth of the allegations in Disney's Complaint? What relevant "correspondence, memoranda, interoffice papers, ledgers, profit and loss statements, bank statements, receipts, invoices, canceled checks... [and] other documents, records or papers" did they possess? Where did they bank?

Laveroni granted the Pirates' attorneys three extensions of time to answer his questions. By November 20, none had, so he asked Judge Wollenberg to order them to — and to pay sanctions, including his fee ($150) and costs ($50) for the bringing of his motion, for their failure to comply.

On December 20, before Wollenberg issued any order, Morse and Stepanian filed Hallgren's and Richards's answers. Both were equally replete with "Unknown"s and "Not applicable"s. Both described the Air Pirates as "a loose confederation of cartoonists." Each disclosed his own address in San Francisco and said London was in Seattle and O'Neill's whereabouts were unknown. Both denied any knowledge of or involvement with the business end of their comics' publication. All they did, they said, was draw cartoons. Last Gasp was their publisher, promoter and distributor. They denied any malice toward or intent to injure Disney. They advised Disney to read their affidavits already on file to learn why they had denied its allegations. Hallgren stated that his labors had earned him $350. Richards said he made $20, plus room and board. They had no documents — and no bank.

Judge Wollenberg ordered London and O'Neill to file their answers by January 20, 1974, or have judgment entered against them.

On January 16, Kennedy filed nearly identical sets of answers for London and O'Neill. Neither added much to what Hallgren and Richards had said. Each identified the Pirates as a "loose-knit organization of friends." Each denied any knowledge of or involvement with the business end of their comics publication and referred Laveroni to Ron Turner, whom they identified as their publisher. Their comics, they said, had neither harmed Disney nor confused the public. Indeed, they had been the only people damaged because their work, "namely excellent parodies... was suppressed." Each said he had made fifty cents — and O'Neill revealed prior earnings of $179 a month from the *Chronicle* for "Odd Bodkins" in the six-and-a-half years before the formation of the Air Pirates and another $1000 from Glide Publications for a 1969 edition of *Hear the Sound...*

Five *hours* later, Laveroni moved to have judgment entered against O'Neill and London. Their answers, he said, were inadequate because neither had signed them under oath, which the Federal Rules of Civil Procedure required, and because their similarities showed them to be "joint answers," which the rules forbade. Moreover, the answers came entirely from Kennedy, who didn't even represent London. They were, Laveroni wrote — adopting a prose style that remained throughout the proceedings the legalese equivalent of an M.P. striding into a bar and laying into its revelers with his truncheon — a "charade," "inadequate," "incomplete and evasive," "misleading," "flippant... and almost devoid of meaningful information," "[non-compliant] with the letter or spirit of the rules," "patently frivolous at best and, at worst, contemptuous of the entire

Federal discovery process..."[112] He demanded that judgment be entered against O'Neill and London.

Kennedy responded February 27. When he and O'Neill had dropped their appeal, allowing the preliminary injunction to become permanent, he stated, they had assumed Disney would not pursue the case. When the interrogatories arrived, he could not locate O'Neill. Phillips, still officially London's attorney, had moved to the east coast.[113] Kennedy had also "broken" contact with the other Pirates and their lawyers. When O'Neill fortuitously called him about another matter, they tried to answer the questions with information on hand for both him and London. He signed them because O'Neill was out of town and the deadline was approaching. Kennedy says now, "We felt totally sandbagged. We felt we had an agreement that, if the Pirates wouldn't draw similar characters behaving inappropriately, the whole thing would lie fallow." Both Tatum and Laveroni say no such agreement was made.[114]

Simultaneously, O'Neill filed "supplemental" answers. The only new information was that he placed Hallgren on Cape Cod, working as a "caricature artist"; London in Seattle, doing a strip for *National Lampoon*;[115] and Richards attending San Francisco State on the G.I. bill, earning $15 a week drawing cartoons for the school paper. He described himself as "an unemployed cartoonist," teaching cartooning part-time at the University of California Extension in San Francisco, earning $200 a month.

These responses were sufficient to have Disney's motion dropped from the court's calendar.

Ron Turner had been neither surprised nor disappointed when Disney had sued the Pirates. "I knew it would happen," he says now, "and I thought it would be nice

---

[112] When I raised Laveroni's language with Stepanian, he laughed. "That's a Downtown Thing. If you have the copyright, you talk tough. You don't say, 'Oh please, Mr. Infringer, stop what you're doing.' When we represented Crumb, we were, 'Fuck you, if you use "Keep On Truckin."' We'd come down like Thor on these fucking little t-shirt guys."

[113] Actually, Phillips says, "I had been doing a lot of acid and speed; and, one morning, I realized my briefcase was full, and I wasn't interested in one thing in it. I thought, What you're doing is stupid! I closed my office and didn't practice law for seventeen years."

[114] I am no expert on federal procedure, but the Tatum-Laveroni version seems persuasive. Without a final decision or stipulated judgment to resolve the suit, Disney would have been vulnerable to a motion to have it dismissed for a lack of prosecution, leaving the Pirates free to resume their bedevilment.

[115] The *Lampoon,* which debuted April 1970 with a special "Sex" issue — followed by "Greed," "Blight," "Bad Taste," and "Paranoia" — had quickly become the country's top humor magazine. London says that, when he began working for it, he was castigated by other UG cartoonists for selling out. Then, when he left, they fell over themselves trying to replace him.

to get things into the next phase." He believed he could afford this detached curiosity because the Pirates had promised to keep his role secret. But when a process server subpoenaed him to Cooley, Crowley's to give a deposition, his first thought was to arm himself with a lawyer tough enough to stand up to Disney. His choice was Jim Woods, of the Berkeley firm Cake and Woods, who had represented his dope dealer-financial backer.[116]

Cooley, Crowley's offices were in the twenty-five story, block-wide Alcoa Building, at Front and Clay, at the north end of San Francisco's financial district, an ingot's throw from the TransAmerica pyramid, the Bank of America's black obelisk, the Golden Gateway. The building's glass exterior is fixed with X-bracing, fourteen vari-lengthed steel beams, seven ascending left-to-right, seven right-to-left, so that it seems, if you are partial to symbolic thought, to have been constructed from mammoth diamonds, monstrously pricey, enormously hard. Cooley's suite was on the twentieth floor. The floors were polished hardwood, the view of Telegraph Hill and the Bay.

A deposition is a proceeding in which an attorney questions a party or potential witness, who has been placed under oath by a court reporter, to find out what he might testify to at trial. Depositions are known for their repetitious, mind-numbing, butt-aching, same-questions-in, same-answers-out, many-haystacks-searched, few-needles-found quality. Turner planned to portray himself as "a big, hairy freak, an acid-dropping hippie who couldn't care less what was going on" to convince Disney the cost of pursuing a case against him would far exceed any judgment they could hope to collect. The result was 107 pages of testimony that are still recalled with wonder by those present. There were the standard issue evasions: "I don't remember"; "I don't recall"; "I don't know"; "I have no idea"; "Beats me"; accented by an exemplary rococo "I don't know what my categories were then but whatever it was, you know, that was a lot of — $700 would have been — I don't know. Fifteen cents for each book? I don't remember"; and a Hall of Fame, custom-tailored-for-the-occasion "I was doing a lot of psychedelics in that period. I can't remember too much of what was going on then."

Much of what Turner did recall began with whimsy and devolved into moonshine. Last Gasp's origins, he related, lay with twenty to thirty — or thirty to forty — people, none of whom he could any longer name, who passed in and out of a non-structured "commune or collective or something," called The Visual Yo-Yo Tribe. ("Three words," he helpfully explained, "with a dash in the

---

[116] While almost all the attorneys involved in the case were delighted to revisit this piece of their past, Woods, now an assistant district attorney in Trinity County, was not. "You called about a case of Walt Disney versus somebody," he said in response to my phone message. "I have absolutely no idea what you're talking about."

"Let me refresh your recollection..."

"No, you won't. You can't. I have no memory that can be refreshed. You got the right guy. I was Lee Cake's partner. But I don't remember a thing. Got it?"

Every word.

middle of the 'Yo-Yo.'") The Tribe printed comic books — without the aid of any formal business status, license, or tax I.D. number — whenever it could find a willing printer.

After the Tribe split up, Turner and whoever was living with him at the time — also unrecollectable — decided to go into business. That business, Last Gasp, incorporated September 11, 1971. It published comics and, as a community service, advised others how to do the same. This was all he had done for the Air Pirates: counseled them about technical matters; suggested printers who might do their books. He denied writing or editing their books or consulting with them about content or marketing. When told the Pirates had fingered him as their publisher, wholesaler, promoter, and distributer, Turner replied, "That's indeed an honor... [But] I had absolutely no control over what they did. They wanted to be Air Pirates, and they did it; and they wanted to battle Disney, and they did that. The trip they were on was their own trip. It wasn't my trip. Every suggestion I made was turned down." The Pirates, he said, were their own publisher. John Lowe, who had worked for Co. & Sons under the name Pentagram Press, had printed the covers and jobbed out the interiors. (This was correct as far as it went. Lowe *had* worked for Bagley. He *did* print the covers. But Turner did not volunteer that, between the "had" and the "did," he had lured Lowe away from Bagley, and Lowe had set up his press in Last Gasp's building.)

Turner's picture of the UG business world in 1971 must have felt about as familiar to corporate attorneys as Oz to Dorothy. "Our culture," he said, "was based on the American Indian, which is you have a kiva — it's like a storehouse, a grainery. You put into it what you produce and you take out of it what you need." He, for instance, had gifted various Pirates with $1-2000, "bought a lot of groceries," paid for some supplies, and received 5-10,000 copies of each issue of *Air Pirates Funnies*, which he sold for twenty or thirty cents apiece or swapped for merchandise. Other people who had put up money or provided services, along with each Pirate, received copies to sell as well. The number each received was decided collectively, according to "whatever seemed right," based on each person's recollection of what he had done or donated to the operation.

While Woods kicked him repeatedly under the table, Turner's creative juices flowed. He found himself unable to recall the names of anyone who had contributed money or services to the Air Pirates, except "some guy named Joe," who hauled things in his truck. (Alert readers who wish to provide a more complete answer to this question may now raise their hands.) He could not remember anyone to whom he had sold or swapped any books. He no longer had his mailing list of potential customers or any other records, except for a couple of flyers, a few canceled checks, and some invoices from Lowe that were "worth about as much as the paper they're printed on," since Lowe was well known for fudging the count of how many books he was handing over, botching his work so thoroughly many copies were thrown out before being shipped, and being vulnerable to having boxes of completed comics mysteriously disappear between shipment and delivery. (Lowe, Turner revealed, had unfortunately vanished two years earlier; and his only known employee, as luck would have it, had relocated "somewhere in the midwest.") Turner conceded he was "a very, very poor record keeper.... We really didn't like records much. It was just very organic. It was all kept in our heads." He'd had a bookkeeper who might have been more detail-oriented, but that fellow was no more available than Lowe or anyone else in his narrative, since he had pulled up stakes and become a ranch hand in Sonoma County.[117]

Turner's deposition, deft and charming as it was, lacked the desired result. Disney amended its complaint and joined him and Last Gasp as defendants.

This was not a good time for Turner. In a few years, his company had gone from being his sole proprietorship, to a partnership, to a corporation of which he owned only twelve percent. As a corporation, Last Gasp's reputation had suffered from the dilution of his personal touch. Cartoonists often felt they were being short-changed when accountings rolled around; and Turner, who still valued the community of spirit that once infused the UG world, was in the process of reacquiring complete control of the business, "so I could pay royalties and not screw the artists."

"I wanted out," he says. "I was never supposed to be in, and I couldn't afford to be liable because it would put me out of business."

On December 3, 1974, an informal settlement conference was held before Judge Wollenberg. Stepanian, Morse, and Kennedy, now representing both O'Neill and London, appeared for the Pirates. Turner was represented by Woods. Wollenberg ordered the defendants to provide Disney with information about their financial status so meaningful negotiations could take place.

The following April, Laveroni notified the court that a settlement had been reached with Turner. Less than two weeks later, Hallgren settled too. "I felt guilty breaking solidarity," he says, "but Albert [Morse] told me I was being stupid. We had no chance." Both agreed to refrain from printing, making, manufacturing, publishing, selling, marketing, displaying, or otherwise making any use or deriving any benefit from any of the Air Pirates' comics. Both agreed to turn over any plates, molds or prints from which copies of these comics could be made. Both agreed to refrain from further infringements upon Disney trademarked or copyrighted property. And both allowed judgement to be entered against them for $85,000. It was understood, without being memorialized in the official record, that as long as they abided by the other conditions, Disney would not attempt to collect. Turner also had to destroy the unsold Air Pirates books he had in stock. He was out the money he had paid for them, as well as

---

[117] This particular detail does not strike me as outlandish as it might some, since my own accountant in those years worked as a carpenter in Marin County before abandoning both gigs to write sitcoms in L.A.

for the never-completed third issue, and his legal fees.[118] O'Neill, Richards and London were set for a three-day court trial before Judge Wollenberg on June 23.

O'Neill says London and Richards were also supposed to settle. "They had done what they were supposed to, which was create this comic book company; and it was planned, if there was a fall, to eliminate them. It was my idea, and they weren't supposed to take the rap." Richards says he didn't settle because he still believed the Pigs to be part of a common heritage and he wanted to protect his rights to Zeke Wolf. He also felt a commitment to O'Neill. "I was a warrior. I had received great training; and, in return, I would stay in the battle. But it was a mistake. I should've taken the deal." London says, "I vaguely recall O'Neill saying 'Gary's settling. If you want to, go ahead,'" but, he told Ringgenberg, Flenniken gave him "this whole lecture about the First Amendment, my loyalty to Dan O'Neill, Lenny Bruce, Dick Gregory [and]... talked me out of it." Their marriage was in trouble and, not wanting to increase tensions, he followed her advice.

[118] Turner believes the agreement only barred him from infringing upon Disney's copyrights for ten years, which rankled him because he expected some to be expiring shortly, and he had wanted a shot at them when they fell into the public domain. The judgment on file, however, is unlimited in duration; and, as noted earlier, all of Disney's copyrights remain good.

Chapter Twelve:
While C.J. Masturbated With the Towel Rack

By 1975, America had become a vastly different place from when Robert Crumb had rolled his baby carriage down Haight Street. Its combat troops had been gone from Vietnam for over a year. Richard Nixon had crushed the progressives' last great hope, George McGovern — and then been driven from the White House in disgrace. *Penthouse* and *Hustler* were for sale at the corner newsstand. *Deep Throat* and *The Devil in Miss Jones* were pulling boffo crowds to the local multiplex. National best seller lists had featured a serial masturbator, "zipless fucks," and sex's *Joy*. Pop music had cleared room for androgyny, bestiality, cross-dressing, live-animal abuse, sheriff-shooting, God-dissing, every drug and/or fetish you could imagine, and sixteen minutes of a diva sounding like she was being planked. Hollywood had made heroes out of a fratricidal Mafioso, a sexually impaired bank robber, a psychopathic cab driver, and a drug dealer named "Captain America." It had depicted full frontal nudity, simulated oral and anal sex, and introduced the first X-rated, feature-length cartoon.[119] Cocaine had replaced marijuana and LSD as the younger generation's drug of choice. And the hippie, whom the next wave of adolescent rebels, the Punks, would treat with about as much respect as their predecessors had Suzie Creamcheese and Mr. Jones, retained the cultural clout of flappers and teddy boys.

The superhero renaissance of the 1960s had resulted in the domination

---

[119] *Fritz the Cat*, the work in question, was based upon a character of Crumb's creation. He so loathed the film, he had his name stricken from the credits and dispatched the feline with an ice-pick to the spine at his next opportunity.

of the comic book industry by two companies, Marvel and DC, both of which now thrashed about to accommodate themselves to the changes that decade had wrought. DC sought social relevance — particularly through those issues of *Green Lantern/ Green Arrow* written by Denny (no relation to Dan) O'Neil — by pitting its heroes against racism and sexism, as well as radioactive mutants and intergalactic monstrosities. Marvel tried black superheroes, Asian superheroes, American Indian superheroes, and female superheroes — including Shanna the She-Devil, who was not only female but a "veterinarian and ecologist." Aping E.C. — and duplicating its lack of success — it introduced a series of black-and-white "magazines" to escape the box the Comics Code continued to place over violence, sex and horror. And after his company was denied Code approval for a Spider-Man trilogy in which Peter Parker's best friend became a speed freak — which had been prepared at the request of the Department of Health, Education and Welfare to warn teenagers about the dangers of drugs — on the grounds that comics ought not mention the vile things even negatively, Stan Lee protested the strictures imposed on creators and published the books anyway. (DC then topped him by hooking Green Arrow's ward, Roy Harper, on heroin.)

The industry revised the code in 1971. But unlike motion pictures, which had establish a rating system that provided room for an adult audience, it had reaffirmed its pledge to provide only "wholesome entertainment" and demonstrate no "disrespect for established authority." In concession to contemporary tastes, though, ghouls, vampires and werewolves were re-admitted to books if presented within "the classic tradition." Drug use could be portrayed — but only as a "vicious habit." Drops — but not pools — of blood could be shown. Seduction could be inferred; but actual sexual acts remained off-limits — and homosexuality was absolutely forbidden. The governing premise continued to be that comics must be suitable for children.

The publishers' efforts to work within these limitations resulted in their scaling never-again surpassed levels of weirdness. New titles like *Giant-Size Man-Thing* and *Super-Heroes Battle Super-Gorillas* resulted. Books featured guest appearances by Uri Geller, Alice Cooper, the cast of *Saturday Night Live*, Don Rickles and his evil twin Goody. But sales continued to plummet. Half the new comics launched in the 1970s lasted less than ten issues. Two-thirds lasted under fifteen. Only seven were still being published in 1980.

The UGs' own problems had driven them from their high water mark on the American cultural front, leaving behind only a few pearls among the fish heads.

Anti-drug paraphernalia laws had shut 20,000 of the head shops, which had remained the UGs major point of distribution.[120] In 1973, in *Miller v. California*, the United States Supreme Court had redefined pornography and ruled that local standards, rather than national ones, could be used to determine if material was obscene, leaving publishers, vendors and creators vulnerable to the dislikes of every evangelical assistant district attorney.[121] Promoters had rolled through the scene, promising creators fortunes, delivering little, absorbing energy, and exacerbating cynicism. A newsprint shortage had increased the cost of printing books. The oil embargo of 1973 had touched off the biggest recession since World War II, leaving customers with less discretionary income to spend. "Either they're not smoking as much dope," one UG cartoonist said, contemplating his sales figures, "or they've developed taste."

Finally, the industry had seen its share of shit-in-its-own-well behavior. A glance at the racks made it seem like a No. 2 pencil, a taste for bizarre sex and/or graphic violence, and you were in business. No one disagreed that there were too many books on the market, though what about this glut was problematic was a subject for debate. Robert Williams, one of the select six cartoonists Crumb had invited to become his co-equals in *Zap* — Griffin, Moscoso, Rodriguez, Shelton and Wilson were the others — said it was the words' fault. "[A]n awful lot of people that had no fuckin' skill [were] putting out underground comics and their justification was that they're more intellectually into the literary end of it than the old, shitty, physical drawing of it. So you had a lot of bohemian crap killing the market." Bill Griffith, creator of Zippy, blamed the pictures: "[W]hat's so 'underground' about rotting corpses!" he wrote in the *San Francisco Phoenix*, "...and inflated rubber women with bulbous 48-inch chests. And all that half-baked crackpot science-fiction...? There's no distance from the

~~~~~~

[120] The industry responded by hopping aboard the newly developing "direct sales" method of business. Traditionally, comics had been sold on newsstands, in drug stores, or at groceries, one item among many, along with the *National Enquirer*, cherry Cokes, and rutabagas. The 1960s had seen the emergence of the first stores devoted to comics; but, by the early 1970s, there were still less than two dozen — and most concentrated on back issues. However, publishers now began allowing stores to order a specific number of books prior to publication at below wholesale cost if they agreed to pay up-front and waive their right to return unsold copies. The publishers gained new outlets and the ability to cut costs by tailoring print runs to demand; and retailers, confident of their abilities to evaluate comics and anticipate their customers' desires, rushed to fill the void left by the shuttered lava lamp purveyors.

[121] Prosecutors had been striving to protect America from the UGs almost since their inception. In 1969, a Berkeley art gallery owner, arrested for selling obscene material in the form of *Snatch* and *Cunt*, was acquitted following testimony from Peter Selz, curator of the University Art Museum, that the books had redeeming social merit. (Selz ascribes the turning point in the case to the D.A. waving a comic at him and demanding he admit it depicted an unnatural sexual act. "'Of course, it's an unnatural sexual act,' I told him. 'That's what makes it funny. Don't you think it's funny?'") In Encino, a judge had dismissed similar charges against a bookstore owner who sold *Zap* #2 with a

material... No movement is undercut with humor or exaggeration."[122]

Whatever the reason, the UGs no longer met an audience's needs. Their public had found other means of satisfying what desires the comics had met; and the cartoonists had not developed other themes, subjects or approaches to win it back. "Vietnam, the great rallying point, was gone. The images that had defined the culture no longer fit," said Turner, whose business had fallen eighty percent. The once "truly revolutionary" books, said Art Spiegelman — whose *Maus* would grow out of a three page story in the UG *Funny Aminals* [sic]— were "stuffed back into the closet along with the bong pipes and love beads." Rip Off Press's Ron Baumgart, quoted in *The New Comics*, summed it up: "[T]he initial impact was shock. 'My God, here are people doing something that nobody's done before. Here's sex! Here's violence! Here's anti-Americanism!... Here's vagrants smoking marijuana!' It's like someone's jumping out of a closet and scaring you. It only works once in a while and then you have to find something of real substance if you're going to continue to be published."

In 1973, in an effort to reverse their fortunes, Griffith, Murphy, Kim Deitch, and Jay Lynch established the Cartoonists' Co-Operative Press. Members would present their books to a printer simultaneously to negotiate a bulk discount and act as their own distributor to eliminate the profits of a middleman. The Co-Op also proposed to certify comics with its own Seal of Approval in an effort to marginalize those its members regarded as unworthy. (It turned out four comics, lasted a year, and folded.) In 1975, Griffith, Murphy and Spiegelman started *Arcade*, an anthology magazine designed to keep the work of the best UG creators before the public in a more respectable format. (It lasted seven issues.) And in perhaps the most unlikely venture of all, a number of artists, including Denis Kitchen, Trina Robbins, and Justin Green, contributed to Marvel's even shorter-lived *Comix Book* ("It's New! It's Strange! It's Subterranean!"), which drew reactions from other UG cartoonists that ranged from "It's the only way to survive" to "Boy! We must really be in trouble."

Co. & Sons went out of business. The San Francisco Comic Book

Wilson story in which one sailor lopped off the head of another's penis and ate it, saying he didn't see how *that* could arouse anyone's prurient interest. But in New York City, clerks at two different stores went down for selling *Zap # 4*, despite testimony by the curator of the Whitney Museum that *it* was redeeming as all get-out, when that redemption occurred amidst Crumb's "Joe Blow," in which family togetherness was skewered with panels of Sis sucking off Dad and a bare-breasted Mom offering herself to Junior.

[122] Both Roger Sabin ("the causes of the American underground's decline [included]...") and R. C. Harvey ("a frost settled on the underground [when]...") list Disney's suit against the Pirates among the Causes of Death. This seems unfair. Few UGs had copyright violations as their mainspring. (No similar cases are cited by these authors.) The UGs thrived after this litigation commenced and were moribund before it resolved. And most of the Pirates had more successful careers — above and below ground — see below — after they were in the dock than they'd had before.

Company, California Comics, Do City, Golden Gate, People's Comix, Star*Reach, Yahoo, vanished. The Print Mint began a decline that, by decade's end, saw it abandoning comics for commercial jobs. Apex Novelties was soon issuing no more than an occasional reprint. Only Rip Off and Last Gasp, among the San Francisco stalwarts, continued strong.

The times had not been kind to — no-sex, no-violence, no-profanity — Walt Disney Productions either. While its theme parks continued to be profitable — Disney World, which had opened on 28,000 acres outside Orlando, Florida in October 1971, had become the most visited vacation spot on earth — and its merchandise sales reached $50,000,000 a year, it had not produced a money-making movie since *The Love Bug* in 1969. "The world had shifted," the journalist Joe Flower wrote, "The tectonic plates of the American psychology had ruptured"; and Disney proved incapable of adapting to the reconfigured terrain. Persisting in pumping out such efforts as *The Million Dollar Duck*, *Unidentified Flying Oddballs*, *The Apple Dumpling Gang*, and not one but three talking Volkswagen sequels, its film division would continue to lose money for a decade.

I believe it appropriate — at the risk of re-enraging those critics who already flog my work for being "annoyingly self-referential" — to interject something about myself here. Any writer, like any expert testifying in court, is trying to sell you something. It may be the standard of care required of a neurosurgeon or the reliability of blood-alcohol testing. It may be the nature of truth or the mysteries of the heart. But it is something. The law recognizes the more you know about the expert's angles, biases, loyalties, the better you can judge his credibility. The same is true for writers.[123]

By 1975, my life had achieved a level of stability it would not lose. Adele and I had been married four years. I'd had my own law practice for five. She had gone from teaching Esperanto, myth, and "Creating Your Own Door" at an alternative high school in Larkspur[124] to graduate school in psychotherapy at UC. We owned the

---

[123] I began putting this belief to work in a series of articles for *The Comics Journal* which, a year ago, resulted in a discussion on its Message Board: "Why Do You Keep Running Articles by Bob Levin?" The thread's initiator — and his gaggle of cretins — hated everything about me: my ignorance of comic books (I had admittedly, not read a comic in forty years when I began these contributions); my writing style; my insistence on blithering details of my deplorable life. When I mentioned the brouhaha to my friend Marilyn, who teaches film at UC, she said, "There's a name for what you do, Bob. Autocritography, in which the writer abandons all pretense that who-he-is has nothing to do with what-he-writes. It's very cutting edge."

"And people hate it."

[124] The district had two alternative high schools. One was for especially gifted students. The other — where Adele taught — was for students no other school would have. Its aim was to keep them on campus long enough to pass out enough credits so they could graduate. Its curriculum was based on whatever someone would take. My favorite course was "Breakfast with Mary," where students learned how to sit around a table, drink coffee, and read the paper.

once-scorned house and two cars. But this stasis had been achieved amidst chaos. When I had been in law school, I had associated primarily with fellows who were not. With some my relationship was casual and new, but others I had known for half my life. We drank at the same bars; we hoped to get lucky at the same parties; they did, as Mick Jagger sang, "smoke the same cigarette as me." What held me to them was their seemingly hellbent intent on carving out lives of admirably un-"anybody" distinction. To me, law school loomed as a dreadful threat — I feared, I once wrote, that I was being laid upon "a conveyor belt that would drop me off the other end with everything about me regimented, from my sideburns (short) to my shoes (wing-tipped)" — and my proximity to these raging others promised an inoculation against exposures to come. Now, one was dead in a car wreck, one fallen from a cliff, one killed in prison. One had been institutionalized twice, and two or three others held hard-earned slots on the waiting list. Then, Max Garden, my oldest friend among them — and the beneficiary of those institutionalizations — told me that Dave Peters had committed suicide after nearly murdering his girlfriend.

When the three of us had been in elementary school, Davey possessed more E.C.s than anyone we knew. The summer after he was booted out of Antioch — "For trying," he claimed, "to start a fraternity" — Davey and I had driven cross-country, Martha, The Vandellas, "Heat Wave" blaring all the way. Davey and I had seen Georgie Benton knock Slim Jim Robinson through the ropes at Connie Mack Stadium — and Bennie Briscoe beat The Champ of Columbia Avenue bloody some years after that. ("Ain't no George Benton," the man beside us had said.) We had seen Joe Tex belt out "All-I-could-do, all-I-could-do, all-I-could-do...," dive from the stage at the Uptown, disappear from view, re-emerge at the back of the theater, and race down the center aisle "... all I could do WAS CRY!"

That Davey Peters was dead.[125]

As for the Pirates...

Funnies had provided them an outlaw swagger that had set them apart from the crowd. ("Mythic characters," Clay Geerdes called them in *Graphic Story World*.) But to maintain this stance, they needed a win; and no banner hung

---

[125] How I received this news was itself instructive.

When Max got out of the nut house, he had moved to San Diego to pursue a career as a percussionist — and deal a little this-and-that. Davey had already sought refuge in Los Angeles, writing pornography while waiting for his screenplays to sell. Max wanted to contact Davey, but I had had no word from him in months. Then a fat envelope arrived from a p.o. box in L.A. Maybe, I thought, a journal I did not remember was returning a story I had forgotten I had submitted. But the manuscript inside had no structure, no order, no logic. It was uncontrolled stops-and-starts, bits-and-pieces, all rant, all shriek, all invectives hurled at one enemy or another. Maybe, I thought, *Madman's Quarterly* was sending me a sample to review. Then I realized the handwriting was Davey's.

So I sent Davey's p.o. box in L.A. to Max's p.o. box in San Diego, and Max wrote to Davey. In the return mail, in what he thought was a birthday card, a lawyer told him about Davey. "I guess

from their rafters. Instead, their litigation dragged on, no longer in harmony with the dominant themes of the times, not even a minor arpeggio to what most of them wished for their lives, threatening to reduce them to answers on a Trivial Pursuit card: "What once nearly famous cartoonists now work as dishwashers to pay off their debt to what well-known Hollywood corporation?" The idea of owing someone hundreds of thousands of dollars was unreal. They had no way to pay any portion of that sum. For the most part, they were tired of the suit and wished it would disappear. They wanted to get on with things.

Ted Richards was completing his degree at S.F. State. A creative writing major, he was compiling a collection of short stories, sharpening his narrative skills, learning how to hook a reader and lead him along. Bobby London remained in Seattle, publishing in the *Lampoon* and what remained of the underground press, still striving for success as a cartoonist. His refusal to settle with Disney had not helped his domestic situation, though. On December 31, 1975, he and Flenniken separated. A year later, she served him with divorce papers.

Only Dan O'Neill seemed thoroughly at ease with their old "*épatez-le-bourgeois*" spirit. He had been publishing in *City Magazine*, *New West*, and the *Lampoon* (where he and Hallgren placed some gorgeous full-color "Odd Bodkins" strips). With his parents, he co-authored *The Big Yellow Drawing Book*, a how-to primer bringing a reader from drawing circles to human beings within sixty pages. (It would prove a popular number with right-wing, learn-at-home, survivalist groups.) For the Mitchells, his largest account, he drew cartoon ads ("Make a night of it, kids... Dinner and the movies at the O'Farrell"), posters (*Hot Nazis* was his favorite), and helped with scripts. (David McCumber, in *Rated X*, gives him a solo credit for *Beyond the Green Door*, but O'Neill says he only story-boarded some of Artie Mitchell's stranger fantasies.) He even acted, debuting in *Resurrection of Eve* as a priest who ad-libbed Latin poetry:

All around is desolation.

Things are quiet as a tomb.

Sister missed her menstruation.

Mother has a fallen womb....

his translation begins. Following that triumph, the Mitchells offered him the role of Jehovah in *Sodom and Gomorrah*, but, out of modesty, he declined, and they cast a chimpanzee — augmented by the voice of John Wayne — instead. Then

I'm handling Davey's thing all right," Max wrote me, "with a wake of green herb and red wine. After all, killing himself really didn't add any problems to my situation. Just some more sadness & as you get older you get better at dealing with sadness & there is sort of a Permanent sad spot in your head where you can put it all & you don't have to think about it all the time except when you have to like now."

One morning, Max showed up in my office, eyes wild, body jumping, electric sweat flashing, boots rotting on his feet. He had hitchhiked all night, clinging to his conga drums like they were buoys. I was glad to have him in town.

the owners of Comics and Comix, a four-outlet chain of comic book stores strung between Berkeley and San Jose, offered to publish a new comic by him.

Dan O'Neill's Comics and Stories, Vol. 2 draws from Northern Ireland, Wounded Knee, and the Disney suit. The artwork is often cramped or smudgingly reproduced, but the wit and intelligence remain sharp. And the stories, unrestrained by the fetters of a mainstream newspaper or the limits of a "funny animal" format, no longer required to court an advertisement-consuming public or accommodate the often less-than-fully-engaged attention span of UG readers, were unsparing in their level of engagement and humored harshness.

"The average freak will trade his pet monkey for a hit of acid."

"People who keep both feet on the ground never get their trousers off."

"The world is not safe for the harmless."

The stories are a Pandora's box of what is bedeviling a particular mind at a particular moment: corporate domination; repression of individualism; planetary endangerment. O'Neill delivered a children's story (an Indian boy is instructed by wild creatures to rejoin his people's struggle), a fable (God is so disappointed by Earth he abandons it), some American history (Abraham Lincoln and Jesse James). He revived "Odd Bodkins" and introduced Cub Calloway, a reporter-*noir* who, prowling San Francisco's SoMa alleys and bars, encounters a Satan who argues there is no free will, only responses manipulated by those who control distribution; a Holy Mugger who plants cash on his victims to destroy their incentive to earn or vote; and a future where the Chinese (and Mexicans, Filipinos, and Eskimos) are hunted to near extinction and ground into burgers. He discusses his court case ("I say 'Poo-poo,' your honor, because I can't say 'Bullshit' in court"), quotes Josef Goebbels to his advantage ("Jokes cease to be funny when they deal with the holiest goods of the nation"), and advocates spraying poison oak extract on the toilet seats of one's enemies.

O'Neill says that Comics and Comix had promised him a monthly but pulled the plug after two issues. Bud Plant, one of the owners, laughs when told this. "It doesn't sound like anything we would've done. Nobody in the underground was putting out a monthly. My memory is we paid O'Neill $1000 for another issue, and it never happened." His partner Robert Beerbohm agrees. "Dan was caught up in the post-court imbroglio with Disney, and there was no way he could have concentrated on, much less completed, a monthly book. We fronted hard-earned bucks, and Dan did not deliver."

O'Neill would not work in comic books again.

The same year his comic book career ended, O'Neill received cartooning's highest award, the Yellow Kid, at the 11th International Congress of Cartoonists and Animators in Lucca, Italy. Vaughn Bodé had won the year previously. Flenniken and London won later, which, O'Neill computes, gave the Pirates four. "They got it for being great artists. I got it because I was stupid. I took on Disney. I took comics into places they'd never been. Belfast. South Dakota.

Took 'em to combat situations where, you do a cartoon right, you get shot. It was great. Here you are without a dime, and a taxi picks you up in Oakland, drives you to the airport; they fly you to New York, New York to Milan, Milan to Pisa, for fourteen days, free, hanging out with these incredible cartoonists. Then they fly you back, and you've got the same dollar ninety-five you had before you went on this trip."

That year, too, O'Neill received his first extended salute in a national magazine when Richard Milner, later a senior editor of *Natural History* but then a freelancer trying to break into the men's market, profiled him in *Gallery* as "Patriarch of the Underfunnies."[126] Milner lauded O'Neill for bringing "a disturbing dimension" to the newspaper comics page by changing "styles, stories and characters as [he] grew and changed" and applauded the "many-leveled metaphysical musings" that made his the first syndicated strip "to deal with the consciousness revolution."[127]

The populace, alerted to this diviner in its midst, decided, for disturbance, it preferred *Jaws*.

---

[126] Milner, whose proposed thesis, *Black Players: the Secret World of Black Pimps*, "a pioneering work of ethnography of the Bay Area prostitution scene," had gotten him booted out of the Ph.D. program of the Anthropology Department at UC Berkeley — published by Little, Brown, it went on to sell 280,000 copies — had known O'Neill for several years. He illustrated their relationship — and illuminated O'Neill (in the event more illumination is deemed necessary) — with the following story. A rainy day had cooped them inside discussing "interesting things" when O'Neill took out a bottle of Irish Mist and a bag of Columbian beans and offered Irish coffees. Milner replied he neither drank alcohol nor caffeine. O'Neill pondered the problem. Then he said, "Here's what you do. Take a little bit of the whiskey. Take a little bit of the coffee. And think of it as a drug experience."

[127] Milner also offered me this anecdote which, I assume, he believed I could make better use of than *Natural History*. "After the article came out, I was in New York, editing *Who's Who in X-Rated Films*, when I heard the Mitchells were coming to town to promote *Sodom and Gomorrah*. I asked to interview them. They said, 'Okay.' When they arrived, I called their hotel to set a time. They said O'Neill had told them not to talk to me. 'You made him look bad in *Gallery*.' 'That's ridiculous,' I said. 'He read every draft. He fed me punch lines. He wrote entire sections.' 'You betrayed him.' 'I didn't say one bad thing about him. Let me show you the article.'

"The next morning, I went to their hotel and buzzed the room. No answer. I go up and knock on the door. No answer. I pound on the door. Still no answer. So I turn the knob. There's tons of weed and coke all over the place. The Mitchells and two young ladies, all nude, are passed out on the bed. Well, I'd come that far. I woke one of them, Jim or Artie, and reminded him of our appointment. He comes to, 'Oh yeah,' and starts pushing his brother. 'Wake up. We've got to read this.' They're totally bleary-eyed, passing pages back and forth, while one of the girls, C.J. Lang, trying to shake me up, is sticking a high-heeled shoe up her kazoo. 'Fucking O'Neill,' they say, 'should kiss your ass for this.' They gave me the interview while C.J. masturbated with the towel rack."

Cover, *Air Pirates Funnies* #1, July, 1971

Cover, *Air Pirates Funnies* #2, August, 1971

Back Cover, *Air Pirates Funnies* #2, August, 1971

Fund Raiser jam painting, circa 1977

Fund Raiser drawing by Dan O'Neill, 1977

Cover, *Air Pirates Pirate Edition*, 1971: "Presented for historical and satirical purposes only by the New Mouse Liberation Front, a renegade operation in no way affiliated with the original Air Pirates Studio or its members. ... This special Air Pirates Edition inspired by the importance and rarity of the original defiant gesture. Obtain and enjoy at your own risk." [from the indicia]

Lead story from the Mouse Liberation Front's *Air Pirates
Pirate Edition*. Artist unknown.

147

Page from "Silly Sympathies Presents The Mouse,"
Air Pirates Funnies #1

Page from "Silly Sympathies," *Air Pirates Funnies* #1; by Dan O'Neill

149

Splash page from "Zeke Wolf," *Air Pirates Funnies # 2*;
by Ted Richards

Page from "Bucky Goes West,"
Air Pirates Funnies #2

Page from "Silly Sympathies Presents The Mouse,"
Air Pirates Funnies #2

Page from "The Tortoise and the Hare,"
The Tortoise and the Hare #1, 1971;
by Gary Hallgren

Page from "Tales of Ezekiel Wolf," *The Tortoise and the Hare* #1; Ted Richards

Half page "Dopin' Dan" and "Zeke Wolf"
from *Air Pirates Funnies* #1

"Air Pirates Comics Page!" from *The San Francisco Bay Guardian*, August 5, 1972; individual strips copyright © 1972 Dan O'Neill, Bobby London, Shary Flenniken, Gary Hallgren

Dan O'Neill, 1971
Photo: Clay Geerdes

Bobby London, 1971
Photo: Clay Geerdes

Gary Hallgren, 1973
Photo: Clay Geerdes

Roger May, Shary Flenniken, 1973
Photo: Clay Geerdes

Michael Kennedy (today)

Michael Stepanian, 2000

David F. Phillips (today)

Ted Richards, 1971

Gilbert Shelton [l], Albert Morse [r],
1973
Photo: Clay Geerdes

Dan O'Neill [l], Harvey Kurtzman [r],
1979
Photo: Clay Geerdes

Air Pirates Fund Raiser [l to r]: Gary Hallgren, Dan O'Neill,
Shary Flenniken, Ted Richards. Photo: Clay Geerdes

Air Pirates Defense Fund promotional poster,
1976
Photo: Clay Geerdes

Shary Flenniken, 1977
Photo: Clay Geerdes

Dan O'Neill at the Walt Disney
Studios, 1979
Photo by Jim Mitchell

Sergio Aragonés [l], Dan O'Neill [r] [top]
Photo: Clay Geerdes

Ted Richards, 1971
Photo: Clay Geerdes

Self portraits by Gary Hallgren
Copyright © 2003 Gary Hallgren

Mickey and Minnie model sheet; art by Gary Hallgren

Goofy model sheet

Ezekiel Wolf model sheet; art by Ted Richards

Ezekiel Wolf model sheet;
art by Ted Richards

Horace Horsecollar model sheet; art by Gary Hallgren

"Communique #1 from the M.L.F.," *The CoEvolution Quarterly* #21, Spring, 1979; by Dan O'Neill

"YOU SHOULD TELL THE FOLKS WHERE YOU FOUND THE AIR PIRATES"

"AMATEUR CARTOONISTS LINED UP EVERY DAY IN FRONT OF DISNEY STUDIOS.. ALL TRYING TO BREAK INTO BIG LEAGUE FILM.."

"WE SIMPLY HIRED THE HUNGRIEST"

"SUDDENLY, MICKEY AND I WERE BEGINNING THE MOST WONDERFUL ADVENTURE OF OUR LIVES"

"ONCE THEY WERE SAFELY UNDER LOCK AND KEY THE PROGRAM STARTED.. FIRST WE HIT THEM WITH THE PSYCHEDELICS.. KNOCKED OUT THEIR CONDITIONED RESPONSES ..THE VIDEOTAPES OF THEIR SEXUALITY SEMINARS MADE ALL THE NETWORKS.. EXCEPT THEY WERE CALLED "PORNOGRAPHIC".. REMEMBER?

IT WAS MY RELUCTANCE TO ACCEPT MY OWN SEXUALITY THAT WAS PORNOGRAPHY!

WE WERE FIVE MONTHS IN THE OLD SKINNER BOX.. ALL I CAN TELL YOU IS AS SKINNER'S PIGEON FEELS TOWARDS HIS CORN..THAT'S ME AND MINNIE...

" WE WOULDN'T LET THEM SLEEP TOGETHER UNTIL THEY WERE MARRIED.. "

WE WEREN'T UPTIGHT ABOUT PREMARITAL SEX..

WE JUST WANTED THEM TO BE CRAZY ABOUT EACH OTHER..

I ALWAYS THOUGHT OF MY SEXUALITY AS A COMMODITY.. IT WAS HOLLYWOOD ATTITUDES, REALLY..

WE WOULDN'T BE HERE IF IT WASN'T FOR PREMARITAL SEX!

IT WAS RADICAL PSYCH.. BUT WITHIN THE LAW.. DRUGS.. SEX THERAPY.. ALL OF IT! I'M NOT THE FIRST MOUSE TO BE GOONED OUT ON EXOTIC DRUGS.. IT'S NOT ILLEGAL TO GIVE MICE DRUGS..

"AT THIS MOMENT THERE ARE PROBABLY SIX MILLION STONED MICE IN RESEARCH LABS AROUND THE COUNTRY.. FEELING REAL WEIRD.. NEWS COVERAGE AFTER THE RESCUE MADE IT SOUND LIKE MOM AND DAD WERE MAINLINING HEROIN !

SO, WITH THE AIR PIRATES IN CUSTODY, WE WENT BACK TO HOLLYWOOD..

POLICE

WE WERE AN EMBARRASSMENT BEFORE WE LEFT, WHAT WITH MY DRINKING AND MINNIE'S PILL-CRAZED TANTRUMS.. AND NOW WE WERE RETURNING AS SUPPOSED DRUG ADDICTS AND SEX FREAKS.. SO THERE WAS NOT MUCH OF A WELCOME AND NO NEW FILM OFFERS..

DISNEY STUDIOS DIDN'T BELIEVE ME AND FERDIE SET UP THE SNATCH.. AND INSISTED ON PROSECUTING THE AIR PIRATES..

WE TOLD THEM WE WERE MARRIED.. THEY SAID "SO IS ZSA ZSA GABOR"!

Chapter Thirteen:
You Don't Just Go Off Shooting Fish

Judge Wollenberg, now seventy-five years old and carrying a reduced work load as a "senior judge," had postponed the trial until August 11, 1975.

In its pretrial statement, Disney summarized the case as one of copyright infringement, trademark infringement, and unfair competition in the form of trade disparagement and intentional interference with business. It added Toby Tortoise and Max Hare to its list of copyrighted characters infringed upon and *The Tortoise and the Hare* to the publications that did this infringing. It alleged the Pirates threatened its profits from more than 100 licensees who used its characters to market over 600 products. It requested damages of $5,000 per copyright infringement (or, alternatively, one dollar for each infringement in each comic made or sold); all of the Pirates' profits; treble damages for its infringed trademark; compensatory damages for the unfair competition; punitive damages of $100,000 from each defendant; and reimbursement of its attorneys' fees and costs. It identified as potential witnesses the defendants, a representative from Walt Disney Productions, and a James Foster of Consolidated Fibres, Inc. Otherwise, it would rely on exhibits and affidavits already on file and clippings from various underground publications to prove its case. It said settlement remained possible but, if that failed, offered to submit the case for decision on a statement of facts agreed to by both parties. It estimated the trial would take one or two days.

The Pirates' pretrial statement identified several issues for the court to resolve. Were Disney's works protected by valid copyrights or had they fallen into the public domain? Was their own work protected either by the fair use doctrine or the First Amendment? Was this work likely to confuse the public into thinking it was by Disney? Had it infringed upon Disney's copyrights or trademarks or disparaged or unfairly competed with Disney? If it had, was this done intentionally? And, finally, had it harmed Disney in any way? The Pirates asked to have the injunction against them dissolved and to be reimbursed their own attorneys' fees and costs. Their witnesses were to be Hoppe; McCabe; Sales; Fred Crews, a UC Berkeley English professor and author of *The Pooh Perplex*; John Wasserman, the *Chronicle*'s popular arts critic; Nicholas Von Hoffman, a political columnist and author of *Don't Shoot! We are Your Children*; the novelist Blair Fuller; G.B. Trudeau, creator of "Doonesbury"; and a Ms. Vanasek. They thought the trial would last two to three days and that no settlement was likely.

On July 3, Laveroni dropped a small bomb, a motion for summary judgment, requesting Judge Wollenberg to rule that the documents on file — the pleadings, affidavits, admissions, interrogatory answers, and Turner's deposition — established that no genuine dispute existed as to any material fact. The only dispute was how the law applied to these facts. The court could resolve this on the existing record without additional testimony, avoiding the costs and delays of a formal trial; and, Laveroni said, the only decision it could reach must favor Disney.

The facts, as Laveroni saw them, were that Disney had copyrighted cartoon characters which the Air Pirates admitted copying. The Pirates denied this copying constituted an infringement, but the court had already found it did when it granted Disney its preliminary injunction. Disney also had a valid trademark in the name "Silly Symphonies," which the Pirates had used without permission. While the Pirates denied this use resulted in public confusion, confusion was a matter of law, not fact; and when similar names are seen on similar products, confusion about the origin of these products may be inferred to establish that an infringement has occurred. Finally, Disney had spent forty years developing these characters and fostering their reputations through appearances in books and magazines, in movies and on television, at parades and theme parks, resulting in their acquiring a popularity which had made them valuable commodities. The Pirates denied an intent to destroy these characters' reputations, but they could hardly have portrayed them "in a more perverted and offensive manner" or created works "more antithetical to the image of wholesome family entertainment" for which Disney strived. The Pirates' "base and grotesque" actions constituted an "'aggravated assault,'" motivated by an intent "to steal what did not belong to them," "carried out with premeditation and malicious intent." They had to be stopped.

The legal issues in dispute — the copyrightability of cartoon characters, the Pirates' entitlement to a fair use defense or the protection of the First Amendment — remained as when the court had previously ruled. The only relevant cases decided since supported the conclusions it had arrived at, most notably in *Robert Stigwood Group Ltd v. O'Reilly*. That court had rejected arguments by a group of Catholic priests that the First Amendment allowed them to mount an alternative version of *Jesus Christ, Superstar* in order to counter the show's "sick, distorted, perverted version of the Gospel." If the priests' arguments had failed, so must the Pirates'.

Laveroni requested that Disney's injunction be made permanent, that all copies of the Pirates' comics be destroyed, and that it be awarded compensatory and punitive damages and reimbursement for its fees and costs.

The hearing on this motion took place August 1. Disney was represented by Laveroni and Tatum, Richards by Stepanian, and O'Neill and London by Joseph L. Matthews, a junior member of Kennedy's office. George Gilmour, a thin, bespectacled, chain-smoking, self-described "180-proof Irish" friend of O'Neill's for fifteen years, also appeared on his behalf. His presence denoted a problem in the Pirates' broth. Due to "a little failure in communication," they had failed to file the written response due ten days earlier.

Gilmour was a dedicated political activist. After a stint registering black voters and participating in sit-ins in Mississippi in the early 1960s had landed him in Parchmen Farm prison with a shattered arm and fractured skull — a trip unnavigated by anything remotely resembling a trial — he had returned to San Francisco to pursue a Ph.D. in social psychology. But hearing Charles Garry, chief counsel for the Black Panther Party, speak had convinced him the law afforded a way to work for social justice — and avoid jails and hospitals. He attended San Francisco Law School at night, while teaching sociology, raising a daughter, and falling by the Pirates' warehouse after class for occasional silliness-es. After graduation, he went to work for TURN, a public interest entity, as its first and only attorney, battling the phone company and major utilities. He had been in practice less than a year when O'Neill mentioned over lunch that Kennedy's busy calendar was keeping him from attending to the brief on Disney's summary judgment motion. Gilmour offered to help.

Stepanian, believing that Kennedy would be responding to the motion for them both, had gone to Hawaii to collect fish for San Francisco's Steinhart Aquarium. And when Gilmour met with Kennedy, Kennedy spent much of the time on the phone discussing a murder case in which he was involved. As a result, Gilmour left not realizing he had assumed sole responsibility for the reply brief and that the extension of time he had heard Kennedy mention was for the trial, not the brief. "I knew Michael and Joe Rhine were really good guys and excellent attorneys," Gilmour recalls. "I couldn't figure out, if there was a crisis of this magnitude — a summary judgment motion — why they hadn't done something about it. I certainly was under the impression that this was not of significance. Otherwise, they wouldn't have left the case with someone obviously so ill-equipped to deal with it as I was."

But Kennedy, assuming Gilmour had everything under control, took off for a five-week sabbatical. Three days before the hearing on the motion, Gilmour received a call from Kennedy's office asking if he had filed the response. "I was taken aback. All I had was the moving papers. I didn't even have the file. I knew absolutely nothing about copyright law. I moved into Kennedy's building and grabbed a multi-volume treatise, and started plagiarizing like crazy. I didn't know what the hell I was doing. My girlfriend did all the typing. We worked all night, non-stop, for two days; and it was a bitch."

The morning of the hearing, Gilmour, Matthews and their hot-from-the-photocopier brief arrived at the federal building in your classic Young Lawyer's Moment — we have all had them — when your most fervent wish is that you be allowed to leave the courtroom without having your Bar card snatched for impersonating an attorney. "I had never even been in federal court before," Gilmour says. "It was a relatively new building with ceilings fifty feet high, like a church. I knew Stepanian's partner, Brian Rohan — a beautiful man, a pussy-cat — very well, but I had never met Stepanian; and, all of a sudden, he came walking out of the elevator on the seventeenth floor with a cigar in his mouth, with this aura of arrogance like a Mafioso. He walked into the courtroom with the cigar still in his mouth. It wasn't lit, but it reeked. The judge was very clearly irked; and I was like, 'Oh, God...'"

Having learned from another lawyer in his office that things were in disar-ray, Stepanian had flown back from Hawaii the day before to argue the motion. He arrived late for court and, realizing neither Matthews nor Gilmour had any idea what to do, thrust himself front-and-center. "I mean, summary judgment! Give me a fucking break," he says now. "My main thing was, 'Fuck you! It was late. At least look at it.' I just didn't want to leave these two kids there alone." He urged Judge Wollenberg to accept Gilmour's reply brief. He pointed out that the Pirates had made all previous appearances, responded to all previous motions, had been prepared to try the case the month before, wanted to try the case now — and had been surprised by Disney's motion coming at so late a date. Laveroni replied that the defendants' failure to follow the court's rules was characteristic of their behavior throughout the litigation. He objected to their arguments being considered. "He was," Gilmour says, "the prince of the fucking darkness. I mean, really, this guy enjoyed doing evil."

Judge Wollenberg was put out. Laveroni, who recalls him as a low-key, "grandfatherly type" — "They were fortunate to have drawn Judge Wollenberg. Other judges would have thrown them in jail" — says it was the only time dur-ing the entire case he saw him irritated. He dismissed Gilmour as "not of record" and Stepanian as "completely unprepared." "You are in this position through your own neglect," he admonished. "You don't just walk out to go shooting fish..." He allowed Gilmour's memorandum to be "lodged" but not "filed." The trial was delayed until November 3 while he considered his ruling.

Gilmour's brief, which Judge Wollenberg may or may not have considered, began by reminding him that summary judgment was a drastic remedy because it deprived a litigant of his right to a trial. He should, therefore, proceed with extreme caution before granting Disney's motion. He should view its witnesses' affidavits skeptically, since they had not been subjected to cross-examination as they would be in court. He should give all documents filed by the Pirates the interpretation most favorable to them. Because of the importance of the ques-tions before him — Was a parody of copyrighted material a fair use? Did the First Amendment protect the Pirates' work? — and the inevitable appeal that would follow his decision, he should assure the existence of a complete record for the reviewing court to consider. He should grant Disney's motion only if absolutely convinced that no genuine issue of material fact was in dispute and that the Pirates could not prevail at trial under any circumstances.

It would be improper, Gilmour went on, for Wollenberg to rely on the conclusions he reached when granting the preliminary injunction. Then he had only to decide the "probability" of Disney prevailing at trial. He had not been asked to make any ultimate factual determinations. Now he had to decide matters of "actuality," which demanded a full hearing.

Finally, Gilmour said, the record established that genuine factual disputes existed. Whether a copyrighted work-component has been copied, a trademark infringed, or an unfair business practice committed were questions of fact, not law. Whether too much of a copyrighted work has been copied was a matter of fact. Whether a parody can be a fair use is a question of fact. For Disney to argue that the Pirates' admission that they parodied Disney was equivalent to admitting they had infringed its copyrights was "not only intellectually dishonest but... a serious misrepresentation to this Court."

Five days later, Judge Wollenberg granted Disney summary judgment.

He ruled that Disney's copyrights on its cartoon characters gave it the sole right to decide how they were to be portrayed. He rejected the Pirates' arguments that the characters were not component parts of copyrighted works or that, if they were, copying of them was protected by the First Amendment "for the reasons stated in... [my] opinion on the preliminary injunction." While the question of "fair use" was normally one of fact, in this instance "the material facts are not controverted..." The Pirates had admitted copying Disney's characters' visual representations as closely as they could. While the Pirates may have altered the characters' personalities and presented them in stories of their own creation, this similarity of likeness alone made their copying excessive. Under *Benny*, their copying was not a fair use because a parody may not consist of a "substantial" taking or "outright copying" of a copyrighted work. This copying also constituted a trademark infringement, and the derogatory manner in which these infringements had been carried out constituted trade disparagement.

In his opinion's only footnote, Judge Wollenberg addressed a potentially Pirate-friendly proposition that had come to his attention. Melville B. Nimmer, a law professor at UCLA, in *Nimmer on Copyright*, the leading treatise in the field, had proposed that the test for determining whether a parody was a fair use should be "whether the defendant's work tends to diminish or prejudice the potential sale of plaintiff's work." While Wollenberg recognized it was unlikely *Air Pirates Funnies* would satisfy a Disney-craving buyer, the Pirates' goal "of undermining the public image of the Disney characters" would sufficiently damage their marketability to deny them a safe haven even under this standard. Besides, he said, in the Ninth Circuit, *Benny*'s "substantiality" test was all that mattered.

Wollenberg ordered O'Neill, Richards and London permanently enjoined from infringing Disney's copyrights and trademarks. He ordered them to surrender to Disney's lawyers all "infringing material" in their possession or control. He ordered a hearing before a federal magistrate, Owen E. Woodruff, Jr., to determine the amount of damages and attorneys' fees Disney should receive. And he awarded it reimbursed its costs of suit. Laveroni then filed a costs bill of $508.05: fifteen dollars for the filing fee; $324.35 for Turner's deposition; and $168.70 for "exemplification and copies of papers..." (Disney had also incurred $2154.64 in non-recoverable costs.)

Because an injunction was part of the requested relief, Wollenberg, rather than a jury, would have decided the case anyway. His granting judgment without sitting through three days of testimony when the parties' positions were already spelled out may have just hastened the inevitable; but the Pirates had hoped to impress him with the value of parody by having live witnesses espouse its artistic and social worth. Richards' reaction summed up his co-defendants': "WHAAAT! The attorneys must've messed up." "If we were going to lose," he says, "it should have been on the field with a proper beating, not for stupid stuff."

On September 15, Stepanian filed his notice of appeal to the Ninth Circuit on behalf of Richards. Two days later, Kennedy filed his for O'Neill and London. Laveroni asked that each Pirate be required to post a costs bond of $500, rather than the minimum $250, because of the "extensive and complex legal issues" that were to require briefings. (The bonds only cost $20, but Laveroni must have wanted to apply every bit of pressure he could.)

Chapter Fourteen:
Outrageous, Inappropriate, Incredible, Preposterous, and Without Mreit

Magistrates are attorneys hired by the federal court to lighten a judge's burden by performing quasi-judicial functions ancillary to a case-in-chief. Owen Woodruff, to whom Judge Wollenberg had assigned the damages-and-fees issue, had defended criminals for much of his professional life. "A sweet guy," Stepanian says, "who once tried twenty straight, court-appointed, pieces-of-shit, disgusting murder cases at the Hall." Any expectation that such prolonged exposure to the societally askew would incline him toward other, incalculably more modest offenders against decency would prove unfounded. He would act, instead, like he could not wait to scrape them from his shoe.

Woodruff set oral arguments for October 21, 1975. He ordered each side to submit its position in writing before then. On October 6, Kennedy filed a motion with Judge Wollenberg to postpone the damages hearing until after the Ninth Circuit ruled on the Pirates' appeal. If its ruling was favorable, he pointed out, the hearing would have been unnecessary.

Laveroni objected. Kennedy's motion, he said, was not made in the interests of "judicial economy" but was a "maneuver" to gain him time to prepare his brief. He could have waited until after the damages hearing to file his appeal. Instead, he had filed it and then waited until a few days before the hearing to object. Four years litigation was enough; it was time for resolution. Damages was the last issue pending; deciding it would take "minimal" time compared to all that had gone before; postponing this decision would prejudice Disney.

Wollenburg denied Kennedy's motion; but because of the time required to hear it, the arguments on damages did not take place until December 11.

At the hearing, Laveroni urged Woodruff to consider "the extent and breadth" of the infringements and the "malicious intent" behind them in determining how much to award Disney. The Pirates, he pointed out, had published three separate copyright-infringing comic books in editions of 15-20,000 copies each, the third of which while already restrained from further infringements. They had copied twenty-one different Disney characters, intending with each portrayal "to undermine" Disney's property rights.

The United States Code — 17 USC 101b, to be precise — gave courts two methods to assess damages for copyright infringements. The first, ordering the Pirates to turn over their profits to Disney and to reimburse Disney for its losses, would not work, Laveroni said, because the Pirates had made no profits and Disney could not measure its loss. The second method, which he pressed upon Woodruff, applicable when either profit or loss is unknown, is to award *in lieu* damages of between $250 and $5000 for each infringement, according to considerations of what is "just" and not a "penalty."

Laveroni counted sixteen copyrighted Disney characters in each issue of *Air Pirates Funnies* and six more in *The Tortoise and the Hare,* for a total of thirty-eight infringements. Since the characters had been shown "in a degrading, lewd and offensive manner for the avowed intention of disparaging and ridiculing [Disney]," he requested an award of $5000 for each. It would be difficult, he wrote, to imagine a case more worthy of maximum damages. To hold otherwise would not only fail to discourage others from acting in a similar manner, it would "promote" continued outrages. Besides this $190,000, Laveroni requested $27,292.50 for attorneys' fees to date, $1500 for future work, and reimbursement of his firm's costs.

Kennedy's reply, on behalf of O'Neill and London — Stepanian filed no opposing papers for Richards — asserted that Woodruff could not award *in lieu* damages because Judge Wollenberg's order referring the case to him had limited his determination to "the amount of actual money damages."

Even if Woodruff were to treat "actual" as a slip of the pen, Kennedy argued, *in lieu* damages were inappropriate. If either profit or loss was known, courts had discretion to award that amount in order to prevent unjust results. In this instance, both had been established. The Pirates' unrebutted evidence showed their profits to be nil; and Disney had presented no evidence of any loss — neither a decline in sales nor a diminution of its public image. Disney, therefore, deserved only a nominal award. To give it more than it had lost or the Pirates had made would be "impermissibly punitive." The law was not meant to disproportionately enrich copyright holders or sadistically punish infringers, particularly when, as here, they had acted in good faith, believing themselves protected by the First Amendment and the fair use doctrine, to express socially and politically important ideas.

If Woodruff concluded *in lieu* damages were warranted, Kennedy proposed he calculate them differently than Laveroni. Several of the copied characters appeared within the same copyrighted work, so the maximum number of actually infringed copyrights for which Disney could be compensated was seventeen. And if the Pirates' three comics were treated as a single, infringing work, which was fitting since they appeared close together in time as part of one continuous story (and since one group of infringements — those in *The Tortoise and the Hare* — was merely a reprinting of an earlier one), the total was reduced to eight. Finally, Kennedy said, attorney's fees being discretionary and the Pirates free of "moral blame," none should be awarded; or, if they were, the amount should be minimal.

Laveroni's response began by saying that Stepanian's failure to object meant that Disney was entitled to all its requested damages from Richards. Then he turned to Kennedy's "incredible assertion" that Disney was not entitled to *in lieu* damages. He found this position "amusing," "facetious," "querulous," "without merit," "pure sophistry," full of "red herring[s]," and "tortured reasoning," the product of "defective logic," factually inaccurate and ignorant of the law. Of course, *in lieu* damages were appropriate. The code, the United States Supreme Court, and, in decision after decision, the Ninth Circuit said so. Judge Wollenberg had sent Woodruff the case within the context of this matrix of authority. He had ruled that Disney had been damaged by the Pirates but that a precise dollar figure could not be placed on the amount, so that determination was up to Woodruff.

The Pirates' willful, malicious, "blatant and outrageous" conduct demanded that this award be significant. To award less than the maximum would deny Disney adequate relief for its "great expense and inconvenience" and would encourage others "who, like the Pirates, have little respect for the rights of others" to act similarly. In fact, the Pirates' publication of *Tortoise*, while already restrained from infringing upon Disney's property rights, an act which bordered upon contempt of court, if not outright criminality, called for Woodruff to award even greater damages than the statute authorized.

Woodruff found that he could award *in lieu* damages. He accepted Laveroni's argument that *The Tortoise and the Hare*'s deliberate violation of the restraining order justified the maximum award. He instructed him to draft finding of facts and recommendations in accordance with his conclusions to present to Judge Wollenberg for ratification. When Tom Steel, a twenty-five-year-old recent addition to Kennedy's staff — (He would go on to a distinguished career as an activist attorney in San Francisco in the areas of criminal defense, police brutality, and tenants' rights before dying of AIDS in 1998) — objected that these findings did not accurately reflect Woodruff's conclusions, Laveroni replied that Steel's objections were "outrageous," "inappropriate," "incredible," "preposterous," and "without merit" — and took the opportunity to instruct him that "Personal attacks upon counsel... have no place in the law."

On March 5, 1976, Judge Wollenberg ordered O'Neill, London and Richards to pay Disney the full amount that Laveroni had requested.

The Pirates' opening brief with the Ninth Circuit Court of Appeal was due December 28, 1975; but Kennedy obtained an extension because of the work required to prepare for the damages hearing, his busy trial schedule, and the intervention of the Christmas holidays. (He also mentioned that his services to date had gone "largely uncompensated.") When he filed it, three weeks later, his points were familiar: the Pirates had not copied anything copyrightable; if they had, they were protected by fair use and/or the First Amendment; the granting of summary judgment was improper; the Pirates has not infringed any trademarks or committed any unfair business practices.

Kennedy's arguments on trademark infringement and unfair competition either actually or virtually repeated those in his office's earlier opposition to Disney's motion for the preliminary injunction. His argument that the granting of summary judgment was improper was new but perfunctory. Since the existence of any "conceivable" dispute over a material fact should have sufficed to defeat it, he said, the question of whether the Pirates had committed a substantial taking made the decision erroneous. This matter should not have been resolved by merely comparing pictures. All elements of the works should have been considered in order to evaluate the "total impression" each created. On the copyrightability of characters question, Kennedy added only a rebuttal to Wollenberg's "story-itself" test. How, he asked, could a creation whose very name — "mickeymouse" — had become synonymous with "trivial" and "shallow" be considered a strong enough personality to overshadow entire narratives?

Kennedy's treatment of the fair use defense, however, broke new ground. Specifically, he asked the Ninth Circuit to overrule *Benny*'s substantiality standard, on which Judge Wollenberg had based his decision. Parodists had to be able to copy substantially, he argued, in order to deliver "the shock of the unexpected..." To hold otherwise "disemboweled parody as an art form." He urged the court to adopt Professor Nimmer's approach and assess whether the infringing work was apt to satisfy a potential customer's desire for the original. And, he pointed out, Wollenberg had misunderstood Nimmer. Considering how the mocking of characters might effect sales of products promoted by them would negate a fair use defense by any parodist who intended to diminish his target in the public's eye, which is to say all of them. For Nimmer, it was not "criticism" that mattered but "substitution." The Pirates' work was not going to replace Disney's in any of its markets. And it was unlikely to preclude Disney, which had never parodied itself during its entire existence, from entering any new ones. Finally, Kennedy referred approvingly to the Second Circuit's recognition in *Berlin* of a parodist's right to take as much as was needed to "recall or conjure up" the object of his satire. That is what the Pirates did, he said. They copied only the image of the characters they intended to parody, which was the minimum necessary for their work to succeed; everything else they wrought was original.

Kennedy also used Nimmer to counter Wollenberg's concern that applying the First Amendment's shield to the Pirates' publications would obliterate the Copyright Act's protection of Disney's property rights. As parodists, the Pirates' aim was social and political criticism, he argued, not passing their books off as Disney's. The First Amendment guaranteed them the freedom to make their points. The Copyright Act only secured Disney against those who hoped to steal its customers.

Laveroni's response wasted no time alerting the Court to his feelings. The Air Pirates, he began, "glorying in the apt name they have chosen... [have behaved as] modern buccaneers... [feeling] free to seize what is not theirs and to turn [it]... into gain for themselves." Through their "degrading and offensive" work, they had plundered and pillaged Disney's characters, destroying their reputations and good will.

Laveroni then sought to immunize Disney from any noxious non-copyrightability-of-characters fumes still leaking out of the Ninth Circuit's earlier decision in *Warner Brothers*. He invoked Learned Hand again for the proposition that any well-defined fictional character warranted protection. Even if *Warner Brothers* said otherwise — and Laveroni denied that it did, arguing that its language to that effect was irrelevant *dicta* and its actual ruling determined by contractual terms specific to its contending parties — it explicitly exempted from its application characters copied in a "degrading or cheapening" manner likely to diminish public interest in them. In any event, *Warner's* holding could not apply to Disney because it concerned literary, not cartoon, characters. Every case that had dealt with cartoon characters, from Betty Boop to Superman, had found them copyrightable; and in considering whether these copyrights had been infringed, these cases had looked to the similarity of the likenesses alone. The postures or situations the characters were placed in were irrelevant.

Once the Ninth Circuit recognized that cartoon characters could be copyrighted, it would not matter what standard it adopted for determining a fair use. The Pirates' books would satisfy none of them. Fair use was a judge-made doctrine, arising not from actual legislation but general equitable considerations. And no equity worth its name would countenance the conduct here: the defamation of characters beloved by children worldwide in works "so perverted that when Appellants' counsel feels compelled to quote from their contents" — the "Why won't anybody fuck me?" panel — "he feels equally compelled to apologize to this court."

The Pirates' cries of "Parody" and "First Amendment" entitled them to no relief. Their work was not a parody but a close-as-possible copying. They had appropriated "the entire subject of the copyright," the graphic representation of the characters and their names, and used them for their own commercial purposes in a way no reasonable copyright holder would have authorized. Disney did not care what views the Pirates espoused, but it did not want its characters associated with them.

The granting of summary judgment was proper for no material facts were in dispute. Disney need not prove actual confusion in the mind of the public to prevail on either its claim of trademark infringement or trade disparagement. *Air Pirates Funnies* looked so much like a Disney comic confusion was "inevitable." It was equally clear that if the Pirates continued to publish their books, the negative associations they would build up about Disney's characters would diminish their reputations and dilute their value.

Tom Steel opened the Pirates' rebuttal by trying to strip the Disney characters of the cloak of invulnerability Laveroni had tailored for them. Even if characters were a copyrightable component part of a copyrighted work, Steel argued, this did not mean they could not be copied. Every individual work bore only one copyright. This work should not then be "dissected into as many 'copyrightable component parts' as imaginative counsel can conjure up" — good choice of words there — with each part evaluated individually and in isolation to see if too much of it had been copied to be a fair use. If that were permitted, any couplet, sentence, phrase, or name could be the subject of an infringement claim. Courts should consider the totality of the copyrighted work in question — plots, themes, dialogue, settings, subjects, ideas — to see if an infringing "substantial similarity" existed between it and the work that borrowed from it.

Steel, then, sought to expose what the defense believed to be Disney's true purpose in bringing suit. The Pirates' books were too erratically distributed and ineffectually advertised to threaten Disney economically, he said. But Laveroni's language — his argument's reliance on pejoratives like "perverted," "offensive," "degrading," and "defamatory," rather than the evidence of monetary damage or public confusion expected to lie at the heart of a copyright dispute — revealed what the case was really about. Laveroni hoped to inflame the court into a "climate of passion and prejudice," where it would take more extreme action than affording Disney financial relief. Disney wanted all criticism of its world view extinguished. It wanted the Pirates' tongues torn out; their pens ground into dust; their pages burned; salt plowed into their fields.

While their case had been winding through the courts — and while they now waited for the Ninth Circuit to hear the oral arguments of their appeal — the Air Pirates had sought to focus public attention on the issues it presented. They solicited donations to a Defense Fund through flyers showing O'Neill panhandling. ("Help! A 50-ton mouse is trying to step on my fingers.") They sold original art at cooperative galleries. (Invitations show O'Neill fleeing a gigantic, enraged Mickey.) They issued press releases ("IF THIS INJUNCTION IS MADE PERMANENT... THE FREEDOM OF ALL HUMORISTS, SATIRISTS, AND PARODISTS WILL BE SERIOUSLY CURTAILED") accompanied by reprints of magazine articles favorable to their cause, copies of their "experts'" affidavits from the hearing on the preliminary injunction motion, and copies of their own. Most of these actions centered around a relatively new phenomenon: the comic book convention, itself a portion of the not-too-elderly world of comic fandom.

In the 1950s, comic book aficionados, who saw the objects of their affections rarely discussed by the media except in terms of calls for their abolition, began to publish their own "fanzines." The authors were usually teenagers. Their works might be devoted to a single character — Ted White's *The Story of Superman* — or an entire line — Bhob Stewart's *E.C. Fan Bulletin.* They were reproduced by ditto, hectograph, or mimeograph machine. They contained historical information, industry news and gossip, biographies of artists, amateur strips, and never-before-available (or, for that matter, much missed) compilations of assorted comics-related esoterica of incalculable — or zero, depending on your point of view — value. Their work had the intellectual weight of a high school term paper that might not thoroughly humiliate its propounder but would raise a teacher's eyebrow or two, salved by the fervor of passionate belief. A circulation in three figures was Lucean. A run of six issues duration positively bordered on the *Collier's*-esque. By the mid-1960s, there were nearly 200 fanzines.[129] In 1971, there were more than three times that, and some circulations reached (not too far) into the thousands.

In mid-1964, 400 people came to a small hotel in New York City for the first convention devoted solely to comic books. That crowd was sufficient to make such conventions a regular part of the entertainment/separate-the-suckers-from-their-dollars circuit. Conventions brought together fans and professionals, collectors and dealers. Films were shown; panel discussions held; books, art and *tchotchkes* sold. In 1973, the UGs entered this world with a convention of their own in Pauley Ballroom of the student union building on the UC Berkeley campus.[130] A year or two later, a delegation of Pirates made an unofficial, unscheduled appearance at one of its successors. They were so well received that Phil Seuling, an English teacher at Brooklyn's Lafayette High School — alma mater to such luminaries as Larry King, Sandy Koufax and Gary David Goldberg, creator of *Family Ties* and legend of North Berkeley pick-up basketball games in the early '70s — who ran a large comic book convention in New York City every July 4th weekend, invited them to make a formal presentation about their case. Seuling also offered them free lodging and free table space in his exhibition area to sell whatever material they wished.

London and Flenniken took the train to Oakland, joined O'Neill, and, with money provided by Seuling and Comics and Comix, flew to New York. Hallgren, who now summered in Provincetown, drawing caricatures that earned him enough to carry him through a Bay Area winter, where he contributed to comics, motorcycle magazines, or whatever else came his way, gave up the lucrative holiday weekend and met them. With no one else selling artwork created

---

[129] At the same time, there were reportedly only 500 people "actively" engaged in comic fandom, which means almost every other one had printers' ink on his fingers.

[130] This event constituted, the official program noted, "the historical moment in which underground artists... have assembled together to affirm the validity of their art, to declare comic art to be the people's fine art, and to celebrate the victory of human fantasy over the comic code authority and all other attempts to limit artistic range, scope and imagination."

on the spot — and the attention-catching draw of the noise from Hallgren's air-brush — they attracted a crowd. (Since other artists were asking as much as $1000 for their work, the Pirates, who wanted less than $50, were also price-competitive.)

After New York, the Pirates — in various configurations, though never all together and never without O'Neill — appeared at several more conventions.[131] They participated in panel discussions about the case. They distributed fund-soliciting pamphlets. (A 1976 edition depicted Hugh, Fred the Bird, Dirty Duck, Annie Rat, Trots, Bonnie, and the Tortoise and Hare trying to chop down the beanstalk before an ogrish Mickey, descending, can reach them.) They also defied the injunction by selling "federal crime drawings," numbered sequentially to record how many violations they had committed. With support-ers like Murphy, Todd, Denis Kitchen of Milwaukee's Kitchen Sink Press (and creator of the first 3-D underground comic), *MAD*'s Sergio Aragonés, and Vaughn Bodé, who spent several hours on one drawing, which he sold for $300 — or $400 — or $450, accounts vary — they sat at tables, drawing as fast as they could while fans lined up to make requests and negotiate prices. Usually they did Disney characters, but they were open to other suggestions.[132] Hallgren says, "We met a lot of interesting people with a lot of interesting requests" — which should come as no surprise to anyone who has ever attended a comic book convention.

O'Neill says each appearance brought in about $5000; but, according to London, what money they made "went up in smoke." Kennedy confirms this. "I don't think my office ever saw a dime. If somebody says we did, they may be right; but I don't recall it." Stepanian only laughs when asked if he was paid.) Flenniken says, "The money paid for meals, the trips, supplies. It wasn't intend-ed for the lawyers. It was to help the cartoonists survive while fighting the case."

---

[131] Hallgren recalls being at three (1975-77), all in New York. London says he stopped appearing after '76 and was never at any with Richards. Richards says he didn't participate in many because he was married, had a child, and was putting his efforts into trying to market a daily strip to a major syndicate.

[132] London says he never drew Disney characters, only his own.

Chapter Fifteen:
Once You Say You've Copied Directly You Have a Problem

The Ninth Circuit Court of Appeals roosts in caliphal splendor at Seventh and Mission, one block from San Francisco's blackest hole. On Sixth Street swarm humanoid predators and victims, carrion and scavengers, carcasses and maggots. Here, festering, ragged, filth-caked, drift those clinging to SSI checks by their ulcerated fingertips. Here stumble and rave the diseased, the maimed, the mind-rotted, the soul-damned. They beat each others' brains out with sawed-off pool cues in vomit-soaked alleys. They filet each others' innards with friction-taped shanks in piss-sodden stairwells. They huddle and shriek in SRO rooms where their own defecation may occur as the only adornment. They spill, besides the empty crack vials and used condoms, into the gutters, embracing whatever form deliverance may manifest.[133]

But on Seventh Street — according to the pamphlet the Office of the Circuit Executive presses upon juxtapositionally shell-shocked visitors — sits the *Sunset Magazine*-dubbed "Palace." "[This] fine and early example of Beaux

---

[133] Excuse my overheated prose; but it was in a Sixth Street hotel room — a bed, a chair, a broken mirror, a bureau with syringes and bleach in open display — that after two-plus decades in the Bay Area — some ups, some downs, some lifts and falls that only the outlaw life provides — my friend Max Garden had come to ground. We had maintained regular contact — though, in later years, most of our visits coincided with his requiring money from me. At one of the most recent, he'd wanted to do something special for me for my birthday.

"You've never done crack cocaine, have you, Bob?"

"No," I said.

"You'd really like it."

I looked at him. He looked as bad as anyone asleep in any doorway. "Tell you the truth, I'm afraid of catching some disease."

He laughed. "I'll get you your own pipe. You can keep it for a souvenir."

Arts Classical or American Renaissance... [was built of] rusticated ashlar granite... [with] pilastered colonnades... [and] triangular pediments... [beneath] a granite cornice and ballustrade," at the last century's turn for $2,500,000. It was expanded during the Depression, refurbished in the '60s, and rehabilitated — all at taxpayers' expense — for nearly fifty times its original cost, ten years ago. The doors are bronze or mahogany. The hall floors are porcelain mosaic tile or marble — pink Tennessee, gray Georgia, rouge Languedoc. The walls are marble too — green Vermont, white Carerra and white Sienese. The ceilings are groin or cross-vaulted, the transom windows arched, the chandeliers spun bronze, the skylights varicolored.

The five courtrooms, though limited to use by appellate attorneys and jurists — no witnesses or actual litigants, no public lingers here — do not suffer by comparison. Their walls — white pavonazzo or yellow California marble or bronzed, acoustic cork — are augmented by oak piers, Corinthian columns, Venetian glass. The benches are oak, finished in red Numidian marble. There are Art Deco light fixtures (star-and-artichoke pattern), a travertine marble dias, gilded plaster eagles behind each judge. Ceramic tile murals honor Science and Art, Freedom, Majesty and Wisdom. The ceilings bear plaster fruit and — I cannot help mentioning, cheap shot though it is — swastikas.

The Ninth Circuit scheduled oral arguments on the Pirates' appeal February 17, 1978. Steel requested a postponement. Kennedy was already committed to depositions in India, and he was booked for a seminar in Puerto Rico.

Laveroni objected. The parties had been litigating this case for over six years, he said. They had been waiting two to argue this appeal. Disney wanted the case decided now. Defense counsel should rearrange their calendars and make themselves available. Besides, he pointed out, Steel's declaration did not even state he or Kennedy would be making the arguments the court was being asked to postpone.

The court rejected Steel's request.

The oral arguments took place before a three-judge panel: Richard Chambers; Aldon Anderson; and Walter J. Cummings. Chambers was seventy-one. A graduate of the University of Arizona and Stanford Law School, he had been in private practice in Tucson when Eisenhower named him to the federal bench in 1954. Anderson was born January 13, 1917, in Salt Lake City. He had received his undergraduate and law degrees from the University of Utah and had been a state court judge when Nixon elevated him in 1971. (He also had eight children, which must have floated a lot of Disney under his household's bridge.) Cummings, who sat on assignment from the Seventh Circuit, was sixty. He had a B.A. from Yale and an LL.B. from Harvard. A former Assistant United States Solicitor General, he had been a senior partner in a Chicago corporate law firm when Johnson had appointed him on July 4, 1966.[134]

Tatum argued for Disney, Stepanian for Richards, and A. Kirk McKenzie, an anti-trust lawyer and securities litigation specialist, stood in for Kennedy on behalf of O'Neill and London. "I always enjoyed First Amendment work," McKenzie says. "This was a cutting-edge case, legally and intellectually fascinating; and with Mutt and Jeff, Jack Benny, and Sid Caesar for precedents, how could I refuse?" Disney corporate headquarters was interested enough that its general counsel attended — and brought his family to observe.

McKenzie centered his argument around changes in the law wrought by the recently enacted Copyright Act of 1976, where Congress, for the first time, had specified factors for courts to consider in determining what constituted a fair use: the nature and purpose — commercial or non-commercial — of the infringing work; the nature of the copyrighted work; the amount and substantiality of the copied portion in relation to the whole; and the effect of the infringing work upon the potential market for, or value of, the copyrighted work. While that last clause seemed particularly Pirate-friendly, its embrace was cooled by the act's exclusion from its coverage of all cases that had arisen before its passage. McKenzie also felt the nature of the work he was defending had him arguing into a chilly wind. "Certainly some of it was crude," he concedes, "but some of it was clever; and it was an obvious parody. It couldn't be confused with an actual Disney comic, and it caused Disney no commercial damage. I tried to emphasize the economic-use approach, but the court wasn't willing to look at the issue. Sure, the Pirates copied the characters, but get real. There was no damage."

"McKenzie argued very well," Laveroni recalls. "He laid out the law, the precedents, the free speech issue smoothly. He was very effective in his presentation. But Stepanian was out of his element. I know Michael. I've played rugby with him. He's a fine criminal lawyer; but when he was explaining to these three judges how this Wolf character represented a stereotype of Southern whites, their eyes glazed. They couldn't believe this argument was being made." Then he paused. "And, you know, once you say you copied directly, you have a problem."

Stepanian rejoins, "Whatever Richards said, I said. If they didn't like it, that's life."

McKenzie admits Stepanian's approach might have been "a little over the top" but recalls being taken to task himself by one of the judges who believed he had "misrepresented" the legislative history behind the 1976 act. "And Sandy Tatum was very good. Quite good. He was very well prepared. And Cooley, Crowley always did excellent paperwork. The argument was presented

---

[134] Including Wollenberg, the average age of the four men who rendered judgment on the Pirates was sixty-seven. The Pirates' average age at the time of their roguery was twenty-five. The moral is: "The wisdom of age does not always square with the exuberance of youth."

as well as it could have been. In fact, the caliber of all the lawyering remained high long after the case ceased to be a paying proposition. It was great fun."

On September 5, 1978, in an opinion by Judge Cummings, the Ninth Circuit Court of Appeal ruled three to zero that the Pirates were guilty of copyright infringement.[135] Because it was *the* Ninth Circuit, it did not have to be troubled, as Judge Wollenberg had been, by what an earlier incarnation of itself had written. What the Ninth Circuit said in *Warner Brothers* was what Cummings said it said now. The result of this Rosetta-worthy deciphering was that *Warners* did not imply cartoon characters uncopyrightable after all. It only spoke to the literary characters it addressed. Cartoon characters, because they have "physical as well as conceptual qualities... likely to contain some unique elements of expression," were different and deserved to be treated so. (In reaching this conclusion, the Court of Appeal rejected Wollenberg's "constitute-the-story" test for his failure to recognize it would only protect characters in works "devoid of plot.")

The Ninth Circuit agreed with Wollenberg that because the Pirates had other means of expressing their ideas, the First Amendment did not allow them to infringe Disney's copyrights. But, discussing fair use, it accepted Kennedy's argument that the bi-partite "substantiality" test Wollenberg had derived from *Benny* should be abandoned. (In point of fact, it called his interpretation, which equated "the substantiality of the taking" with "the substantiality necessary to constitute an infringement," an "absurdity," for it would limit a successful fair use defense to cases where the portion copied was an insignificant part of the work it was copied from.) *Benny*, it said, merely established a "threshold" that denied a fair use defense to any "virtually complete or verbatim" copying. For less extensive copying, the issue became did it take more than was necessary to meet *Berlin*'s "conjure up" standard.

But this shift helped the Pirates less than Kennedy had hoped. Though the court recognized that the question of whether the copying of the visual representation of a cartoon character was excessive *per se*, or if other factors, like plot, personality and speech, should be considered had never been answered and that an answer might help parodists conduct themselves in the future, it concluded it need not provide one. No matter how you looked at it, the Pirates had taken too much "of both the conceptual and the physical aspects of the characters."

The court's analysis, however, limited itself to the physical. Mickey

<hr />

[135] "The Ninth Circuit Court of Appeals ruled..." sounds infinitely more impressive than "Three guys named Moe said..."; but, really, isn't that what it comes down to? Three men — lots of degrees — *mucho* eminence — seriousness up the gee-gee; but how do they put their pants on? Three Moes. But for the rest of the country, until this question got this far again: "The Ninth Circuit Court of Appeals ruled..."

Mouse, it said, was so recognizable any rough likeness would identify him.[136] The essence of parody was behavior, not likeness; and a comic book required less mimicking than a work of pure prose to produce "a recognizable caricature." Instead of utilizing this freedom, the Pirates had "track[ed] Disney's work... as closely as possible." This might sharpen their satire's bite, but it exceeded the permissible. They were not entitled to a "best parody" standard but a "what is necessary..." one. "[E]xcessive copying," it concluded, "precludes fair use." Therefore, summary judgment on the copyright infringement cause of action was proper.

The decision held some good news for the Pirates. Because Disney had produced no evidence of actual public confusion about the source of their books, the court reversed Wollenberg's findings of trademark infringement and trade disparagement and remanded the case to him for further proceedings on those issues. But since the monetary damages and injunction stood — and because Disney had also been awarded another $1628.77 for costs incurred in connection with the appeal — Laveroni's brief had been professionally printed, rather than typed like Kennedy's — Kennedy petioned the United States Supreme Court for a writ of certiorari on behalf of O'Neill and London. Stepanian did not join in this request.

The petition was primarily McKenzie's work.

His argument again emphasized economics. The Copyright Act of 1976, he wrote, following Nimmer's wise counsel, had made market value diminishment the prime requisite for denying a claim of fair use. Even though it did not apply to cases that arose before its passage, the act expressed Congress's view. The Ninth Circuit should have paid "greater deference" to this view, because judicial bodies ought not substitute their will for that of legislative ones. Making economic loss, which could be fixed through expert evaluation, the key to an infringement case would also provide an objective standard by which parodists could govern their behavior. Leaving them measured by the subjective "conjure up" test put their judgments at the mercy of second-guessing by judges whose

---

[136] A point of minor interest is how many Mickeys there have been. His eyes, which began as ovals with black pupils, became black spots, added "pie-slice" highlights, then resumed their original form. He donned shoes, gloves, loosened his shorts, then swapped them for pants. He became "streamlined," with an elongated nose, tucked-in mouth, and swept-back ears. His legs, which had dropped straight down from his torso, were hinged and set outside it. He grew chubby-cheeked and, once, even lost and regained his tail. And the percentages of his eye size to head length increased by one-half, his head length to total length five percent, and his nose-to-ear distance by more than a third.

Ub Iwerks, who first drew Mickey, once said, intending to share credit with Walt Disney for the Mouse's success, "It isn't creating it, it's what you do with it." If Iwerks is correct, the physical representation of a cartoon character may not be so important after all in defining who he is and what he is about.

power to impose large damage awards would make parodists fearful of exercising their First Amendment rights.

On January 22, 1979, the Supreme Court, without comment, refused to hear the Air Pirates' appeal.

Chapter Sixteen:
My Chance To Be Sued for a Million Dollars and Jailed

Doing something stupid once is just plain stupid.
Doing something stupid twice is a philosophy.
Dan O'Neill[137]

"I got the news sitting in the bathtub in this tiny house with no foundation," Dan O'Neill remembers. "The bathtub is tilted; the water is cock-eyed; and Farley, my neighbor, hollers in the window, 'O'Neill, you just lost nine-zip.' I was feeling pretty low at this point. My second divorce had just hit. I had 700 pounds of hollering children and 340 pounds of mothers of those children attached to 3000 pounds of district attorneys after me. I was kind of blacklisted. I was thinking of jumping off a bridge. And suddenly I'm 'Ahhh, good! One more fight. Renewed life. I can work with this.'"

To a man with O'Neill's perspective — "When you're down $190,000 in a poker game, you have to raise" — the next step was obvious: commit a new crime. He had piped London and Richards aboard initially; he had swept them along in his wake to this goal. Now, unasked, he assumed responsibility to free them.

O'Neill has said he had always planned to lose all the way to the Supreme Court, lose there — and do it again. (He just hadn't thought it would take eight years to reach that point.) Now, he reasoned, those losses had placed Disney where he wanted it. If he defied its injunction, its only recourse would be to have him held in contempt of court. "And then they have to put you in jail. For drawing a mouse? In the land of the free? No way. And any storm that came

---

[137] Compare with Voltaire: "Once, a philosopher; twice, a pervert."

down would force them to change their interpretation." As a legal strategy, this seems less likely to have been formulated by the Hon. Arthur Goldberg than the cartoonist Rube. O'Neill wouldn't have needed to appeal if all he wanted was to defy an injunction. He could have done that in 1972. However...[138]

O'Neill called Stewart Brand.

As one of Ken Kesey's Merry Pranksters, Brand had dreamed up the Trips Festival of January 1966, which Tom Wolfe, in *The Electric Kool-Aid Acid Test,* anointed "the first national convention [of acid heads]." In 1968, he had attained a less feloniously inclined celebrity with his launching of *The Whole Earth Catalog.* Since 1974, through POINT, the Sausalito-based non-profit corporation he'd founded with its profits, he had published *The Co-Evolution Quarterly.* The nearly advertisement-free *CQ* drew contributions from Gregory Bateson, Paul Ehrlich, Gary Snyder, and Admiral Hyman Rickover. It had about 16,000, more-or-less alternative-living enthusiast subscribers and was devoted to explorations of the benefits of underground housing, holistic health, wood cookstoves, and the dangers of genetic mutations.

O'Neill had met Brand through Paul Krassner,[139] who had briefly been his roommate in an apartment noteworthy for the Kali-esque, eight-armed Donald Duck that roosted on its mantlepiece.[140] Brand, an admirer of "Odd Bodkins," had taken O'Neill's cartooning course at UC Extension and joined him now and then for the release from the rigors of academia available back-stage at the O'Farrell. "The girls would be doing their stuff, having fun, acting friendly," Brand recalls, "and Dan would be having an Irish-Catholic crisis, enjoying himself one moment and banging his head against the wall the next."

Over the next few years, O'Neill had contributed numerous pieces to the *Quarterly,* some commissioned by it and some he had been unable to place elsewhere. Brand knew about the Air Pirates case; and when O'Neill

---

[138] This may be a good time to note other ornaments with which O'Neill has trimmed the tree of his account, whose apparent fragility, while enchanting, has dissuaded me from too close an inspection: (1) Disney's failure to sue him for his use of their characters in "Odd Bodkins" means he now owns thirty of them; (2) the outcome of the Air Pirates suit forced Disney to return rights to Winnie the Pooh, Bambi, Pinocchio and other characters it had misappropriated; and (3) he is consulted regularly as an expert in copyright law.

[139] In yet another bit of counterculture synchronicity, in September 1965, Brand had presented one of San Francisco's first multi-media shows. The place was the Committee Theater and the subject "America Needs Indians."

[140] Overzealous fact-checking forces me to concede that, while technically correct — Krassner did have such a waterfowl on his mantle — it was not the one he shared with Brand but that of a separate abode he maintained in Watsonville.

approached him, he put four pages in the Spring issue at his disposal in a sort-of toss-the-drowning-man-a-torpedo gesture. O'Neill says Brand's motivation was: "Here I am, forty years old, and all my friends have been sued for a million dollars. They've been in jail, and I haven't. This is my chance." Brand says, "Sure, I was aware of the injunction. That's why we did it. We always went to bat for our contributors when they were in trouble. And I'd absolutely do it again. It's always a pleasure to come to the defense of creativity being squashed unfairly and inappropriately — to come down on the side of the lone creator against the machine."

Seventeen drafts later, O'Neill, spinning off from what had been planned as the third installment of the Mouse story, presented the *Quarterly* with "Communique #1 from the M.L.F." (Mouse Liberation Front). Brand provided a brief introduction, in which he summarized the litigation and called Disney "the General Motors of the cartoon world, immense, inescapable, admirable, despicable..." "Prodigious success...," he concluded, "draws parody. That's how a culture defends itself. Especially from institutions so large that they lose track of where they stop and the world begins so that they try to exercise their internal model of control on outside activities."

"Communique" opens with Mickey and Minnie happily married and living on a small farm in Mendocino County. They explain that, after forty years in Hollywood, they had hit bottom, careers going nowhere, hooked on alcohol (him) and diet pills (her), having affairs, so jealous and embittered they had once almost put out a contract on Donald Duck. (A nod to "Mickey Rodent" again.) Their children (Mortie and Ferdie) had been so concerned they hired "these bozo artists" (the Air Pirates) to kidnap and recondition them. Dosed with psychedelics and indoctrinated through sexuality seminars, Mickey and Minnie recommitted to each other; but Disney had the Pirates arrested and prosecuted and, unable to revive the careers of their former stars, offered them "a modest retirement" if they'd leave town.

Now Mickey and Minnie want to speak out. (They weren't, they say, surprised by what transpired in court. "It's taken the court over 200 years to discover Negroes are people and they're only half sure about women... so how can we expect them to understand mice.") They credit the Pirates for turning their lives around. They defend their right to parody Disney by *exactly* copying its characters. They demand that Disney cease all legal actions against the Pirates and work with them in "a joint venture [...rebuilding Cleveland, making films, whatever]" and that the Pirates cease all "mouse-eating-snot jokes [and start] making big bucks for Disney..."

"Communique #1" is delightful — and brilliant. From the double-width opening panel, a long shot of Mickey, Minnie, their house, farm and surrounding countryside, to the smallest detail (a Mickey Mouse cookie jar being my favorite), O'Neill's skills as a draftsman have never been more fully displayed.[141] The mice positively glow with "innocent delight." The page pops with comic clutter when clutter is appropriate. The visuals soothe or jar, reflect or incite, depending on the text's demands. The language mingles the humorous and the instructive, the honed and the outrageous. Nowhere else, in print or conversation, does he analyze the Court of Appeal's holding as insightfully. Mickey and Minnie report that, while the court said "some" copying is permissible and "too much" is not, "No one, including the court, is sure how much is 'some.'" O'Neill demonstrates the absurdity of this standard in a way that Louis Dembitz Brandeis with a Ryder van full of footnotes could not. "Is this 'some'?" he asks of a Minnie with an extra-fingered left mitt. "Is this 'some'?" he inquires of a hairy-torsoed Mickey with a lengthy, naked, articulated tail.[142]

Neither pure prose nor pure pictures could have made this point so well. Only through this cuttingly accurate, affectionate but bracing, respectful but confrontational treatment could he lay down what he had been arguing all along. While mocking Disney, he was making political points. He was tackling social issues. He was a cartoon-drawing parodist, not a pamphlet-pushing polemicist; but he demanded the same First Amendment that shielded the most astute, the most erudite, the most thoughtful among us. And by so doing, he asserted his middle-finger-extended self into the face of the most august, blackest-robed nay-sayers in the land. (I mean, three freaking tiers of the federal judiciary had already told him to bloody well behave without a dissenting vote.) O'Neill championed defiance, license, and pedal-to-the-metal liberty when, from sea-to-shining-sea, the powerful and pious were urging order, demanding decorum, struggling to reinstate a landscape of buttoned-down, buckled-up, "Just Say 'No'" repressiveness and denial, whose primacy a decade's unruliness had cast in doubt.

On April 20, 1979, Disney petitioned to dismiss its causes of action for

---

[141] It was, one cartoonist-commentator wrote, "the sharpest, funniest and most substantive Disney parody [O'Neill] had yet produced." This may have been, in part, because the art was Gary Hallgren's — with supplemental inking by Larry Todd. In 1979, Hallgren had moved to New York. He had already created the "Weird Wheels" bubblegum card series for Topps, for which he had been recruited by Art Spiegelman, its "creative consultant," and was contributing regularly to the *Lampoon* when O'Neill called. "He told me Disney was a signature away from collecting, and he wanted to do an in-their-face Mouse story. He wanted it drawn well and would protect me from prosecution. The scheme of a secret identity had a mischievous attraction. I didn't care if I got credit. I just wanted to prove to myself I could rip off Disney with style."

[142] O'Neill's concern was not misplaced. Over the next few years, cartoonist-parodying cartoonists found themselves being asked, on the advice of their publishers' attorneys, to lengthen noses, shorten ears, re-cut hair, re-fashion wardrobes. But often nothing they did satisfied the concern that they still might have copied more than was necessary. The standard was too amorphous and the risk of abuse too costly. Magazines ceased parodying comic books and strips.

trademark infringement, unfair competition, and trade disparagement. With its injunction in force and its award of damages sustained, it was content to let things conclude. The Pirates did not object.

Then the *Quarterly* hit the stands.

On May 2, Disney moved to have Judge Wolllenberg hold O'Neill, Brand and POINT in contempt of court, fined $10,000 each, and ordered to pay its attorneys' fees and costs. The next day, it asked to have the United States Attorney's office prosecute them criminally.

Disney's motions were accompanied by affidavits from Craig H. Casebeer and Charles S. Paul, two junior attorneys at Cooley, Crowley, that they had purchased copies of the *Quarterly* — three for Casebeer, one for Paul — at City Lights Books in San Francisco and the Real Food Company in Sausalito. An affidavit of Laveroni's summed up the consequences of these acquisitions. By drawing Mickey, Minnie, and other Disney characters, O'Neill had "knowingly and intentionally violated the injunction of this Court and... openly defied the dignity and authority of the Courts of the United States." "Indeed," he wrote, "[O'Neill] boasts that this latest work amounts to 'contempt of the Supreme Court of the United States.' And while defendant may have misconstrued the target... he is correct that this work is contempt." He has shown "utter disdain and disregard for the judicial process... Unless strong action is taken, he will continue to defy the Court and perhaps encourage others to emulate his conduct." Brand, Laveroni went on, by helping O'Neill market his defiance while fully aware of the injunction and the appellate decisions sustaining it, had "aided, abetted and assisted" this outrage. Without this help, Laveroni said, O'Neill's transgressions "would have been extremely difficult or... more limited in scope" — as if delivery to those 16,000, solar-heated, yurt-dwelling *Quarterly* readers had power-boosted the impact of O'Neill's defilements — as if this previously judiciary-respecting, Disney-adoring troupe had been shaken from its tree of grace.

Brand replied with a "letter" in the *Quarterly*. (It also ran as a half-page ad in *Variety*.) He called the "Communique" an "insightful," good-humored, tasteful comment upon the Supreme Court's ruling. While it might displease Disney, it did not harm it. If Disney wanted to complain, he would give it equal space. Pointing out his magazine could be bankrupted by his legal fees even if he won, Brand wrote, "Parody is a fragile right, all too susceptible to overzealous suing.... [Ask yourself] [h]ow would Mickey handle a situation like this? He'd come up with some good-hearted solution no doubt."

Disney ignored Brand's offer.

Kennedy and McKenzie responded to "Communique" and Laveroni's broadside by petitioning the court to be discharged as attorneys for O'Neill and London. They had recently learned, they said, of a potential conflict of interest between their clients. Disputes had arisen over how to proceed with the case and, due to their differing roles within the Air Pirates, how responsibility for Disney's damage award should be allocated between them. In addition, while they had repeatedly asked their clients for money — and repeatedly been promised it by them — aside from $1350 received from groups interested in the case's First Amendment issues, they had not been paid in several years and should not be required to continue financing the case from their own pockets.

Disney did not oppose this motion.

The reactions of those to whose rescue O'Neill had ridden were mixed.

Bobby London, after separating from Flenniken, had lived in San Francisco, Washington, D.C., and Provincetown, before settling in Manhattan. With the underground behind him, his career was progressing nicely. His work had appeared in *Esquire*, *Playboy*, and on the Op-Ed page of *The New York Times*. In 1978, he had won his own Yellow Kid award as the best writer-cartoonist of the year.

London viewed the Disney suit as an embarrassing — perhaps, virulent — stain on his resume. In early 1977, he had asked Sherman S. Saiger, an attorney in New York City, to whom he had been referred by Dik ("Hagar the Horrible") Browne's son, to cut a deal for its removal. Saiger learned the terms of Hallgren's settlement from Albert Morse and called Laveroni. Laveroni did not exactly salivate with excitement. Since 1975, he pointed out, Disney had been forced to fight its case through the obtaining of summary judgment. It had battled over damages. It had warred to the portals of the Ninth Circuit. "In sum," he wrote, "we are just not interested in letting your client... simply walk away from a situation which has already cost our client a substantial amount of money." If London wanted a settlement, he must dismiss his appeal with prejudice, agree to abide by the injunction, *and* pay Disney $5000. Disney, in turn, would not execute the judgment it had against him.

Saiger replied that the conceptual framework to the settlement was fine, but one of its particulars appeared a deal-breaker. As a freelance artist, London did not have and could not raise $5000. Since he had been only a "passive" participant in the recent court proceedings, not a "prime mover," would Disney accept $250 from him? Laveroni responded that Disney was not a plaintiff with which to nickel-dime, so Saiger asked London for authority to offer a take-it or leave-it thousand or two. On March 31, he wrote Laveroni that, through "various borrowings," London had come up with $1500. If that was not acceptable, he would file bankruptcy. Laveroni sent Saiger a formal settlement agreement, but Saiger advised London not to sign it, since it did not discharge the judgment but kept it on file for twenty years.

London continued to halfheartedly pursue a settlement with Disney;

but when "Communique" appeared, it assumed he was involved and broke off talks.[143]

Ted Richards had returned to comics in 1976, when he co-authored two books: *Two Fools*, with Willy Murphy and Justin Green; and *Give Me Liberty*, with Gilbert Shelton, and lesser contributions from Murphy and Hallgren. *Fools* was strongly influenced by French cartoonists, who had to appeal to the multilingual European market.[144] It relied heavily on visual gags, with long stretches of pantomime — the exception being "The Origins of the Two Fools," a tribute to Murphy, who died prior to its completion ("They'll always be two fools trying to write and draw funny stories," it poignantly concluded) — and sold much better abroad than domestically. *Liberty* was a Kurtzmanesque take on the American Revolution, replete with exploding manure wagons, dotty patriots, and debaucheries. Rich in myth-puncturing — Paul Revere never made it to Concord; John Paul Jones sold captured stores back to the British — and deflating fibs — Jefferson copped the phrase "created equal" from a black janitor — it portrayed a war won by blunders and luck and concluded "...[R]evolution is a vicious circle and an illusion. Nothing is going to change and we must lay down our arms." Intended as counter-programming for the Bicentennial fever sweeping the country, in quintessential UG fashion, it appeared too close to the actual celebration to attract much attention.

Later that year, when his old space became available, Richards re-opened Fast Draw, with J.M. Leonard, a fellow southerner, and Larry Gonick, creator of *Cartoon History of the Universe*. Through Rip Off, Richards syndicated two strips to college and alternative newspapers: "E.Z. Wolf" (collected in the comics *E.Z. Wolf* and *E.Z. Wolf's Astral Outhouse*) and "The Forty Year Old Hippie" (collected in *The Forty Year Old Hippie* and *The Whole Forty Year Old Hippie Catalog*). "E.Z." was set near the town of Terminus, in Chitterland County. It championed the "common man" (E.Z., Slick Fox, Brer Bill Goat) and mocked the wealthy (P.J. Pigman), the corrupt (Sheriff George C. Alabama), pretentious politicians (Jimmy Otter), the New York media (Walter J. Weasel), food additives, modern art, and all manifestations of the "Spiritual Consciousness Business."

"Hippie" was perhaps Richards's finest work, wide in range and deep, if dark, in vision. "I felt old," he says, when asked how it came about. "I was sober, raising a family, making a living. I saw people, like myself, who'd done all this weird stuff and now had to figure out what to do with themselves." His protagonist panhandles, deals

[143] According to "Mark's Very Large *National Lampoon* Site," in 1979, London's parents had him incorporated "to protect him from the M.L.F." Probably, the protection sought was from Disney, though, coming after the judgment was already in place, if I remember my Corporations I, it would have done him little good.

[144] The French had shown a demand for adult comics existed in the early 1960s with the satirical newspaper *Hara-Kiri* and, later, through graphic novels like *Barbarella*. By the 1970s, a large, UG-appreciative audience existed throughout western Europe, only a small corner of which could be knocked for its veneration of Jerry Lewis as a cinematic genius.

dope, runs a holistic kazoo workshop. He floats between San Francisco, a pot farm in Deadboldt County, and the stomach of a whale he is trying to save. He collides with pyramid power, parquet-contaminated weed, falling sky-labs — not usually to his betterment. "I've always felt like I don't belong here," he says. "I don't see anything I recognize." "We stumble about like burned out casualties. Taunts and abuse spew forth from every street corner and rock concert." In the then-futuristic "Year 2000 Story," the Hippie's daughter, ChildPerson, abides on an Earth where anarchy rages; energy sources are depleted; murders are videotaped for entertainment; drugs and sex fail to cope with the void; the spirit of annihilation fills the planet. But, she offers, "[A]s long as we survive, we got a chance."[145]

Shortly before "Communique" appeared, Richards's newest strip, "Mellow Cat," about a "skateboard guru," debuted in *Skateboarder Magazine*. Its million-plus readership, primarily among nine-to-fourteen-year-olds, had led Hanna-Barbera to approach him about developing it as a Saturday morning television cartoon show. For H-B to acquire the strip, Richards needed it freed of any encumbrances — like a $190,000 judgment. If London took "Communique" as further evidence of O'Neill's lunacy and efforts to destroy his life, Richards thought it inspired — and fortuitous. Disney had been unresponsive to the efforts of Lloyd Crenna, a commercial law specialist who worked with Stepanian, to negotiate a settlement on his behalf. Now Richards called Laveroni and arranged a meeting.

Laveroni was furious about "Communique." "That sonovabitch," he said, "is going to get it."

"Calm down," Richards said. "'Sixty Minutes' is pretty hot right now, and I can just see Mike Wallace dropping in to interview O'Neill with Mickey Mouse painted behind him on some cell block wall. And O'Neill loves to draw on walls."

"Can you talk to him?" Laveroni said.

"No one can influence Dan. He has his own thing going. It's artistic and intellectual, and it's revolutionary. You'll have to work out your own deal. But if this goes on, and I have to file bankruptcy, you'll have two of us out there; and I am someone who can draw the other characters."[146]

---

[145] The parallel between this conclusion and that expressed by O'Neill in Bucky and Rollo's last conversation in his *The Collected Unconscience...* is noteworthy. Life will hurl its traumas at you, both cartoonists maintain. That is the nature of life. But if a person can endure — without being driven mad or pounded numb — the mere fact of this endurance is itself an affirmation.

[146] I was literally halfway through printing out my final draft when Richards told me that Disney did not learn of "Communique" until he showed it to Laveroni. That so fucked this chapter's carefully constructed narrative line I decided not to mention it. (Also, Laveroni — while saying he found Richards to be "an intelligent, responsible person" whose memory might outshine his own — recalls neither this meeting nor this conversation.) To partially make up for any oversight, I have promised to plug Richards's web site: tedrichards.net. (And while I'm at it: garyhallgren.com; DirtyDuck.com; sharyflenniken.com; and oddbodkins.com.)

Chapter Seventeen:
By Now You Should Have Figured Out He's Irish

Dan O'Neill had no trouble finding new counsel. John Keker, a graduate of Princeton and Yale Law School, who had served as a Marine in Vietnam, clerked for United States Supreme Court Chief Justice Earl Warren, been a Federal Public Defender, and was developing a reputation as a top-flight litigator in private practice in San Francisco, agreed to defend him against the contempt charge *pro bono*. "I don't remember how I got involved," Keker says, "but I found Dan absolutely charming and the situation suitably ridiculous; and I had a great relationship with Wollenberg."

Brand and POINT retained Lawrence A. Klein, a specialist in corporate tax law with the firm of Blase, Valentine & Klein in Palo Alto, which handled their legal affairs, to represent them.

Keker's response to the contempt motion reintroduced his client to Judge Wollenberg as "an indigent cartoonist against whom Walt Disney Productions has a $190,000 judgment and whom Disney is now trying to put in jail [and have ordered to]... pay Disney's lawyers for putting him there." Klein presented Brand as a Stanford graduate (B.A. in Biology, 1960), a U.S. Army infantry lieutenant (1960-62), a National Book Award Winner (*The Last Whole Earth Catalog*, 1972), and a special consultant to Governor Jerry Brown. (The Prankster/Trips Festival portions of Brand's resume were omitted.) The two denied that their clients had violated any court order — or shown anyone contempt. Disney's suit should be dismissed, they said; and it should be ordered to reimburse O'Neill and Brand their attorneys' fees and costs for the trouble to which it had put them.

Keker and Klein pointed out that the order which the defendants stood accused of violating forbade O'Neill only from *infringing* upon Disney's copyrights. Under the present state of the law, as defined by the Copyright Act of 1976, however, "Communique" was not an infringement but a fair use. That statute's four-factor measuring rod had knocked the "conjure-up" test ass-over-teakettle, and applying those factors to this case left O'Neill and Brand blameless. Theirs were "different caricatures expressing different themes in dissimilar contexts fulfilling dissimilar purposes" than any drawings Disney had ever issued.

The *purpose* of "Communique," a trenchant critique of the litigation in which the Air Pirates had been embroiled, was far different than Disney's frolicsome entertainments. The *nature* of the *Quarterly*, a non-profit publication devoted to the serious discussion of weighty matters, directed toward a limited audience of adult readers, was equally dissimilar from Disney's mass-marketed, utterly commercial juvenilia. O'Neill had not taken a *substantial* part of Disney's property. He had only copied one of Mickey's many pictorial representations, which had to be done exactly in order to demonstrate, through the later alteration of some of these features, the absurdity of the "more than enough" standard. O'Neill had then added original dialogue, locales, personalities, and story lines. No Disney Mouse had ever lived in Humboldt County, been angst-ridden, or espoused such bitterness at his employer or the legal system. And, most importantly, O'Neill had caused Disney no *economic harm.* It was "ludicrous" for Disney, which had not even asked to have the *Quarterly* taken off the market, to suggest otherwise. "Communique" competed with Disney, Keker wrote — in words reminiscent of Anatole France on sleeping under bridges — "in the same way rich people compete with poor people for the right to spend the night on a bench in a public park — not at all."

If O'Neill and Brand were not protected by fair use, the respondents went on, they certainly were by the First Amendment. "Communique" was a "political essay," exploring the "metaphysical distinctions" underpinning copyright law and dramatizing Disney's "draconian efforts" to muzzle O'Neill, stamp out parody, and "prevent defamation of a cartoon Mouse called Mickey." Far removed from O'Neill's earlier "bawdy 'counterculture'" transgressions, it was "an expose of the consequences of transgressing imaginary lines constructed by Disney's lawyers..." Like any citizen, O'Neill had the right to mock Disney's prosecution of him. As a cartoonist, he had the right to use pictures to do so. Since even the most offensive expression of the most unpopular ideas deserve First Amendment protection, the Court should stand up to Disney and protect the American public's right to honest, heartfelt satire. To sanction O'Neill and Brand would frighten other publishers away from works even "remotely close to parodying Disney."

Finally, even if O'Neill and Brand had done wrong, neither civil nor criminal contempt proceedings were proper remedies. The defendants had criticized a decision; they had not defied a court. Civil contempt was inappropriate because it was intended to compensate individuals financially for wrongs done them, but Disney had suffered no economic loss. It simply wished to stop O'Neill from poking fun at it, and the court should not help Disney affect a "private censorship." Criminal

contempt was inappropriate because it served no public interest to punish a litigant for what may have been, at worst, disobedience of a court order rendered in
the context of a trivial, private dispute. If Disney wanted redress, it should be
ordered to do as a New York judge had recently ordered the cartoonist David
Levine. Levine had sought an injunction against a politician who had framed
unauthorized reproductions of an unflattering caricature he had drawn of him and
sold them at a fund-raiser. The judge complimented the politician on his sense of
humor and directed Levine to sue for copyright infringement.

Laveroni's reply blistered the defendants' "incredible," "overextended," and
"*ad hominem*" arguments as "unworthy of consideration." He sneered at their
"irrelevant" insertions into the record of Brand's military record, "political connections," and O'Neill's indigence, except to posit the latter as an explanation for
"why he so cavalierly ignores the orders of this Court and the rights of others."
And Laveroni dismissed the defendants' view of the law as "either misconstrued or
intentionally misstated..."

Disney's motion, he reminded all concerned, was an "integral part" of its
original 1971 action. O'Neill had already been a defendant in a copyright action
for eight years. He had been enjoined from infringing upon Disney copyrights *for
seven*. The only questions now were: Did he? Did Brand help? Under the doctrine
of *res judicata*, O'Neill could not re-litigate whether his drawings of Disney characters were infringements, if they qualified as a fair use, or if they were protected
by the First Amendment. All these escape exits had already been nailed shut
against him. If O'Neill had copied Disney's characters, he had infringed Disney's
copyrights. If he had infringed Disney's copyrights, he had violated the injunction.
To follow defense counsel's proposal and require Disney to file a new action for
copyright infringement would encourage people to violate injunction after injunction in order to gain opportunity after opportunity to re-try their case.[147]

The inapplicability of the reheated First Amendment/fair use arguments,
Laveroni argued, was obvious. The law remained firm that plagiarism was not a
protected form of free speech. The Copyright Act of 1909 still governed this case.
The 1976 act's legislative history documented its intent to restate existing law, not
reform it. Even Nimmer agreed it had left courts "almost complete discretion" to
determine if a fair use of copyrighted material had occurred. Even if Judge
Wollenberg were to measure "Communique" by the '76 act's four factors, he would
find it came up short. The *nature* of the copyrighted and infringing works — car-

---

[147] Lawyers are fond of arguing by examples *in extremis*. (Courts are presumed to practically shudder when they hear "floodgates of litigation" are about to be swept open.) But while one can sym-
pathize with Disney's position — and smile at Keker and Klein's *chutzpah* — to hold, as Laveroni
argued, that *any* drawing of something too similar to a Disney character by O'Neill was automatically a contemptuous injunction-defier would mean that he could be tossed in the slammer for
doodling Mickey-like on a cocktail napkin to amuse, for example, a visiting author or delight a
grandchild.

toon stories — was identical. The *purpose* of both Disney's books and the *Quarterly* — despite the alleged "nobility" of the latter's intent — was to make money. The argument that the copying of a cartoon character's likeness was not a *substantial* taking had already been rejected by every judge who had considered the question. (The fact that O'Neill had now toned down his characters' "obscene actions and scatological speech," Laveroni said, only made them more like Disney's.) And this court had already determined that O'Neill's efforts "to cheapen and tarnish the image of Disney and of its creations" posed a threat of serious *economic harm* to it.

Criminal contempt was a suitable response to O'Neill's and Brand's actions because of the "important public interest in having the orders and judgments of its courts obeyed." Civil contempt was appropriate, even if it did not directly reimburse Disney for economic loss, because it would coerce the defendants into refraining from further copyright violations. O'Neill knowingly violated a court order; Brand knowingly helped him; they should be sanctioned accordingly. "They can only be stopped by such... remedies, for they have demonstrated that they will not govern their actions under the rule of law," Laveroni said. "They have no respect for law, for the Court, or for the private property of others. They have only contempt."[148]

At the same time Disney was seeking to have O'Neill held in contempt, the Pirates were petitioning to have the damages against them reduced. On June 15, 1979, Stepanian, filing first, argued that, since no formal business relationship bound the wrong-doers together, each should be liable only for the number of infringements he authored. Richards had drawn The Big Bad Wolf, Li'l Bad Wolf, and The Three Little Pigs, who, since Disney treated them "as one persona by its choice of name," should only count as one copyrighted character. The total number of their appearances — Li'l Bad having been absent from the second issue of *Funnies* — made him liable for only five infringements of the thirty-eight.[149]

London's new attorney, Linda E. Shostak, a graduate of Vassar and Harvard Law School employed by the prestigious San Francisco firm of Morrison & Foerster, who was representing him without charge, based her argument upon a new affidavit he had provided. It stated that, as a nineteen-(actually, I believe, twenty)-year-old inexperienced cartoonist, he had apprenticed himself to the older, more experienced

---

[148] At this point, with two sets of such fine intellects having looked at identical facts, applied identical law, and come up with such heartfelt, anguished-even, opposite conclusions, one could expect Judge Wollenberg to throw up his arms and weep. "Is there no correct answer to any question? Can you not even agree Tuesday follows Monday?" I know the adversary system is based upon the premise that two parties contesting a case as hard as they can will best lead an impartial arbiter to truth; but, sometimes, it seems truth has been lashed to the cabooses of two trains, and each engineer is heading in an opposite direction at full throttle.

[149] In private, counsel-to-counsel negotiations, Stepanian had also argued that each cartoonist's infringements should be evaluated individually. "Richards's weren't as explosive. They weren't as outrageous. But they wouldn't look at what each artist was doing. They wouldn't look at the Wolf alone."

O'Neill. He assisted O'Neill on "Odd Bodkins" in return for room and board. O'Neill taught him to draw more professionally and instructed him to learn his craft by copying several prominent cartoonists, one of whom was Disney. In early 1971, O'Neill organized a studio to publish adult comic books. The idea and plot for *Air Pirate Funnies* were O'Neill's. Everything he drew or wrote was at O'Neill's direction and "like all of my projects for O'Neill, I did as I was told." When he expressed concern about copying Disney's work, O'Neill assured him their activities were protected by the First Amendment. After learning of the injunction, he had left the studio, leaving a four-page Dirty Duck story with Gary Hallgren for inclusion in what he believed would be a non-Disney comic. Over his objections and without his permission, this story was used in *The Tortoise and the Hare.* He had left California in 1972 and had been working as a freelance cartoonist since. His association with the Pirates, London concluded, "has been a severe professional setback and has tarnished my reputation as an artist/writer."[150]

Shostak argued that Disney's inability to prove it had suffered any actual economic harm showed that magistrate Woodruff's imposition of the maximum statutory damage award had been intended to punish those who had deliberately published *Tortoise* while the TRO was in effect. This was improper since copyright damages are to be compensatory, not punitive. Even if a maximum award was justified, none of it should be charged to London. Because he was a youth, ignorant of the law, acting "under O'Neill's complete supervision and control," he should not be held liable for his work on *Funnies.* Because he had left the studio and played no part in the release of *Tortoise,* he was not a "willful or malicious" TRO-violator but an "innocent infringer," who should escape liability entirely.

O'Neill was represented in this phase of the case by Richard Harris, a Stanford graduate who had spent ten months in Vietnam with the 25th Division, worked as a newspaper reporter in Humboldt County, and gone to law school at Boalt Hall.[151] He was in his second year of practice with Hancock,

---

[150] London says that when O'Neill read his declaration, "He went berserk, calling me up at all hours…, saying not nice things about me and trashing my reputation by painting me as some Judas." O'Neill says, "It could've happened. I mean, I was at the *Chronicle* trying to saw off the editor's leg with a chainsaw. I was a known berserker. And that was the worst thing about the Air Pirates. I loved Bobby. He's an immense talent. He was my first pal as a cartoonist, and he took a lot of flak and got all twisted and screwed up. People who know us say if Bobby put ten bullets in me nobody'd be surprised."

[151] Harris had prior experience with one of the defense's featured performers. As a reporter, he had been part of a media pack assembled by the Sheriff's Department to accompany a raid on a meth lab in the hills near Guerneville. Federal AFT agents helicoptered in first; and when the alleged crank-manufacturer had seen these heavily armed, long-haired-for-cover crazies coming, he'd bolted, and one shot him fatally in the back. The County D.A. tried to prosecute the agent for murder, but the case was removed to federal court, where charges were dropped. Stepanian had been the deceased's significant other's attorney throughout.

Rothert & Bunshoft, a San Francisco firm whose primary client was Lloyds of London, when McKenzie, whom he knew from college, asked him to take his place in a case which, as a former reporter, he might find of interest. Harris was happy to join this "*pro bono* relay team." "I'd always loved O'Neill's cartoons. I thought he was a genius; and he turned out to be a fun, cooperative, pleasant guy, with a good sense of humor — just a great client."

Harris moved to reduce the fine per infringement to the minimum $250, shrinking the total damages for the thirty-eight to $9500. He argued, as had Shostak, that the size of the award showed Woodruff intended to punish the Pirates for deliberately violating the law. But the Ninth Circuit, by replacing Wollenberg's "substantial taking" test with *Berlin*'s "conjure-up" one, had recognized the fair use doctrine needed clarification; and if it had accepted Nimmer's "market demand" approach, the Pirates might have escaped liability entirely. With so much uncertainty about when, why and how much copying was permissible clouding men's minds and so much guidance through this fog required that even federal judges needed refocusing, O'Neill could reasonably have concluded he was doing nothing wrong. His sins may have been accidental, and he should not have been sanctioned so severely. Second, even if O'Neill had acted as willfully as John Wilkes Booth, Murph the Surf, and the Committee to Re-Elect the President combined, the sheer size of the award made it improper. It bore no reasonable relationship to any loss suffered by Disney and completely ignored what the Pirates could afford to pay. O'Neill's affidavit, documenting this last point, indicates he had taken A.J. Liebling's proposition that "A man who works for newspapers and hasn't been broke is no newspaperman" to extremes. He was already under court orders to pay $100 a month support for each of his four children, and his rent alone cost him $130. But in the last five years, his combined earnings as a cartoonist and UC Extension teacher had never exceeded $4000. He got by only because a publishing company had fronted him six months' rent as an advance for a still-owed book.

On June 27, the morning of the court appearance on Disney's contempt motion, the press reported resumption of "one of the goofier cases in the annals of American justice." O'Neill, visited in a "rundown East Oakland cottage," is quoted: "This hasn't been my decade.... Why can't I satirize Mickey Mouse, when I can the Flag, Apple Pie, Presidents, Christ, and the Virgin Mary?" About Disney, he says, "They're so big they don't even know what they're doing. They've sued everything that even looks like a mouse."

The next day's *Chronicle* announced a settlement seemed likely. The terms were rumored to include no admission of guilt by — and no jail time for — O'Neill, though the damage award would remain in place. Asked if he would continue to draw Mickey, O'Neill said, "I can't stand the damn thing. I only got involved out of a vague interest in the First Amendment. There are other people in the country who can draw mice. I won't. I hate mice. I found four of them in my kitchen last week."

O'Neill's recollection of the proceeding is more positive. "It was great. The judge told 'em, 'I'm not gonna welcome this case into my court. If you bring him in on criminal contempt, he will bring up the First Amendment because that's his only protection. I will not end my legal career as a judge that weakened the First Amendment, and you're forcing him to where we'll have to. Now you knocked him down once, and he got up and hit you back. You knocked him down twice, and he got up and hit you back. You knocked him down three times, and he got up and hit you back. By now, you should have figured out he's Irish ' I mean, the judge said that. I'm declared Irish by the Supreme Court of the United States. [Author's Note: Actually, a United States District Court.] 'You got yourself a Quixote here, and you're his favorite windmill. Settle it.' And they still wouldn't."

Laveroni remembers no such admonition. ("It would have been very unlike Wollenberg.") He does say, when he met with Keker and O'Neill in his office to discuss settlement, O'Neill, who continually referred to himself as "Mousecrazed," picked a tablet off his desk and drew one on it. "'Keep it,' John [Keker] told me. 'It's probably going to be worth something.'"

Keker says, " It's what Judge Wollenberg should have said. I have no recollection, so I can't deny it was said. There are some facts too good to check." And he recalls that, during settlement discussions in the judge's chambers, Disney's lawyers insisted on a written promise from O'Neill to no longer draw Mickey Mouse. "So I said, 'All right' and went out to Dan; and he drew a picture of himself in a barrel, with no clothes on, saying 'I won't draw Mickey Mouse.' I thought it was terrific. Wollenberg, who was a wonderful old guy, laughed and thought it was great; but Disney's lawyers went crazy, behaving like a bunch of pompous assholes. 'This shows how contemptuous he's being... Blah blah...'"

On July 2, Keker filed a supplemental memorandum, a photostatic reproduction from the *Chronicle*'s editorial page of Mickey Mouse centered on a one-dollar bill "without comment... except to note Dan O'Neill did not draw it."

CHAPTER EIGHTEEN:
THEY CAN'T HANG EVERYONE

The M.L.F. now swung off the page and into the streets. The impetus for this counter-attack came from a twenty-six-year-old from Fremont, Nebraska, who had settled in the Bay Area after stops in Africa, India, and along the Arabian peninsula.

Robert Beerbohm had been obsessed with comic books since childhood. "I was," he says, "a comic book John the Baptist: 'Read more comics'; 'Comics are a way of life'; 'Comics are recyclable; they're better than TV.'" As a teenager, he rode busses hundreds of miles a day to enhance his holdings, eventually becoming one of an elite group of dealers caravaning from convention to convention to sell-buy-trade-and-amass more comics. At one of these conventions, he met Bud Plant and joined with him and John Barrett to form Comics & Comix, which had published *O'Neill's Comics and Stories,* Vol. II.

In 1975, Beerbohm sold his interest in the partnership. But after a year of college, trying unsuccessfully to ingratiate himself to his parents, he returned to the field with a vengeance. By 1979, he owned comic book stores in Santa Rosa; on Telegraph Avenue in Berkeley; and in San Francisco, on Fisherman's Wharf, in the Mission and the Haight. After "Communique" appeared, he "had gotten word of Dan hiding out in Oakland from Disney goon squads." He tracked O'Neill down, living in an old silver trailer, so paranoid he feared Disney operatives had followed him. After they'd talked a little — and smoked a bit more — O'Neill lamented Disney had taken everything he earned. He was almost beaten.

Beerbohm asked him if he'd seen *Spartacus.*

O'Neill said he had.

"They can't hang everyone," Beerbohm said.[152]

---

[152] O'Neill says of this account: "Beerbohm has a crappy memory." He also says he was living in a gardener's shack, not a trailer.

The idea was to create a presence at conventions, trade shows and exhibitions, where Disney representatives might be expected to appear, that would harass or embarrass them. The media was certain to jump on the story and — to quote that old Biblical scholar Wilton Norman Chamberlain — "No one roots for Goliath."

Beerbohm put up $1200.[153] Hallgren was enlisted to handle the artwork. ("At first," Beerbohm says, "the M.L.F. was Dan, Gary and me. That's about it.") O'Neill, drawing upon his experiences in Northern Ireland, busied himself organizing support "cells" from coast to coast.

By the time of the 1979 New York Comic Book Convention, July 4th weekend,[154] the Gang of Three had 300 M.L.F. T-shirts for sale for $10 each. (A typical creation portrayed Mickey as the vampire "Mikula.") It had 1000 M.L.F. buttons at a dollar apiece. (One showed a Lone Ranger-masked O'Neill drawing Mickey. Another, captioned "Free Mickey," had the mask on him.) It had M.L.F. rings; M.L.F. belt buckles; an M.L.F. Flying Machine (a paper airplane adorned by Mickey, the Jolly Roger, and the M.L.F. philosophy: "It's a Mickey Mouse world so raise hell and don't take no for an answer"); and M.L.F. malted milk balls ("You know it's bad for you"), called "Mouse Drops." (The wrapper pictured Mickey on the toilet and listed ingredients of "Sugar, chocolax, partially hydrogenated rodent guano, cobwebs, bat hairs, insect fragments, drano, assorted carcinogenics.")

The Front also dealt art. O'Neill had contacted cartoonists, fine artists and ex-Disney employees on the West Coast, assured them the court had said anyone was entitled to parody any copyrighted character once (it had said no such thing), and asked them to donate a Mouse-centered work of their choice. Hallgren had made a similar pitch to artists in the East. (Among those he asked was London. His reply — "You must have peanut butter for brains" — suggested a continued lack of appreciation for O'Neill's efforts.)

The result was several crates' of individually framed creations, including a pastel portrait of an actual mouse with Mickey Mouse cap-and-ears; a Mickey in Mona Lisa drag; Velazquez's "Juan de Parejo" in a Mickey Mouse T-shirt; a painting of a human-sized Minnie flashing two small boys; and a photograph of a masked woman, nude, with Mickey painted on her breast, her nipple his nose. These works were displayed as a "Mouse Liberation Art Show" and later shipped to conventions in Philadelphia and San Diego. (Each contributing artist received an M.L.F. Secret Agent identity card,

---

[153] There is also a dispute as to how much of this investment was repaid. Estimates range from all of it to not a blooming farthing.

[154] In Beerbohm's version of events, the Front first struck in San Diego (see below). All other indications are it was up and running before them.

depicting Mickey, torch in hand, robed like the Statue of Liberty, and signed by O'Neill as chairman.)

"We had thirty tons of art moving around the country," O'Neill says. "We had Rembrandt; we had Gilbert Stuart; we had all the dead artists doing Mickey Mouse. We sold $15-20,000 worth of stuff off the walls. We were running comics like marijuana. We also stepped into radio. I had guys from the Committee doing Mickey and Donald voices about drugs and the Grateful Dead doing tapes:

The night they drove old Disney down,
All the lawyers were freaking.
The night they drove old Disney down,
All the mouses were squeaking.

The San Diego Comic-Con, which drew 4000 fans over the Labor Day weekend, was — and is — the nation's largest. O'Neill put forth his position on close-as-possible copying on a Satire and Parody panel which included Harvey Kurtzman and Mort Walker, who were about as receptive to it as a beehive to a bear's paw. (O'Neill recalls responding to one testy exchange by accidentally knocking over a water pitcher onto a microphone "and almost electrocuting the creator of Beetle Bailey.") Another panel, ostensibly devoted to the current state of underground comics, which included Greg Irons, Denis Kitchen, and Larry Todd, evolved into a discussion of the Pirates' case and awarded the audience with the following misinformation: (1) Mickey Mouse was no longer protected by copyright but had "passed into the public domain"; (2) a federal court had "ruled in favor" of "Communique" and found O'Neill "not guilty"; and (3) fair use meant "you could get away with almost anything if you're not directly making money off somebody else's characters."

At San Diego, O'Neill and Beerbohm enticed sixty other cartoonists, drawn to their flame like prankish moths, to do their own Mickey Mouse comics. The finished products took two forms. The first was a four-by-five inch booklet, *M.L.F. Communique 2*, which included a dozen or so "anony-mouse," pen-and-ink, satiric Mickeys — a *Jaws*-Mickey, rising from the deep to attack a cartoonist sketching aboard a raft, a swastika-eared Mickey, an all-skull Mickey, a reefer-toking Mickey, a Mickey Mouse trap snapping down on a cartoonist's fingers.[155] The second were "books," up to eight pages in length, by individual creators that were photocopied for further distribution. The next day, M.L.F. operatives, commanded by O'Neill, delivered a copy of each to the Disney studio in Burbank. A double-agent janitor invited them in, whereupon two dozen Disney artists hosted a small party, crowned by O'Neill smoking a joint with his feet on Walt Disney's desk. Within a week,

---

[155] Art historians of my acquaintance believe they have identified Moscoso, Robbins, Rodriguez, and Wilson among the miscreants.

the Front had shipped Disney another forty books.[156]

"The prospect of having to deal with so many infringement cases," Beerbohm says, "was something Disney did not welcome, so a solution had to be found." "The harder Disney pushed, the more people we got involved and the harder we pushed back," Hallgren says. "We had no difficulty selling the idea to other artists at all." "O'Neill basically wore 'em out," Richards told Howard Cruse. "The whole genius of his thing was that he did it again, in the face of it all. He came back out swinging when they thought they had us trapped."

"Four months later, they're at the table," is how O'Neill remembers the denouement. "'Okay,' I said, 'this is the deal. We have this Mouse disease that's been given us since childhood. It's in the fabric of our being. So if you tell us we can't draw Mickey Mouse, we probably will. If you tell us we can, we probably won't. So everybody shut up, say goodbye to your $190,000, and go home. You go away. I go away. No money, no jail. It never happened.'"

The actual resolution appears to have been not as simple as this Butch Cassidy approach to conflict resolution makes it seem. Negotiations dragged on through the fall. At one point, a frustrated Shostak advised London that Laveroni had said that if Disney could get O'Neill under control, it would not go after him and Richards. "The problem," she wrote, "is that the settlement has to be reduced to writing, rather than Mouse talk. O'Neill continues to talk mice." By Halloween, the attorneys had thrashed out general terms for a settlement, but last-minute haggling and language tweaking dragged things on past Thanksgiving; and the final papers were not ready until December. They provided that the Pirates would abide by the injunction Judge Wollenburg had imposed in August 1975 and neither draw for publication nor public display any Disney cartoon character. The judgment remained in place, but Disney agreed not to collect upon it so long as that first condition held.

On January 18, 1980, Laveroni filed stipulations for entry of judgment against O'Neill, London and Richards for the full amount of Woodruff's recommended award nearly four years earlier: $190,000 in damages; attorneys' fees of $28,792.50; $508.08 in costs. The contempt petition was dismissed with each party bearing its own costs. Judgment was formally entered February 1. No other terms of the agreement were entered into the record. They were to be kept confidential and revealed by the Pirates only to banks, financial institutions, or other prospective business partners who might balk at becoming involved with someone in hock up to his armpits.

The final newspaper accounts of the case reported that "apparently secret

[156] O'Neill's plan to fill the heavens above San Diego with sky-written pamphletering in his favor never got off the ground, but the *San Diego Union* ran a feature article that was sympathetic to his cause; and, a week or two later, a review in the *L.A. Times* of a recently published work on Disney began, "The only book I ever drop-kicked across the room..." and was then given over to a cymbal-clapping congratulation of O'Neill and the M.L.F.

agreements" provided that the contempt charges would be dropped and Disney would not attempt to collect its damages as long as O'Neill didn't "mouse it up any more." Brand, who now says he had found the experience "amusing and depressing," was quoted lamenting the "chilling effect" of having had to spend $11,000 defending himself. O'Neill was unavailable for comment, but Keker said his client had become "sick" of it all and was moving onto better things.[157] Disney was said to be out $2,000,000 but recognized that O'Neill had no assets from which it might collect anything anyway.

Klein, looking back now, thinks the result was fine. "Given the disparity in size, my clients could have been bled dry by Disney in the costs of litigation alone, even if they had ultimately won. Besides, I truly thought Disney felt the only way to get these guys to stop was to throw them in jail."

Shostak says, "My memory is, I said, 'The guy [London] was a kid'; and Laveroni let him out. All I know is, I did something good, and Bobby was happy. We met afterwards at the Elephant & Castle in Greenwich Village, and he drew me a 'Thank you' cartoon on a napkin."

Stepanian remembers little about the specific give-and-take of the negotiations — "I was kind of tired at that point" — but recalls his general approach. "Richards had looked ahead, and his career was going good. He said to me, 'Look, Mike, I'm making money. Mitigate damages.' I said, 'Lemme run this thing out. I don't want to fold, and we're conducting ourselves correctly. They'll get what they want, and no one will go after you for money.' I knew Tatum and Laveroni. Tatum was an elegant guy and a good litigator. Laveroni was a nice guy, a smart guy. They had their injunction, and we weren't going to do it again anyway. They knew we were straight in a way, so my approach was, 'Let's be neighbors and friends. My guy has a career. Have respect for him.'"[158]

Tatum says, "I had very strong feelings that what had been done was fundamentally wrong. The misuse of the Disney characters showed an element of arrogance pervasive in the culture at the time. You don't get many cases where one is so seriously engaged in a professional, intellectual, and emotional level. I received an enormous sense of satisfaction from it."

[157] Two years later, he told a columnist for *Comics Scene*, "The irony is that although Dan lost the case... the individual artist [now] is probably on safer ground when he has clear political and editorial content in a parody. Dan's case crystalized [the] tension between the First Amendment... and [the] right to protect commercial characters... [as] a very difficult tension [to] balance, whereas before it didn't seem as though courts thought it was quite so difficult."

[158] Richards believes that Lloyd Crenna later negotiated a token (one dollar) settlement with Disney to release him from liability entirely. The court file contains no record of this; and Crenna, who claims no recollection, says, "If there was a settlement, it may have had a secrecy clause." Laveroni also professes to not recall any individual settlements but says the absence of any in the file is not determinative. "We may have settled the money damages, but we wouldn't give a dismissal because we wanted the injunction to remain in effect."

Chapter Nineteen:
This Was Not Weird Al

Despite a full-body immersion in a complete Wash-Rinse-Dry cycle of the adversarial process, my view of the litigation remained as muddied as when our hostess-to-be in Nevada City had asked me where I stood. I tend toward First Amendment absolutism. I value highly the outrageous in art. But I doubt I could muster much enthusiasm if I found characters I had created cavorting, satirically or not, between the silky sheets of a Danielle Steel novel. (And I question if O'Neill would be chuckling "Boys will be boys" over the dragooning of Fred and Hugh into the service of strips extolling the blessings afforded our *polis* by John Ashcroft.) While I had problems with the Ninth Circuit's "no exact copying" standard, which seemed to reward the inept parodist over the skilled one, I wasn't convinced *exact* copying was as critical as O'Neill said. Admittedly, I was twelve when I first encountered "Mickey Rodent," an age when my aesthetic judgments still placed whoopee cushions within the Humor Canon; but, stubble and all, he had blown me away. I saw no reason that, if it worked satirically to distort the thoughts and actions of cartoon characters, it would not work to distort them graphically. Two days' whiskers would increase the sniggering, not lessen it. But this was an artistic judgment, not a legal one. For that I required outside, expert help.

Unfortunately, the literature was short on enlightenment. While string-cited perfunctorily or mentioned in passing in several law review articles, *Walt Disney Productions v. The Air Pirates* had been the subject of only one: a brief piece by a law student whose analysis was confined to Judge Wollenberg's initial ruling. The deepest thinkers and most prestigious journals had passed it by when it was vibrant; and, like a starlet who had once turned heads at Cannes but now can't get hit on at the Polo Lounge, all signs were that it had lost its currency. But coincident with my interest, Edward Samuels, a professor at New

York Law School who had taught the case for twenty years, had just ferreted out O'Neill while finalizing his book, *The Illustrated Story of Copyright*; and O'Neill directed me to him as someone who could illuminate the significance of his litigation.

Actually, O'Neill had told me his name was "Levine" and that he taught at New York University Law School, a different institution entirely. After the dozen realining phone calls this misdirection had necessitated, I knew I had the right fellow when, recalling their conversation, his voice took on the starry-eyed, wobble-kneed effect of someone who has stepped off the merry-go-round after a circuit at full acceleration. "I was flabbergasted," Samuels said. "He told me he had won the case. 'No, Dan,' I told him, 'you lost.' 'No,' he said, 'I won.' 'No, you lost.'" There was a pause while I imagined the professor wishing for the steadier terrain of first-year students and The Rule in Shelly's Case. "They set parody back twenty years."

"But do you think the court's decision was correct?" I said.

"It was absolutely correct," he answered. "Even today, when the pendulum has swung back in favor of parody, I don't think the result would be any different. This wasn't *MAD*. This wasn't Weird Al. They went far beyond the acceptable, and they would have kept going too far until they got the response they wanted. They lifted specific frames and story lines practically literally from the original books. They defamed Mickey Mouse. It was part of the culture then. People going too far. People pushing the envelope. They made damn good comics, and reading them gave you the thrill of being a co-conspirator; but did they go too far, yeah."

In his book, Samuels stands firmly astride this conclusion. When comparing the Pirates' comics to the Kurtzman/Elder parody, he explicitly rules out "amount taken" as the factor to have earned the former opprobrium and the latter smiles. "Mickey Rodent," he concludes, was "fairly gentle" fun-making (*Gentle?* Mickey tried to kill Darnold Duck three times before caging him, stripped naked, in a zoo. Amnesty International, not to mention, PETA, would have been all over him) whose joshings could be passed over with a "Tsk-tsk," while *Funnies'* thuggish brutalities called for a hob-nail booted response. "In their lack of subtlety," he said, "they went too far."

They went too far. The phrase, in this context, echoed peculiarly. If we were discussing sacrileges committed... If we were talking icons defiled... But the charge did not seem to naturally reverberate from the threat of potential Disney-buyers lured elsewhere. (No one even semi-seriously claimed that had happened.) It hardly seemed to rebound off the sullying of cartoon characters' reputations. (Satire, after all, had no point *except* the sullying of reputations.) And if neither of these was a true trigger — one because it didn't happen and the other because it couldn't but — why should it ruffle anyone's tweeds how much the Pirates' Mouse looked like Mickey? Five fingers or five heads, who cared if there were no consequences?

"The whole times were about 'going too far,'" Menchy, the Kabbalist-librarian, said when I mentioned my puzzlement over vegi-chicken at the Chinese place on University Ave. between Krishna Copy and Ace Hardware. (He was having his with zucchini and cashews. I went for string beans and black bean sauce.) "Tell-me-why-I-I-I-you-cried...," the radio played in traditional, cheap Chinese restaurant, where-do-they-get-their-programmer-from dining accompaniment fashion, "...and why you lie-I-I-I'd-to-me." "The bastards were always telling us we were 'going too far.' Sitting-in at lunch counters was going too far. Marching against the war was going too far. Smoking pot was going too far when we could have been happy knocking ourselves out chugging quarts, waking up with puke on our shoes."

I shook on extra vinegar. It is the fortunate writer who has insightful friends. All right, the SLA's gunning down of Marcus Foster may have oozed to life from a garbage dump of insane, putrifying monstrosities. Granted, a speed-and-heroin diet might not fit within any AMA-sanctioned body's recommended food pyramid. But "going too far" as a standard for artistic self-regulation within a liberal democracy was about as socially useful a proposition as dousing had proved an effective means for Salem to distinguish true witches from the innocent.[159] Oh, "reasonableness" has its place in the law. I have no quarrel with it determining when a person's speed through a cross-walk rises to negligence or how close the other guy must stand with his crow-bar before you may fire your Glock. But in the area of creativity, to get any-where of interest, the language-governors must be planted out there alongside "clear and present danger."

For the Pirates, it had to have been the sixty-nine that slapped the ruler down. The fifty clitorises going off like Chinese firecrackers. ("It's about sex," Adele had said, when I first described Disney's lawsuit — herself echoing Dale Bumpers defending Bill Clinton on the Senate floor. "When they tell you it's not about money, it's about money. And when they tell you it's not about sex...") In the context of the cultural war that was then raging, the courts were not going to let the *sans-culottes* win this skirmish against this opposition. An entire weave of beliefs and assumptions about how the world was to be — born out of uncountable, over-the-back-fence uttered "Oh, my God"s; nurtured by who-can-say-how-many, country club-bar bandied "You would not believe"s; matured rigid by I-can't-even-guesstimate, boys-in-the-back-room, wise-men-at-the council-table, implicitly understood grins and nods — weighed against them. (I also consider the fact that this engagement was being waged through comic books a factor. I don't believe the judiciary was prepared to take them seriously. Novels, films, fine art — any of that would have had a better shot.)

---

[159] I recently caught the "going-too-far" banner being taken up on a PBS documentary by, of all moderates, Larry Flynt, bemoaning the work of young barbarians who were giving pornography a bad name. (They dismissed him as just another old white guy, trying to hang onto his Cadillac.)

Fair use decisions in parody cases decided after *Air Pirates* only reinforced my opinion. For instance, in *Fisher v. Dees*, the novelty song "When Sonny Sniffs Glue" was held to be an appropriate take-off on the Johnny Mathis ballad "When Sonny Gets Blue"; and in *Elsmere Music, Inc. v. National Broadcasting Company*, the court not only upheld *Saturday Night Live's* transformation of the jingle "I Love New York" into "I Love Sodom," it saluted this appropriation: "In today's world of often unrelieved solemnity, copyright law should be hospitable to the humors of parody." But, in *M.C.A., Inc. v. Wilson*, the doors of that suite were barred to the tunesmith who mocked the 1940 Andrews Sisters hit, "The Boogie-Woogie Bugle Boy of Company B," as "The Cunnilingus Champion of Company C"; and, in *Walt Disney Productions v. Mature Pictures Corp.*, the makers of the film *The Life and Times of the Happy Hooker* were eighty-sixed after they used the Mickey Mouse Club's theme song to accompany that memorable cinematic moment in which their heroine sexually serviced — orally, anally and vaginally — three teenagers in Mouseketeer ears upon a pool table.[160] In all instances, the courts spoke solemnly about substantiality and conjuring-up, public confusion and market replacement (and a new bit of mumbo-jumbo, whether the infringing work was a parody of what it copied or a comment upon a social issue, which made it something else);[161] but none of this turned me from the idea that all this verbiage was meant to conceal a simpler truth. Each court could have reached the same result if its test had been: Would Dick and Pat have let Julie and Tricia watch this on TV?[162]

. . .

[160] The only case I found that contradicts my theory, the barely reported *Pillsbury v. Milky Way Productions*, was decided by a federal district judge in Georgia. *Screw* had commissioned sculptured replicas of the Pillsbury characters, Poppin' and Poppie Fresh, usually seen lolling decorously on cinnamon roll cans, which it then photographed sportively engaged in a bout of fuck-and-suck. In finding this a fair use, the court said it did not matter that it had copied the characters exactly, because this copying was intended to comment upon the values they represented and because Pillsbury had not shown it had been economically harmed.

[161] Judge Richard A. Posner of the Seventh Circuit Court of Appeals, a leading proponent of this satire-as-target "good"; satire-as-weapon "bad" approach, concedes this to be "vague criteria" and admits there may be "a problem both in distinguishing these uses and of overlap between them." With *Air Pirate Funnies*, I submit, this "problem" would have been overpowering.

[162] After writing this, I chanced upon a law review article, published in 1988, by Elliott M. Abramson. Prof. Abramson held "'darker' judicial motives" — to wit, prudery — responsible for denying a fair use defense to a certain class of parodists. "[W]here the alleged infringing work has explicit sexual content," he wrote, "courts have found infringement. There is no legitimate ground for a court to consider sexual content in determining copyright questions, yet courts have repeatedly enjoined parodies due to their sexual content." I immediately felt less lonely on my limb — and less twisted for having clambered out there.

However, my sense of duty to my readers not wanting to allow my bottom-tenth-of-my-first-year-class legal mind the last word on the subject, I sought additional counsel. Wendy J. Gordon, Professor of Law and Paul J. Liacos Scholar at Boston University Law School, had been as one of the most prolific — and most interesting — writers on copyright I had come across. (She also turned out to be an admirer of O'Neill's. "I hope you're a fan," she'd said when I stated the reason for my call.)

"The decision was not incorrect," she cautiously tread, "if you take the perspective of Justice Holmes's 'bad man,' for whom the law is what you can predict will happen.[163] I think you could have foreseen the result the court came to in *Air Pirates*, so from that vantage point the opinion is a legitimate interpretation of fair use. However, I would prefer a more generous interpretation of the doctrine."

"Why is that?" I encouraged.

"There are imaginative works which artists create that become facts in other people's lives, affecting how they think and feel. It could be "White Christmas," the Mona Lisa, the Vietnam War Memorial. I would allow other artists greater latitude to reproduce these works, as long as they are doing it for a different purpose than for which they'd originally been intended, and if the second artist needed the reproduction to make the point he was intending. O'Neill was using Disney's characters to comment upon Disney's effect on him — and everyone in our generation — and that was the only way he could talk about him. A treatise wouldn't have been nearly as effective in loosening Disney's hold on the public imagination."

"Which gains a society what?"

"There is a fundamental importance to guaranteeing people a freedom to discuss the features of the world around them — and to re-conceive the dominant images of their time. I take a Lockean view of property, which calls for an equality of starting points. No creator should be shut out from addressing significant aspects of his world simply because some earlier creator has been there first. The public's right to free speech trumps Disney's right to its intellectual property."

When I hung up, I felt a window had sprung open. The air pricked up my ears and elevated my eyes. My study fronts upon a back yard that appears the recipient of a Back to Wilderness grant. Through snags of blackberry vines and ivy, a gray cat stalked a cabbage moth. I had sat at my desk, seeking revelation, while it — as unconscious of me as the moth the cat — had flitted just ahead, just as unretrievable, out of reach, to the left, the right.

---

[163] As I understand it, Holmes believed laws should be interpreted to mean what a reasonably-minded "bad man" would think they meant, so if he got whacked for violating them he could not claim he hadn't been warned.

In the flats, a siren receded. Closer by, a jay called. Now, I felt the lift of the serendipitously gifted. I had, I thought, the last words for the page. It was only a matter of ordering them. I had, I realized, been honored by having so many fine voices speak to me. I had been privileged to wrap myself around and extend myself through what they had said — subjects and witnesses, experts and friends. Writing is a gift to the writer as well as to his audience if it is to be a gift at all. Above my desk, at eye-level, is a framed flyer from E.C., soliciting subscribers. The flyer, autographed by Kurtzman, Elder, Gaines, some others, has been with me since 1955, when Dave Peters, Max Garden and I made pilgrimage to their headquarters in New York. Even then, I did not welcome others telling me what should be read or written.

So much of who we are depends on who we were. All we believe; all we hope for; all our disappointments; all that leaves us feeling blessed. It shapes what we write — the subjects we summon, the words we choose, the rhythms we adapt — lawyers and parodists, judges and comic journalists.

Chapter Twenty:
Too Much Fun

In 1964, when Dan O'Neill still stood in good stead at the *Chronicle* and Walt Disney was scaling new heights of popularity and acclaim with the release of *Mary Poppins*, Roy Orbison and William Dees wrote "Oh, Pretty Woman." The song, performed by Orbison, sold 7,000,000 copies. Thirty years later, having re-centered in public awareness through the Richard Gere-Julia Roberts film *Pretty Woman*,"[164] it would cause the United States Supreme Court, in the case of *Campbell v. Acuff-Rose Music, Inc.*, to finally address the arguments the Air Pirates had raised.

Orbison and Dees had assigned their rights to "Oh, Pretty Woman" to Acuff-Rose, a leading country-and-western music publisher. In February 1989, the manager of the rap group 2 Live Crew (Luther Campbell, Christopher Wongwon, Mark Ross, and David Hobbs) informed Acuff-Rose that her clients had written a parody of the song which they intended to use on their next album. She offered to pay for this use; but Acuff-Rose, aware of 2 Live Crew's not-too-Nashville reputation — its previous effort, *As Nasty As They Wanna Be*, had resulted in several obscenity convictions — refused. 2 Live Crew included the parody "Pretty Woman" on its new release, *As Clean As They Come*, cheek-by-jowl with the tracks "Me So Horny" and "My Seven Bizzos" anyway. While its version originated verses about "big, hairy," "bald-headed," and "two-timin'" women, it copied the Orbison-Dees first line and well-known bass hook almost exactly.

---

[164] The film was released by Disney, which had purchased the script from a failed production company in Connecticut. Originally a bleak tale of the relationship between a desperate hooker and a ruthless businessman that climaxed around a drug overdose, it became, sweetened with champagne, bubble baths, Rodeo Drive, and redemptive love, the studio's highest grossing film.

Clean sold 250,000 copies, and Acuff-Rose sued Campbell *et al.* for copyright infringement. The District Court granted 2 Live Crew's motion for summary judgment and dismissed Acuff-Rose's suit; but the Sixth Circuit Court of Appeals reversed, saying any infringement for commercial purposes was presumptively unfair and that, by taking "the heart of the original," 2 Live Crew had taken too much. The entire United States Supreme Court, with Justice Kennedy writing a separate concurring opinion, disagreed.[165]

The Court's majority opinion, by Justice Souter, reached its conclusion through a step-by-step analysis of the four factors of fair use set forth in the Copyright Act of 1976. First, it said, the crucial question about the infringing work's "purpose and character" was not whether it was commercial or non-commercial, but whether it copied the original in order to "supersede" it in the market place or to "transform" it into something new. When the infringing work was a parody, this question became did the copying cast new "light" upon the original, enabling the public to view it in a new way, or was it a mere attempt to grab attention but "avoid the drudgery of working up something fresh." (If this fresh, critical slant was present, the Court went on to say, quoting Justice Holmes's recognition that what seems "repulsive" on first viewing often later comes to be viewed as "genius," its good or bad taste is irrelevant.)[166]

Since a parody would almost always be of something well-known, the Court felt the second factor, "the nature of the copyrighted work," would never help much in deciding when a parody was a fair use. While the third factor, "the amount and substantiality" of the copied material was significant, this significance had to be seen in the context of the other factors. Viewed in this light, even the original's "heart" could be copied, so long as the parody did not become "a market substitute" for it. And discussing factor four, "economic harm," the Court made clear that it did not matter if the parody depressed the sales of the original. Even a "lethal" parody that "kills demand" entirely, may be a fair use. "Displacement" could be prohibited; "disparagement" could not. It then remanded the case to the trial court to determine what damages, if any, Acuff-Rose had suffered.

In thirty pages, the Supreme Court mentioned *Walt Disney Productions v. The Air Pirates* only once, then in passing, and, I believe, unfairly, when Kennedy, whose analysis seemed unimpeded by an actual reading of their comics, dismissed the Pirates as "profiteers who [did] no more than... place the characters from a familiar work in novel or eccentric poses." Still, it seems to me, the Court effectively eviscerated the Disney arguments that had swayed Judge Wollenberg and the Ninth Circuit. After *Acuff-Rose*, it no longer seemed

---

[165] The defendants' appeal was also noteworthy for its supporters. For the first time in its history, *The Harvard Lampoon* filed an *amicus* brief.

[166] Holmes's is even a better name to drop than Learned Hand's.

to matter that the Pirates had plucked out Mickey's "heart" (his physical representation). It no longer seemed relevant that they had shredded his aura of "innocent delight." Market displacement, Nimmer wrote, had become "the most important, and, indeed, central fair use factor." If *Air Pirates Funnies* did not "satisfy the same purpose" as *Walt Disney's Comics and Stories*[167] — and how, in God's name, could you conclude it did — it was a fair use.[168]

Judge Wollenberg died April 19, 1981.

Michael Kennedy returned to New York City, where his clients have included Jean Harris, the Scarsdale Diet Doctor murderess; Whitewater's Susan McDougal; Ivana Trump in her divorce from The Donald; and Bill Johnston, the Waco prosecutor who exposed the FBI-Justice Department cover-up of the use of pyrotechnic devices against the Branch Davidians. Their misadventures have brought him an office on Park Avenue, a beach house in the Hamptons, and a cottage in Ireland.

Michael Stepanian remains in San Francisco. His present practice is "one-third federal panel appointments — at $75 an hour — of giant, fucking problems: guys who fire their p.d. and scream at judges; guys the marshals hate. One-third fancy guys in lots of trouble: tax; white collar maniacs; great huge frauds. One-third the new generation of kids in trouble: rock'n'rollers; fancy kids; doctors' sons. Anyone who gets in trouble up here, and any Dream Team doesn't want, I'll come off the bench for."

Albert Morse drifted from the law, publishing, in 1977, *The Tattooists*, a compilation of photographs he had taken and interviews he had conducted. The website Disquieting Muses says he lives on a "decrepit houseboat in northern

---

[167] Judge Posner has suggested "that erotic parodies fill a part of the demand for the parodied work itself and thus reduce the copyright holder's revenues on sales of the original work... [to] that segment of the population that likes its entertainment spread with sex." I have tried to be scrupulously honest in scouring my own memories; but, I must conclude, I would not have purchased any additional copies of *Uncle Scrooge* if he had been portrayed as less successfully sublimating his primal urges. As I recollect, during those years I was busy consuming Disney, I was squirming in my seat at Saturday matinees through all interludes of "mushy stuff," eagerly awaiting the shooting to resume.

So I think the Pirates skate under even his analysis.

[168] My optimism should be tempered. When I asked Professor Gordon if she too thought the Air Pirates likely to prevail today, she replied, "On general principles I would agree with you, except that I think that most courts are too sexually ill at ease to give Air Pirates fair use." And *Acuff-Rose* leaves sufficient room to believe this skepticism apt. The Court stated it was not laying down "bright-line rules" and that future decisions should be made on a case-by-case basis. Its nothing-if-not-vague "light-caster" vs. "drudge-avoider" test for judging "transformative" works, coupled with Kennedy's less-than-sensitive take on *Funnies,* shows that it left about as much room for judicial bias and subjectivity to come into play as there is for centerfielders to snag fly balls in Yankee Stadium. As Nimmer also wrote, parodists "should continue to pay their insurance premiums."

California, inundated with obscure bibelots and bizarre objects," pursuing his art. He has, says an old friend, "stepped away from this world."

David Phillips spent nearly two decades working as a cab driver, typist and librarian, before resuming his practice as a specialist in legal research and writing.

John Keker's abilities were recognized nationwide when he was selected to prosecute Oliver North for his role in the Iran-Contra scandal. He has defended Eldridge Cleaver, Werner Erhard, anti-nuke demonstrators, money launderers, George Lucas (against a charge of stealing the idea for *The Empire Strikes Back*), and Andrew Fastow, the alleged "mastermind" behind Enron. California criminal defense attorneys recently named him the lawyer most would want if facing serious charges.

George Gilmour practices commercial litigation out of his home. He spends half the year in Ireland, where he teaches comparative constitutional law.

Kirk McKenzie is an administrative law judge with the California Public Utilities Commission.

Linda Shostak remains at Morrison & Foerster.

Richard Harris is with the firm of Erskine & Tully.

Lawrence Klein is a partner with Ritchie, Fisher & Klein in Palo Alto. His son is a partner with the Cooley firm, now Cooley Godward, which, with nearly 450 lawyers, has become California's fifth largest.

Sandy Tatum and John Laveroni remain at Cooley as "retired partners." Tatum has represented the University of San Francisco, the Raychem Corporation, Security Pacific Bank, Bankers' Trust, and the United States Golf Association. He has been president of the San Francisco Legal Aid Society, a trustee of Stanford University, and a member of the Mayor's Fiscal Advisory Commission. He has served on the boards of directors of the Youth Law Center, the United Bay Area Crusade, St. Elizabeth's Infant Hospital, and the San Francisco Mental Health Association. At eighty-one, he is working to raise San Francisco's municipal Harding Park Golf Course to PGA tournament level and recently authored the autobiographical *A Love Affair with the Game*.

Laveroni has practiced antitrust, copyright, construction, criminal and trade securities law. He served as an attorney for the Oakland Athletics in contract disputes and the Rand Corporation in the Pentagon Papers case. He litigated claims before the United States-Iran tribunals and the family law courts of Norway. But the career highlight featured above all others in his biography at the Cooley web site is his role as "lead counsel in the case of *Walt Disney Productions v. The Air Pirates*, the seminal case in establishing copyright protection for cartoon characters."

Stewart Brand founded The Well (Whole Earth Lectronic List), became managing director of the Global Business Network, and was on the board of directors of the Electronic Frontier Foundation. He currently leads the All Species Now Foundation's quest to compile a list of every variety of living creature on Earth. He is also a recipient of the San Francisco Media Alliance's Golden Gadfly Lifetime Achievement Award.

Paul Krassner writes regularly for *High Times* and *Playboy* and performs stand-up comedy. His most recent book is *Murder at the Conspiracy Convention.* His most recent CD is "Irony Lives!"[169]

Bud Plant operates a mail order business out of Grass Valley, California, selling comics, illustrated books, and related *objets d'art.*

Robert Beerbohm, after losing most of his stock of comics to a flood, returned to Nebraska. He is writing a history of comic books, tentatively titled *Comics Archaeology,* which will correct many commonly held misconceptions, including several you have read here.

Gary Hallgren, "still and forever" a freelance commercial illustrator, lives on Long Island. He has been married to his second wife, Michelle, for twenty-five years; they have a sixteen-year-old daughter. His work has appeared in *The New York Times, Wall Street Journal, Forbes, MAD*, and *Swank,* for whom he created the monthly, picaresque "Mustang Sally" two-pager. He has drawn greeting cards for Disney, and his "Bad Girls Ride Bad Bikes" logo adorns T-shirts, coffee mugs, and mouse pads; but he has not contributed to a comic book for twenty years. The UGs, he says, "were one of those things that never fulfilled their potential."

Ted Richards left comic books in 1981 to edit the magazine by which Atari instructed customers how to use its products. He went on to become its creative manager and work for several other Internet companies in a similar capacity. In 1996, he was named vice president and creative director for Audio Highway, developing products and promotional formats for clients that included Sony Music, Dreamworks, and Simon & Schuster. Most recently, he has been creative director for DNA Sciences, directing marketing and recruitment for the Gene Trust. He is remarried, has a teenage son, and lives in the Silicon Valley.

Bobby London continued to draw on a freelance basis for "slick" magazines and newspapers. Between 1984 and 1986, he worked for the Disney merchandising division in New York City. From 1986 until 1992, he drew the daily "Popeye" comic strip for King Features. (His stint ended after he took on the Right-to-Life movement by suggesting Olive Oyl had aborted an unwanted pregnancy.) He also helped design the Sonic the Hedgehog video games. He now contributes "Dirty Duck" to *Playboy* and "Cody," a family strip, to *Nickelodeon Magazine.* He lives in Los Angeles.

Shary Flenniken contributed to *The National Lampoon* until 1990; she also served as a freelance editor. Her work has appeared in *MAD, Premiere, American*

---

[169] The disc, a work of "investigative satire" was to have contained an introduction by Dan ("Homer Simpson") Castellaneta; but Fox TV, which claimed ownership of Homer's voice, refused to allow Castellaneta to speak in it.

Lawyer, and *Playgirl*. She contributed to the script of *National Lampoon Goes to the Movies* and wrote *Silicon Valley Guy*, an unproduced film for Disney. She has done advertisements for Burger King and Toys 'R' Us. She authored the books *Seattle Laughs*, *Sexe and Amour*, and *Diving into the Subconscious* and illustrated *Nice Guys Sleep Alone*, *When a Man Loves a Walnut*, and stories in *The Big Book of Martyrs*. She lives in Seattle.

Mickey Mouse has starred in only two motion pictures in the last fifty years. In the 1990 release *The Prince and the Pauper*, he all but made the viewing audience forget Freddy Bartholemew; but his sole subsequent booking, *The Runaway Brain*, saw him reduced to having his brain switched with that of a Frankenstein monster and turned "into a ragged, fanged, menacing wildmouse" — a startlingly O'Neillian vision. (It also — see below — sounds suspiciously like someone was playing subversively with a metaphor for what happened with corporate Disney.) He remains, however, emblazoned as the sole spokescharacter on the stationery upon which the company tells inquiring authors that it receives too many requests to cooperate with books they have in progress.[170]

The Air Pirates comics sell for seventy-five times their original cost. Pages of the original artwork go for four figures. Two of these pages — one each by O'Neill and London — were displayed at San Francisco's Cartoon Art Museum's 2002 show: "ZAP, CRASH AND BURN: Underground Comix and the Bay Area."

The consequences of direct sales on the comic book industry proved profound. Comic book stores, of which there are now 2000 in this country, have become the primary way comics are sold. Because these stores were unable to return unsold books, they fostered the development of a "collectors' market," in which old comics were valued according to such factors as condition, artists, characters introduced, and fetishes catered to, and were treated as investments, rather than mere entertainment or, God forbid, art. Publishers capitalized on this trend by emphasizing the release of "hot" books, featuring the most popular characters drawn by the most popular artists — often with multiple covers (collectors would need one of each) or "pre-bagged" to preserve their full, pristine-condition worth (which meant you had to buy a second copy if you also wanted to read the damn thing) — rather than finding ways to attract a wider, more diverse audience. Coming at a time when comics had dropped from public view on newsstands and magazine racks, this further served to marginalize them from the rest of society.

---

[170] Disney remains protective of Mickey's image. Before it permitted Macy's to erect its "Mickey's Night Before Christmas" show windows display, Macy's had to agree not to depict him and Minnie sharing the same bedroom.

While this marketing shift took place, the Comics Code Authority maintained its thumbs-to-windpipe grip on the industry.[171] Its most recent revision, in 1989, reaffirmed a commitment to "decent and wholesome comic books for children." It mandated the favorable portrayal of governmental bodies; law enforcement agencies; the military; religious, ethnic and social groups; "the economically disadvantaged"; as well as "the economically privileged." It tolerated appropriate and non-excessive violence and substance abuse (including smoking and chewing tobacco), as long as it was not glamorized. Clothing had to conform to "contemporary styles and fashions," and the depiction of graphic sex and "primary human sexual characteristics" was forbidden.

For the most part, mainstream publishers were content to operate within these strictures. While comic book sales dwindled to roughly a quarter of what they once were, the two largest companies, Marvel and DC, still submitted ninety-five percent of their titles for approval.[172] Most of these books recycled tales of bizarrely over-muscled men and equally overly-endowed women engaging grotesquely mutated monsters in never-resolving combat. These battles raged for so long and scorched the earth so severely, they seem to have made it impossible for alternative narratives to take root. The result has been that comic books have become almost entirely a land where only teenage boys of limited imagination and hobbled social skills feel at home.[173]

At present, comics are less important to their publishers for the dimes they generate directly than the dollars their characters attract from elsewhere. Spin-off merchandise and television licensings keep the presses rolling; and, every few years, Hollywood backs up and unloads the Brinks trucks — for Batman, for the X-Men, for Spawn and Blade and Spider-Man and the Hulk — so there is little urgency to rock any dinghies.

The UG scene has also withered. Rip Off weathered the '70s with an infusion of money for the film rights to Shelton's Fabulous Furry Freak Brothers, but the body-blows the Reagan era struck against permissiveness took their toll. After much of its inventory was destroyed by the explosion of an illegal fire-

---

[171] Knowledgeable sources say I overstate the Code's force. In recent years, they point out, direct market books have generally ignored it with no one giving a rip.

[172] In early 2002, Marvel announced it was discontinuing this practice.

[173] Matthew Pustz, in *Comic Book Culture,* argues that mainstream comics are not as devoid of content as they might appear. Frequently, he says, they are rich in "specialized knowledge," allusions and references to not only the entire, often decades-long run of the comic in which they appear, but all of comic book history. Unfortunately, this makes it "almost impossible" for a new reader to pick up some comics and understand them. Publishers have resorted to red-flagging issues where the current is not too swift or debris-clogged for a novice to enter safely or summarizing entire sagas or character case histories inside each volume.

works factory in the building it shared, Rip Off relocated to the wilds of Placer County; and Fred Todd, its chief operating officer, enrolled in junior college to study computer science. He keeps his company's most popular titles in print but, on average, does not issue one new book a year. Don Donahue moved what was left of Apex Novelties into his living space in a south Berkeley warehouse. His walls are lined with storage boxes full of underground work from which he satisfies mail orders; but his schedule of new releases makes Rip Off look like Bertelsman AG.

The cartoonists Joel Beck, Roger Brand, and Jim Osborne were killed by alcohol and Rory Hayes by speed. Rick Griffin died in a motorcycle accident and Greg Irons was hit by a bus.[174] Robert Crumb and Gilbert Shelton moved to France. Justin Green became a sign painter. Bill Griffith syndicated "Zippy." Willie Mendes dedicated her art to Orthodox Judaism. Trina Robbins diverted her feminist coursings first into *Barbie* and *Wonder Woman* and then a ground-breaking series of books on the history of women in comics. Robert Williams built a waiting list for five-figure, original oils of his eyeballs and bathing beauties. And S. Clay Wilson has illustrated — albeit in his own, impeccably tasteless fashion — Hans Christian Andersen and the Brothers Grimm.

Only Ron Turner, his ponytail and beard greyer but still streaming, thrives at the old stand. Last Gasp publishes new comics, old comics, biker books, tattoo and piercing mags. Though his sales are only a fraction of his salad days, he remains proud of the movement of which he was a part. "Everywhere you look graphically today, you see vestiges of underground cartoons," he says. "Young cartoonists read them like a good Muslim reads the Koran. Art students absorb their visuals before they create their art. Modern advertising directly links to them. Sex, drugs, violence — they opened up all of that."[175]

.   And while no second generation of cartoonists sprang up immediately to succeed the UG, the security of having books pre-sold encouraged small, independent companies, who could ignore the code, accept edgier, more experimental, more adult work, and survive on sales of 5-10,000 per issue to enter the field. By the 1980s, a *nouvelle vague* of artists that would come to include Chester Brown, Dan Clowes, Julie Doucet, Phoebe Gloeckner, Roberta Gregory, the Hernandez brothers, Joe Sacco, Seth, Dave Sim, Chris Ware, and Jim

---

[174] In 1998, Malcolm Whyte published *The Underground Comix Family Album*, a collection of photographs taken during the UG's prime. Of the forty-three men pictured — there were also seven women — I counted eleven who were deceased. Assuming their ages to have been twenty-five to thirty when photographed, a normal life expectancy would have had each of them reach seventy-five. They didn't make sixty. Folks exposed to Agent Orange had a better survival rate.

[175] In *Political Fictions*, analyzing the failed Clinton impeachment, Joan Didion credits the American public's recently evolved "non-judgmentalism... in the sexual realm" with immunizing it to the frothings of the rabid Republican right and saving the presidency. Hell, the UGs may have helped alter history.

Woodring, who had absorbed the lesson of the UGs that comic books were suitable vehicles for the expression any form of individual vision, had emerged eager to fill their lists. In books that were autobiographical and fantastic, historical and erotic, magical and political, realistic and surreal, they expanded the comic page far beyond the turf staked out by their predecessors. Their concerns are broader, their viewpoints wider, their approaches more original. There is, simply put, better work being done in comic books today than at any time in the past.[176]

The decline of Walt Disney Productions continued into the 1980s. *The Black Hole* flopped. *Tron* flopped. *The Last Flight of Noah's Ark, The Cat From Outer Space, The Fox and the Hound* flopped. Its production facilities were outmoded and its distribution system poor. (The rumor is not true, however, that Disney ever reached the point that it was swapping film prints for Volkswagens-full of incense.) It trailed all major studios in box office receipts. Its effort to engage contemporary sensibilities by creating a separate division, Touchstone Pictures, to make more adult movies was delayed by internal debate about whether Darryl Hannah, the mermaid in its maiden effort, *Splash*, could be bare-breasted. (The verdict was "No." Her hair was taped across her nipples.) It remained, one critic wrote, enmeshed in the Reaganite "focus on the family and the moral values that, for the far right, defined it."

Disney's theme parks continued to account for most of its revenues, but even their attendance declined; and its stubborn refusal to build additional hotels on its property in Orlando allowed other companies to scoop up the receipts from lodging Disney World's visitors. Its merchandise remained profitable, but Disney barely promoted it. It produced no new shows for network television, and its own cable Disney Channel bled money. Its stock's value dropped from $85 to $45 a share during a period in which the Dow Jones average rose 200 points. By the early '80s, Disney's licensor, Western Publishing, ceased publishing the comics line because of dwindling sales.[177]

Then, June 21, 1984, in a move roughly equivalent to Bob Jones University appointing Dennis Rodman athletic director — or the House of Windsor placing next in the line of succession Mad Man Muntz — or, give me a minute

---

[176] A successful mainstream comic book today has a circulation of about 100,000, ninety percent of which is to boys between the ages of ten and twenty. A successful alternative comic will sell a tenth of that to a readership that is sixty-forty male and generally college age or older. [Ed. Note: these figures of Levin's, like most pertaining to comic books, are highly debatable.]

[177] Gladstone Comics picked up the rights to Disney's comics in 1986. Although Gladstone achieved circulations in the high five to low six figures, Disney ended the license in 1990, convinced that it could better these numbers by taking over the publishing itself. In 1993, confronted with shrinking sales, Disney returned the license to Gladstone, who published them until 1998 when sales of fewer than 10,000 forced them to give it up.

(metaphors are not my strong point), and I will nail this — Disney made Michael Eisner chairman of its board of directors. Eisner came from Paramount Pictures, where he had been president and chief operating officer. During his tenure, through films like *Raiders of the Lost Ark*, *Saturday Night Fever*, and *Terms of Endearment* — nothing too eccentric, nothing too remote or, even, too intelligent — but nothing that was *That Darned Cat* either — Paramount had quadrupled its profits and become the highest grossing studio in Hollywood. (Before that, Eisner had been a senior vice president at ABC, which, leaning on the even more brain-dead *Laverne & Shirley* and *Starsky & Hutch*, had been the country's top-rated television network. His most noted contribution was to insist upon a beefed-up role for the Fonz in *Happy Days*.)

The Eisner Era[178] brought Disney success beyond anything its founder or Horatio Alger or, for that matter, few consciousnesses this side of Alexander the Great might have contemplated. Eisner returned Disney to network television with a Saturday morning children's show based on a popular candy, *Gummi Bears*. (The concept was Eisner's, and, boy, Bill Moyers must have kicked himself for missing that one.) He hired George Lucas to develop *Star Wars*-related theme park rides — and then raised admission price by five dollars — the first of nine price hikes before the decade's end. (Lucas's plan to provide the additional kick of having the drivers appear to be deranged androids did not make the final cut.) He signed Michael Jackson, at a time he was still better known for *Thriller* than the chapter devoted to him in *Psychopathia Sexualis*, for the 3-D movie *Captain EO* — but censored his trademark crotch-grab dance move. (The film's cost, $17,000,000, made it, per minute, the most expensive of all time.) He opened Tokyo and Euro-Disneylands. (Adapting its dress code to deflect current grooming trends, Disney has denied all park employees shaved heads or spiked or oddly colored hair and limited body piercings to one small stud per ear for women.) He revitalized the Disney Channel. He packaged old television shows profitably with new ones for syndication. He saturated the video market so thoroughly that, at one point, Disney had eighteen of the top twenty best-selling children's videos. He advertised at unheard-of-for-Disney levels. The first film script he approved, *Down and Out in Beverly Hills*, resulted in Disney's first R-rating (for one profanity); but it also earned $57,000,000. Fourteen of his first fifteen films were profitable; and with *Aladdin*, *Beauty and the Beast*, *Ernest Goes to Camp*, *The Little Mermaid*, and *Three Men and a Baby*, he made Disney the first studio to gross over $1,000,000,000. (One of Eisner's first moves to make Disney profitable had

---

[178] These achievements were also the work of Frank Wells, Disney's president/CEO, who arrived the same time as Eisner, and Jeffrey Katzenberg, who became head of production of the motion picture division shortly thereafter. (A fellow named Robert Levin took charge of film marketing. From the sound of his name alone, I am sure he deserves some credit for juicing up the old buggy.) Wells died in a helicopter crash in 1994, and Katzenberg left to join DreamWorks. When Disney failed to pay him bonuses to which he felt entitled, he sued, receiving a settlement of $270,000,000 on the eve of trial.

been to lay off 1000 employees. Later, when executives were pocketing lavish bonuses, workers had their health care deductibles doubled.)

When I last looked, Disney's annual revenues exceeded $20,000,000,000, and it had 120,000 employees. It owned Miramax and Merchant-Ivory. It owned ABC, ESPN, the History Channel, Lifetime, A&E. It owned newspapers, television and radio stations, publishing and record companies. It owned cruise ships, residential communities, luxury hotels, vacation clubs, golf courses, a sports complex, a convention center, the Queen Mary (when the captain refused to abide by Disney's "No Facial Hair" policy and shave off his traditional British naval commander's mustache, he was fired), the Spruce Goose, a fast food chain (Mickey's Kitchen), an Indy racetrack, the Anaheim Angels, the Mighty Ducks, and 650 Disney stores in eleven countries, including a monster that helped chase the goblins from Times Square.

This expansion did not come without some bruised feelings. The same literature that credits Disney with being "the most trusted brand name in the history of marketing" notes its reputation for being "cheap," "arrogant," "manipulative," "demanding," and "stifling" of individual creativity. It may be toasted as an "entertainment conglomerate of unparalleled size and breadth," but it remains "puritanical," and a master player of hard-nosed corporate "hardball." While "almost synonymous with the very notion of American culture," Disney is a company "with little respect for free speech and public criticism."

Disney's policies, not to mention its deep pockets, have kept its legal and public relations departments fully employed. It has been in litigation with almost every other major company in Hollywood. It has been sued for refusing to admit a green-haired girl in a halter top to one of its parks and for refusing to allow two gay young men to dance together at another. Home owners at a residential development sued it for property damage from Hurricane Andrew, alleging shoddy construction. Female dancers at Cinderella's Castle sued it for negligently permitting peepholes in their dressing room. Disney has outraged Arab groups with an Israeli exhibit at Disneyworld. It offended keen-eyed Christian fundamentalists who spotted a penis on the Little Mermaid's video box and — with the aid of their freeze-frame buttons — a shot of Jessica Rabbit without panties — or topless, accounts differ. It shocked Southern Baptists by allowing Ellen DeGeneres to come out on *Ellen*. It upset much of the Continent by banning beards and mustaches on employees at Euro-Disneyland. It angered environmentalists by butchering buzzards that were preying on Animal Kingdom. It inflamed Civil War buffs with plans for a 2400-acre Disney America at the site of the Battle of Bull Run. It found itself in (insufficiently) hot water when those who manned its life-size Mickey-Minnie-Goofy costumes charged they were forced to delight and charm while wearing uncleaned underwear. And as it expands globally — it is in China now and opening up the rest of the Far East — it infuriates and terrifies many who believe their native lands' indigenous crafts, arts, traditions and cultures will be destroyed by its Blob-like appetite for market domination.

Meanwhile, Disney continues to be "fanatical" about protecting its own property. ("No company," wrote Ron Grover, the L.A. Bureau Chief for *Business Week*, "has been more vigilant in the protection of [copyright] rights than the Walt Disney Company under Michael Eisner...") It has tripled its legal staff and prioritized combating infringers. (They take, one of these lawyers told *The National Law Journal*, "a more restricted view" of fair use than most.) Its investigators patrol flea markets and survey street corners, searching out poseurs. It files several hundred lawsuits a year, bringing over-reaching T-shirt manufacturers, poster makers, and video distributors to justice. It has forced thousands of stores to abandon unlicenced suppliers — and then taken over most of these accounts.

Disney once sued a fellow who tattooed its characters on his body. It sued a small chain of day care centers that painted Mickey Mouse and Donald Duck on its walls. (The chain replaced them with Yogi Bear, Fred Flintstone, and Scooby Doo.) It sued the Academy of Motion Picture Arts and Sciences for a dance at the Oscars that partnered Rob Lowe — of underage-sex video fame — with Snow White. It sued a Canadian artist who produced "Wishing on a Star" postcards showing Disneyland being destroyed by a nuclear blast. It sued the Italian magazine *Play Man*, for coupling its centerfold with Mickey Mouse. It sued Fox for planning a version of *Peter Pan* that included a Tinkerbell, whose representation it claimed to have created. It forced an émigré Soviet artist to end the display of his painting of Mickey offering a Campbell's soup can to another Russian. It forced Marvel to redraw Howard the Duck — shorter, fatter, yellower, shaggier — and keep his pants on — so he wouldn't be confused with Donald. It threatened to sue Berke Breathed for placing a Mortimer Mouse in his "Outland" strip. When White River, the northern Ontario mill town where the bear cub was captured that became the model for Winnie the Pooh, decided to erect a statue to him, Disney blocked it. When the producers of the Broadway show *Who's Afraid of Virginia Woolf* tried to use the tune "Who's Afraid of the Big Bad Wolf," Disney stopped them. (They used "Here We Go 'Round the Mulberry Bush" instead.) When Random House considered publishing the Marxian *How to Read Donald Duck*, threats by Disney deterred it. When three academics compiled a collection of postmodern essays with the working title *Doing Disney*, Disney scared them into changing it, claiming even this mention of its name was actionable.[179]

Disney has also spent ample time at the other end of the intellectual properties counsels' table. It was sued by Jim Henson's estate for unauthorized use of the Muppets. (Disney settled with an apology.) It was sued by the seventy-year-old, wheel-

---

[179] Disney has not opposed all adaptations. It generally gives editorial cartoonists and non-profit foundations a pass; and I have met fine arts professors who, with a few drinks in them, will swear they have proof that it even paid pop artists, like Roy Lichtenstein, Claes Oldenburg, and Andy Warhol, to use its characters in their work. (In September 2002, Marilyn Manson opened a display of his watercolors, including one of himself as Mickey Mouse, at the Los Angeles Contemporary Exhibitions gallery. As this went to press, Disney's reaction was not available.)

chair-bound Miss Peggy Lee for the unauthorized use of her voice in *The Lady and the Tramp* video. (She won $2,300,000, which led Mary "Sleeping Beauty" Costa, Phil "Baloo the Bear" Harris, and the estate of Louis "King Louis" Prima, among others, to sue for the unauthorized use of theirs. Disney settled with them all.) It was sued by Alan King for stealing an idea he claimed to have shopped to Eisner while playing tennis. It offended Robin Williams by the unauthorized use of his image and voice to promote *Aladdin*. (It apologized with the gift of an original Picasso, though his manager/wife reportedly remained miffed because she'd wanted a Lear jet.) It had to pay $10,000,000 for the unauthorized use of the European cartoon character Marsupilami. It was sued in 2001 for unpaid earnings by Gary K. Wolf, *Roger Rabbit's* author. And it ended 2002 trying to hang onto over $1,000,000,000 in royalties it was alleged to have wrongfully derived from Winnie the Pooh.

While Disney's wealth and power have never been greater, it does not seem to me to any longer command its former revered position within American culture — High or Low. Its products, I suspect, no longer automatically summon forth the attention and respect they did when I was a child. Its appeal, I read, is limited to younger and younger children; and, even there, it is losing ground to Teletubbies. Its efforts at the hipness that would attract an older crowd — a Rock'n'Rollercoaster ride with music by Aerosmith, outfitting Mickey Mouse with a skateboard — seem clueless rather than connected to the *zeitgeist*. When it purchased Fox Family Network from Rupert Murdoch, it elected to rename it ABC-Family, rather than Disney-Family, so as not to risk alienating too much of the audience it hoped to draw.

The term that has been coined to describe the way modern children are seemingly growing up faster and faster is "Age Compression." Disney claims awareness of the phenomenon and espouses confidence in its ability to withstand it. Deciding to explore the depth of its challenge for myself — and eager to share any light I brought forth — I put the following question in my best test-marketing fashion to my twin, ten-year-old nephews, Izzie and Shecky:[180] "What do you think when you hear the name 'Walt Disney': 'Pew!' 'Wow!' or 'Eh?'"

"PEE-YOUUU!!!" they answered, rather too gleefully. "You think of cartoons and children's things. You think of..." They summoned up all the disdain they could muster. "...*The Little Mermaid*. Some of the old movies were good, but the quality has sunk so low the main viewers are kids under six or sick kids with the flu or something who have to stay home and there's nothing on TV. Disney's just a name to sell stuff. Walt Disney has nothing to do with it."

"You sure you guys are only ten?" I said.

In sum, Disney no longer seems to shine as a magic sword to wield against the shoddy nor an enchanted shield with which to deflect the worrisome. It is one

---

[180] Faithful readers may wonder what happened to my twin nephew and niece in my last book. Well, that entire family was a lie. This is the real deal.

more entertainment moguldom among a fleet of many, dragging the public waters. It hooks; it strikes; once in a while it lands a whopper; but Michael Eisner could not, I imagine, appear on evening television, comfy and avuncular, and expect anyone to kneel before him.[181] The soul of Disney, I would respectfully posit, that led it once to produce a steadily expanding realm of wonders, has been stymied by the part of it that demands it glut itself on profits. (Kim Masters, in *Keys to the Kingdom*, damningly summons up the following Eisner quote: "We have no obligation to make history... to make art... to make a statement. To make money is our only objective.")[182] These wonders may have been limited in scope, but they were true wonders, marvelous and, on occasion, inspiring; and if you remain in pursuit of wonders, who knows where you may get to. If your pursuit is of profits, you get to banks, to fancier boardrooms, to showrooms that sell yachts.[183] In one sense, yeah, this squares with what seems to power this country. But in another, one suspects (or hopes or wishes) that while this drive (this greed, it could be called, this hyena-avarice) is met with "You-go-gal!"s, at the same time, there remains a lingering, subliminal shame, a repulsion, a wish of "There-must-be-more-than-this" that withholds the widespread celebration of the Disney company that once fell upon it, warm and constant, like Miami rain.[184]

~~~~~~

[181] Ooops! News has just reached me that, in 1986, Eisner, slimmed down, stylishly clothed, and voice coach-tutored, hosted Disney's return to Sunday night television. Obviously, this made little impression on your local correspondent; but if his appearances imprinted themselves regally upon any of you, I am taking names with which to correct my next edition. (I might add, though, when I concluded the polling of my nephews, "And what do you think of Michael Eisner?" they answered, "Who's he?")

[182] This policy has worked so well that, in 1997, not counting any paper clips he may have filched from the supply cabinet, Eisner brought home $570,000,000. (In the interests of fairness and full disclosure, my campaign adviser, Robert the K, has prevailed upon me to reveal I did not.)

[183] If you find yourself reacting, "Hey, that sounds good to me," you may not be my ideal reader.

[184] In the mid-1990s, an otherwise unidentified New Mouse Liberation Front issued a new comic, *Air Pirates*, in a "Special Pirate Edition." Denying any affiliation with the original Air Pirates but claiming inspiration from "the importance and rarity of [their] original defiant gesture," it reprinted the two Mouse stories from *Air Pirates Funnies*, along with a brief summary of the case. To this "gesture," the New MLF added its own four-pager. That story opens with Mickey — clearly recognizable, masked by no stubble — behind a desk, fuming about "fucking Democrats" revising the tax code and the cost of keeping "that old popsicle" cryogenically preserved. When his secretary, Clarabelle Cow, enters, he exposes himself and demands she relieve his stress by "chew[ing] on something besides your cud." When a man who has tattooed his likeness on his chest is hauled before him, Mickey wields a sword and claims "my cut" for this infringement. To complaints about company trade policies and environmental abuses, he responds, "I am Mickey Mouse and I AM the AMERICAN DREAM!! It's simple... I got mine... FUCK YOU!"

Dan O'Neill, after the Disney settlement, re-emerged — of all unlikely places — at the *Chronicle*. His strip, now titled "O'Neill," ran every Sunday for six years in its "This World" section. Again, the *Chron* hoped to syndicate O'Neill, promoting him as "a genius of the art of comics," and, again, he proved a difficult sell. Other papers regarded a weekly strip skeptically, and his effort was uniquely hard to take in. Its content was that of an editorial cartoon; but its multi-paneled format made it look like it belonged on the comics page, and its oversized scale made that placement impossible. O'Neill, of course, would not change a thing.

He appeared as a character in most installments; but it was a kinder, gentler O'Neill. He sat in his Nevada City cabin, Bud in hand, watching TV, fished in Hennessy's Pond, rooted for the Giants, fought crabgrass, struggled to give up smoking. This did not mean that the legal process had deterred or rehabilitated him into "The Family Circus." His work remained political, but it roiled more with head-shaking bemusement than fist-waving rage. (A basic premise was that Ronald Reagan appeared on his television set one evening and asked him to be his Special Advisor. He also stole O'Neill's watch.) He tweaked the presidential nose here and there but levied none of the savagery one might have expected.[185] Issues of the times flickered across the page — Granada, Beirut, Nicaragua, trickle-down economics, acid rain, nuclear proliferation — but the disappointments of two decades had taken a toll. The inevitable progress that did not occur. The sure-fire winners that faded. The allies that would join you on the victory stand who were gone. By the '80s, political issues had become as flies. You swiped at one and went about your business. You did not chase it around the room, out the door, across the yard, until you had pounded it with a hammer — or been strapped onto a gurney, Thorazine pumping in your head. You recognized there were too many flies.

The one cause to which O'Neill remained committed was removing the British from Northern Ireland. Here, in a sense, he lived his art. This dovetailing began with the Falklands War. In his strip, O'Neill created an Irish Navy, three guys grumbling in a rowboat, to whom he attributed the sinking of a half-dozen ships, though "the Argentines took all the credit." He recalled them to service the next year to intercept the ship which was to bring Queen Elizabeth into San Francisco Bay to entertain the Reagans on their thirty-first anniversary. Over several weeks, he detailed his fleet's journey around Cape Horn, up the Gulf of Mexico, to the Colorado River where, rowboat and all, they traveled the final 600 miles to the Oakland estuary by boxcar. Here, they linked up with a flock of Irish Republican seagulls who dive-bombed the assembled dignitaries,

[185] Expected, that is, if you are the author of "Republic," a short story (*frying pan*, August 1984) whose portrait of Reagan as a senile, child-molesting, trunk-murderer still seems to him among the most accurate assessments of the Great Communicator to see print.

ruining the Queen's suit and Nancy's hair-do and driving the ship into the Berkeley pier. "A Great Day for the Irish!" O'Neill concluded.

O'Neill says that, as the Queen's actual visit neared, he and the Mitchell brothers raised a four-boat armada, rigged with every Irish flag they could find. Then, armed with 750 pounds of illegal herring they had scored from poachers, they lured a 500 foot tall ball of seagulls toward Sausalito's outdoor Trident restaurant, where diners were "having their eggs Benedict and early morning martinis, trying to be Episcopalian." This exhibition of firepower caused a change of plans. "She got off the boat in Santa Barbara and flew in; and it's all over the English papers, 'IRA Tries to Sink *Britannia*.' The British Home Office even declared Northern California a 'No-Go' zone. 'You can never have an official visit again.' Thank you very much. Like we want the bitch."[186]

O'Neill also ventured into civic affairs on other occasions unlikely to rouse *artistes* of a more Proustian temperament. He assumed the editorship of the weekly *Nevada City Independent* and, in a few months, increased its circulation from 200 to 5000 while fighting off developers' plans to double the town's size. He ran for City Council, finishing third in a race for two seats. ("I was the people's third choice for second place," he says. "I didn't spend any money, because I didn't have any, and I wouldn't kiss any babies because they give you diseases.") And when Tom Forcade, the ex-director of the Underground Press Syndicate (best known for concluding his testimony before the U.S. Commission on Obscenity and Pornography by tossing a pie at it) and founder of *High Times* magazine, suicided, a fight for its control erupted between his widow and some reputed mobsters. Michael Kennedy, the estate's trustee, summoned O'Neill to set things straight. "He burnt my clothes, bought me a Brooks Brothers suit, and sent me to New York. I was there a month and fired $140,000 worth of art directors. By the time I got the right people in the right places, I had sixty others looking for me with a gun."

Gary Hallgren, who hosted O'Neill during his mission, recalls him returning one night to their loft, shoving the sofa bed against the door and announcing, "They're after me!" Hallgren suggested the Gramercy Hotel might better suit O'Neill's residency requirements. O'Neill politely decamped, but Hallgren's projected *High Times* cover, a full-color Mickey Mouse, his head blown apart by a joint, never saw print.

Then, the journalist/pornographic film producer Gail Palmer Slater accused Hunter Thompson of interrupting a meeting being taken in his hot tub to discuss her acquiring the film rights to *Fear and Loathing in Las Vegas* by grabbing her tit, and the ensuing police raid turned up LSD, cocaine, marijuana, and

---

[186] Photographs of the event reveal two Boston Whalers, one with one flag, one with, maybe, four. And John Hubner's book on the Mitchells, *Bottom Feeders*, says it was a press party, invited to the Trident, not casual diners, that served as witnesses.

dynamite on the premises. Before PEN had even drafted its first petition protesting the resulting criminal charges, O'Neill and the Mitchells had launched a support caravan bound for their old pal's home in Woody Creek, Colorado.

"It was the Last Ride. Jim and Artie in a red '71 Chevy Caprice convertible, with a buffalo head on the front; two Winnebagos full of naked, dancing girls; freaky looking hippies; and a friend of mine with diabetes we'd sit out beside the road in front of troopers in Utah to shoot up. We held press conferences in whorehouses all across Nevada to show what happens when you mess with the Doctor. It ended with all charges being dropped."

In 1986, O'Neill made another move that, in terms of career advancement, continued his program of taking one step forward, two steps back — and shooting himself in the foot once he had settled in.[187] William Randolph Hearst III, the *Examiner*'s new publisher, sought to hire away talent from its major competition. Since the *Chronicle* was only paying O'Neill $100 a week, he was happy to jump ship. But, it turned out, Hearst was more interested in bigger prizes, like Warren Hinkle, the swashbuckling ex-*Ramparts* editor who was then a *Chron* columnist, than securing O'Neill a plush berth.

Unemployed, O'Neill had moved back to Nevada City when his oldest son died from AIDS. He did not draw a cartoon for a year. But when the Gulf War erupted, he again felt the call. His vehicle was *The War News*, a paper founded by Jim Mitchell, which printed anti-war material the mainstream media would not touch.

O'Neill drew cartoons, solicited contributors, and served as art editor. Daniel Ellsberg, Krassner, Ishmael Reed, and Barbara Ehrenreich delivered articles and Crumb, Shelton, Flenniken, and Spiegelman, cartoons. Looking ahead to when the conflict concluded, the *News* planned to take on AIDS and homelessness. But one night, after only two issues had appeared, Jim Mitchell went to his brother's house to coax him out of an increasingly troublesome pattern of drug-and-alcohol-fueled behavior. Some of this behavior had involved guns, and Jim Mitchell had gone to this meeting armed. Before the night was over, Artie Mitchell was dead, and Jim was under arrest.[188]

---

[187] Richard Milner says of this tendency, "O'Neill once did a strip where, in the first panel, this guy is screaming at the sky, 'Bring it on down, you dumb bunny!'; and, in the second, a giant rabbit's foot mashes him flat. He gets up, screams it again, and gets mashed again. 'Why's he keep doing that?' Hugh asks Fred. The answer is 'He's Irish.' Well, that's O'Neill."

[188] Jim Mitchell was charged with first degree murder. After a three-month trial, defended by Michael Kennedy, he was convicted of voluntary manslaughter. O'Neill and Hinkle covered the case for the rabidly anti-establishment Anderson Valley *Independent* of Mendocino County. "It wasn't jury-tampering exactly," O'Neill says, "but suddenly this paper, normally not seen south of Ukiah, mysteriously appeared at every 7-Eleven a juror was likely to pee."

O'Neill surfaced from his friends' tragedy at the *Bay Guardian*. His weekly strip, "Dan O'Neill" (later, "Odd Bodkins") centered around a Nevada City bar, The End of the Trail Saloon, whose habituees included O'Neill; Aloysius Xavier Magillicuddy, its proprietor; the leggy Miss Lily, who cooked; Hugh, who swept up; Fred the Bird; and Bill the Horse, who flew well enough to travel through time, played piano, and knew all the words to "Hooray for Captain Spaulding."

Much was familiar. Digs at fascism and Richard Nixon, allusions to free will and the Disney suit, conversations with God. But O'Neill still wrote Saturnian rings around most cartoonists. He had not lost his ability to toss off the stride-stopping line.[188] Age had neither blunted his political edge nor reined the flying ponies of his imagination. He continued to assert his thorny, idiosyncratic self — inciting resistance to everything from further U.S. involvement in Colombia to plans to route 180 giant water trucks a day through downtown Nevada City — even if these assertions caused the *Guardian* to inter his work among the classifieds, buried deep among calls for used accordions, ejaculation aids, and Jamie's search for Paul from the #22 Fillmore.

There has always been a lot of America blind to O'Neill, deaf to him, obscuring him. This has never kept him from his best effort to hit the right notes to crumble its walls. Greil Marcus has written, in *Mystery Train*, of those luminous popular artists — rock 'n' rollers, in his case — who, in taking on the risks and responsibilities of dramatizing "what it is to be an American, what it means, what it's worth, what the stakes of life in America might be," struggle to formulate a vision for "a world where we can feel alive...ambitious and free... dispensing with the rest of American reality if we can." They are, Marcus says, striving to "lift America to heaven or drive a stake through its heart." O'Neill, I think, continued to rank with the best of those.

Then, in 2001, the *Guardian*, for "budgetary reasons," let him go.

In late October, Adele and I returned to Nevada City. ("Are you coming for the autumn leaves?" our *hotelier* inquired this time. "Absolutely," I said.) On I-80, past Sacramento, a dark scrim of clouds filled the horizon. Penetration seemed problematic. "Come on down, sweet Virginia," Mick Jagger sang. "Welcome to California," a bumper sticker on a passing pick-up answered, "Now go home." Traffic clotted all lanes. "At this rate," Adele said, "we'll never get there."

The plan was to meet O'Neill the following afternoon. He would take us to the cabin at the gold mine where he lived. He would fill holes my narrative stumbled over. He would resolve contradictions that tied it in knots. I especially

---

[188] My favorites from this period include "All Americans have family overseas... With the neighbors shooting at them"; the query by John Wesley Horowitz (the not-just-a-wandering Hebrew of the Old West) "How come the Ishmaelites got the oil and we got the end of our what cut off?"; and, when Bill is seated at a restaurant ahead of a snooty French philosopher, "You put theez horse before Descartes?" "Exactly."

liked the idea of concluding at a gold mine. I intuited much metaphoric room to bounce about in.

The next day, I called O'Neill's message number at 10:00, 11:00, 12:00, and 1:00. Only an answering machine responded. I noted the progress of our day (to a garage to check an oil leak, to lunch for a club sandwich, to the café for a *doppio...*) and, by my tone, a developing annoyance. At 2:00, when I concluded the day doomed, I did not say what I would be doing.

Which was... pace. Stare at the changing leaves (Overrated!). Stroke the gray cat until my allergy exploded. Throughout, I auditioned the tragic, the reasonable, the semi-crazed for explanations. I was frustrated, mad, not ideal company for a getaway weekend.

Adele suggested a drive. The word in the street — in the parlor of our B and B, actually — had put a name to O'Neill's mine. It was no inescapable conclusion. There were other worthy contenders. Even if correct, there was no chance he would be there. But I sensed a satisfying paragraph.

We rode north forty miles. We traversed a mountain ridge. On one side of us was chasm. On the other, forest rose.

"He never got out of childhood," Adele said, turning pages of my still-in-progress manuscript.

"Who?" I said.

"Latency, actually," she said. "Walt Disney."

"Latency," I said, "had not occurred to me."

"He needed to maintain a child's fairytale view of the world, where only the good and pure are rewarded," she said. "The next step, the step he did not take, the step which turns this world upside down, is adolescence." I hugged the Honda to the center line. It sucked it up for one more ascent. "The Pirates, of course, were great adolescents. They were also talented and smart and in touch with passions that they knew the hand of a Disney would squelch, so they turned their art against him. Disney was talented and smart too, but he was hampered in where his art could go by his abusive childhood."

"His father," I said. "That leather strap. Those newspapers delivered through snow."

"The rage he felt must have been enormous. It would have led him to fantasies more horrible than those in your E.C.s. That's what he fought all his life. That's what gave rise to his zany belief that he had to save America by turning it into a child's land. Otherwise, it would be overrun by the release of forces as terrible and frightening and potentially destructive as those in his fantasies." She looked into the forest. Planning our trip, she had told O'Neill we must return from his cabin before dark because she feared narrow mountain roads. He'd replied the road was fine; then he mentioned weasels, bobcats, red-balling eighteen-wheelers toting timber. "You can tie a six-pack to your bumper," he'd riffed, "and troll for bears. Or go down Sixth and Market and troll for Indians."

"What he did was terrific. Even the Air Pirates enjoyed them when they were children. But, unlike Walt Disney, most people don't remain children all their lives."

"So you had Disney trying to protect everyone from adolescence and the Pirates trying to welcome everyone to it with streamers, confetti, and party balloons — most likely filled with nitrous oxide."

"And in the end, none of it made any difference. People read the Pirates' books, and some were appalled, and some said, 'Oh, wow!'; and some went on to vote Republican and some Democrat."

"And probably all of them let their kids watch Disney."

"Probably. The world is neither a totalitarian state like Disneyland nor a free-floating psychodrama like the Pirates' warehouse. It is not so fragile; it is not so easily changed; in the end, it's not so easy to topple things. The world is pretty stable, for better or for worse. Disney wasn't about to be annihilated by comic books like the Pirates hoped — or as its lawyers feared. The only thing that keeps me from being absolutely furious at the case's outcome is that in the end the Pirates got what they wanted. They did their books; they got attention; and, to someone with O'Neill's turn of mind, they could claim to be victorious."[190]

The sign posted by the town said "POP. 150." The next one was not as over-built. We hung a down-grade right.

A rusted gondola car brimming with crushed rock marked the mine. A plaque saluted a nugget named "Big Whopper." Across the road stood two green-and-white, wood-frame houses, with aging sedans blossoming in the front yards. From the salvage, three skinny dogs yapped toward us. A brindled gray male, an orange-muzzled bitch, a pup with markings of both.

"NO ENTRY," welcomed a sign at the mine's portico, "CAMERA SUR-VEILLANCE." I pocketed a fortune cookie-sized chunk off the gondola, wondering what jack-booted troopers that would set storming my door. The air cut through my leather jacket. The light stung my eyes like chlorine. Throughout our short history, gold mines have centered archetypal American dreams. In our national imagination, they incubated a particular form of personal redefinition and rebirth. The kind that cast off security and comfort. That braved wilderness and renegades. That had room for honky-tonk and hookers and letting it all

[190] This "turn of mind," Adele also once explained to me, when I was sputtering Gale Gordon-like over my inability yet again to match O'Neill's account of an event with what I was learning elsewhere, could be viewed more generously than my nit-picking moments allowed. "Sure, making up stories can be viewed as a deficit. But, with O'Neill, they could be considered a mark of genius. Seeing yourself in the center of a world of events, ideas, causes, where what you do and think make history, is a big vision. It easily justifies elaboration. Like with all visionaries, whatever happens to him becomes the next level of a story by which he instructs social primitives and other comatose individuals who only wake up through a good story to the happenings of the world."

"It is a damn good thing for American letters," I said, "that I have you along."

ride on one spin of the wheel. You took the risk; you battled through the handicaps and odds; and when you raked in your rewards — if you raked them — they filled your pockets and overflowed your arms. The thing about mines, I thought, is you have to have the gold in there. Then you have to dig it out. Then you have to hope people don't decide they'd rather have zirconium.

When we got back, a Post-it announced, "Your guy called. He can meet you anytime."

We settled on the same bar. Adele refused to go. The baseball playoffs were on, and, having suffered formatively as a Red Sox fan, she had recently switched allegiance to the Yankees. "You would not believe the pleasure in rooting for winners," she said.

By the time I arrived, dark had settled. Overhead lights heated the patio. All around us, reconnoitering couples, assaying the evening's materializations, clicked bottles against glasses, exchanged tales of origin, excursion and arrival. O'Neill was abuzz with news. He was organizing a coalition of loggers and environmentalists to save the Sierras. He had uncovered tapes from Belfast ("My mother made me clean my room...") which would prove to the tribunal investigating Bloody Sunday that the British fired first. He planned to re-issue "Odd Bodkins" books and sell them on his website. And, best of all, his strip, while now confined to the *Mountain Messenger,* a Downeyville paper of circumscribed circulation, had been accused of violating a gag order imposed by the Sierra County Superior Court judge presiding over a criminal investigation into the death of a miner in an industrial accident. Then, between sips of cranberry juice and drags on his Camels, he answered my final questions.

"So," I said, two hours later, "what's the ultimate message? How'll we put the kids to bed?"

"Any damn fool can quit." O'Neill lifted his hat and ran a hand through his hair. The smoke from his cigarette ran away into nothing. "My day in the sun may've been a long time ago. It may not happen again. Not that that has anything to do with anything. If I can't do something for myself, I can do it for someone else. A comic strip makes people laugh. And there's nothing more fun than doing a comic strip. It makes for the greatest daydreams. The greatest rides. You're on twenty-four-hours-a-day every day." His face took on the light. Years faded away. "That's what I want on my tombstone: 'He had too much fun.'"

In Memoriam

    While this work was in progress, my friend, Mark Greenfield, died of infections secondary to intravenous drug use. He appeared regularly in my work as "Max Garden." Even unnamed, he was present. (Of the aforementioned *Best Ride*, he once said, accurately, "I drove.") Mark was really really good at being bad with. Being bad, I think, is an important part of childhood and adolescence. It is not so important in an adult, a judgment Mark may have disagreed with but did not hold against me. I — and my work — will miss him.

Acknowledgments

This book could not have been written without the cooperation of Dan O'Neill. He gave openly and generously of his time, his past, his charm, his scars, his vision, his trust. It has been my good fortune to have been permitted to recount his story. Similarly, this book could not have obtained what quality it managed without the other Air Pirates. Shary Flenniken, Gary Hallgren, Bobby London, and Ted Richards freely shared recollections and reflections, anecdotes and analyses, infused with wit, intelligence, and inspiring personal style. It was a delight to portray people who brought so much to the portraying.

I am equally grateful to the attorneys who represented Walt Disney Productions and the Air Pirates for open-heartedly taking time from their present practices to candidly answer queries about this long passed, loopy by-way, in their careers' paths. Michael Kennedy, Michael Stepanian, David Phillips, John Laveroni, Sandy Tatum, George Gilmour, Kirk McKenzie, John Keker, Richard Harris, Linda Shostak, Lawrence Klein, and Lloyd Crenna were patient, courteous, more than professional — and often delightful — in suffering the pesterings of my exuberance.

Gary Arlington, Bob Beerbohm, Stewart Brand, Paul Krassner, Bud Plant, David Smith, Kathe Todd, Larry Todd, and Ron Turner added color, depth, flavor, and spice to my narrative. Don Donahue's knowledge — and his collection of underground comics — was indispensable.

R.C. Harvey and Mark Koenig filled gaps in my record without making me feel too much the fool.

Stuart Dodds pulled a treasure trove of files from his garage — and Carl Nolte and Carol Vernier chipped in valuable facts and recollections — concerning O'Neill's *Chronicle* years.

Edward Samuels helped orient me amidst the whirlpools, reefs, and shoals of copyright law. Wendy Gordon was especially good-hearted and bolstering in assisting me to keep my craft afloat as I tacked through murky waters.

Richard Milner fueled me, not only with his enthusiasm for the Pirates and the times — but with priceless material from his collected papers. Bruce Chrislip, Sam Henderson, Lee Nordling, David Scroggy, and Christopher Stoner graciously opened up other storage boxes and memory banks.

Peter Beren's enthusiasm made me believe this book could happen. Malcolm Whyte's address book helped get me started. Richard Weber's example kept me kicking on doors. Michael Lydon braced me with doses of much-needed journalistic rigor.

David Hoffman delivered clutch insights — when he wasn't trying to get me to write more about West Philly. Danny and Noah Levin, in their only plate appearance, knocked it out of the park.

Rebecca Bowen proofread her way through misspellings, sentence snarls, and punctuation abominations that would have driven lesser mortals over the brink. Tom Spurgeon's belief in my work, during his years as *The Comics Journal*'s managing editor, emboldened my efforts. His help in getting this manuscript shaped and formed was immense. Kim Thompson scoured the globe to correct factual errors only a polymath would have been concerned by in the first place. Patrick Rosenkranz and Eric Sack, historian and philanthropic art collector respectively, graciously contributed to the art section of the book. And Gary Groth has been as courageous and supportive a publisher as any writer could wish. It has been a privilege to work with these people.

I've made clear, I hope, how much Adele means to me; but I want to say it again. Every day, I give thanks.

BIBLIOGRAPHY

I. Books.

Anderson, Terry H. *The Movement and the Sixties.* Oxford University Press. 1995.

Bain, David and Harris, Bruce eds. *Mickey Mouse: Fifty Happy Years.* Harmony Books. 1977.

Ball, Horace G. *Law of Copyright and Literary Properties.* Banks and Company. 1944.

Barker, Martin. *A Haunt of Fears: The Strange History of the British Horror Comics Campaign.* Pluto Press. 1984.

Barrier, Michael and Williams, Martin eds. *A Smithsonian Book of Comic-Book Comics.* Smithsonian Institution and Harry N. Abrams, Inc. 1981.

Beauchamp, Monte ed. *The Life and Times of R. Crumb: Comments from Contemporaries.* St. Martin's Griffin. 1998.

Bell, Elizabeth, Haas, Lynda, and Sells, Laura eds. *From Mouse to Mermaid: The Politics of Film, Gender and Culture.* Indiana University Press. 1995.

Benton, Mike. *Superhero Comics of the Silver Age: The Illustrated History.* Taylor Pub. Co. 1991.

Bondi, Victor ed. *American Decades: 1970-1979.* Gale Research, Inc. 1995.

Daniels, Les. *Comix: A History of Comic Books in America.* Bonanza Books. 1975.

_____. *Marvel: Five Fabulous Decades of the World's Greatest Comics.* Harry N. Abrams, Inc. 1996.

Diehl, Digby. *Tales From the Crypt: The Official Archives.* St. Martin's Press. 1996.

Donahue, Don and Goodrick, Susan eds. *The Apex Treasury of Underground Comics.* Quick Fox. 1974.

Dorfman, Ariel and Mattelhart, Arnaud. *How to Read Donald Duck.* International General. 1991.

Eliot, Marc. *Walt Disney: Hollywood's Dark Prince.* Carol Publishing Group. 1993.

Estren, Mark James. *A History of Underground Comics.* Ronin Publishing. 1987 ed.

Feiffer, Jules. *The Great Comic Book Heroes.* Dial Press. 1977 ed.

Flower, Joe. *Prince of the Magic Kingdom: Michael Eisner and the Re-Making of Disney.* John Wiley & Sons. 1991.

Franz, Ron. *Fandom: Confidential.* Midguard Publishing Co. 2000.

Glessing, Robert J. *The Underground Press in America.* Indiana University Press. 1970.

Goldstein, Paul. *Copyright: Principles, Law and Practice.* Little, Brown and Company. 1989.

_____. *Copyright's Highway: From Gutenberg to the Celestial Jukebox.* Hill and Wang. 1994.

Goulart, Ron. *Comic Book Culture: An Illustrated History.* Collectors Press. 2000.

Griffin, Sean. *Tinker Belles and Evil Queens: The Walt Disney Company From the Inside Out.* New York University Press. 2000.

Groth, Gary and Fiore, Robert. *The New Comics.* Berkeley Books. 1988.

Grover, Ron. *The Disney Touch: How a Daring Management Team Revived an Entertainment Empire.* Business One Irwin. 1991.

Harvey, Robert C. *The Art of the Comic Book.* University Press of Mississippi. 1996.

Heide, Robert and Gilman, John. *Mickey Mouse: The Evolution, The Legend, The Phenomenon.* Welcome Enterprises Inc. 2001.

Hiassen, Carl. *Team Rodent: How Disney Devours the World.* The Library of Contemporary Thought. 1996.

Hubner, John. *Bottom Feeders: From Free Love to Hard Core: The Rise and Fall of Counterculture Heroes Jim and Artie Mitchell.* Doubleday. 1992.

Jaspar, Margaret C. *The Law of Copyright.* 2d ed. Oceana Publications. 2000.

Koenig, Mark. *Mouse Tales: A Behind-the-Ears Look at Disneyland.* Bonaventure Press. 1994.

Krassner, Paul. *Confessions of a Raving, Unconfined Nut: Misadventures in the Counterculture.* Simon & Schuster. 1993.

_____. *Sex, Drugs & the Twinkie Murders.* Loompanics Unlimited. 2000.

_____. ed. *Psychedelic Trips for the Mind.* Trans-High Corporation. 2001.

Lawrence, John Shelton and Timberg, Bernard eds. *Fair Use and Free Inquiry: Copyright Law and the New Media.* 2d ed. Ablex Publishing Corp. 1989.

Lee, Stan. *The Origins of Marvel Comics.* Simon & Schuster. 1974.

Masters, Kim. *The Keys to the Kingdom: How Michael Eisner Lost His Grip.* HarperCollins. 2000.

McCumber, David. *Rated X.* Simon & Schuster. 1992.

Nimmer, Melville B. and Nimmer, David. *Nimmer on Copyright.* Lexus Publishing. 2001.

Nyberg, Amy Kiste. *Seal of Approval: The History of the Comics Code.* University Press of Mississippi. 1998.

O'Brien, Geoffrey. *Dream Time: Chapters from the Sixties.* Penguin Books. 1989.

O'Neill, Dan. *Buy This Book of Odd Bodkins.* No publisher or year given.

_____. *The Collective Unconscious of Odd Bodkins.* Glide Publications. 1973.

_____. *Farewell to the Gipper.* Eclipse Books. 1988.

_____. *Hear the Sound of My Feet Walking, Drown the Sound of My Voice Talking.* Glide Urban Center Publications. 1973

_____. *The Log of the Irish Navy.* Hugh O'Neill & Assoc. 1983.

Peck, Abe. *Uncovering the Sixties.* Pantheon Books. 1985.

Perry, George & Aldridge, Alan eds. *The Penguin Book of Comics.* Penguin Press. Rev. ed. 1971.

Pustz, Matthew. *Comic Book Culture: Fanboys and True Believers.* University Press of Mississippi. 1999.

Reich, Charles. *The Greening of America.* Random House. 1970.

Richardson, Duin. *Comics Between the Panels.* Dark Horse. 1998.

Rosenkranz, Patrick. *Rebel Visions: The Underground Comix Revolution 1963-1975.* Fantagraphics Books. 2002.

Rosenkranz, Patrick and Van Baren, Hugo. *Artsy Fartsy Funnies.* Paranoia. 1974.

Roszak, Theodore. *The Making of a Counter Culture: Reflections on the Technocratic Society and Its Youthful Opposition.* Doubleday & Company. 1969.

Rubin, Jerry. *We Are Everywhere.* Harper & Row. 1971.

Sabin, Roger. *Adult Comics.* Routledge. 1993.

_____. *Comics, Comix & Graphic Novels.* Phaidon Press. 1996.

Salisbury, Harrison E. ed. *The Eloquence of Protest: Voices of the '70s.* Houghton Mifflin. 1972.

Samuels, Edward. *The Illustrated Story of Copyright.* St. Martin's Press. 2000.

Savage, Jr., William W. *Comic Books and America 1945-1954.* University of Oklahoma Press. 1990.

Schelly, Bill. *The Golden Age of Comic Fandom.* Hamster Press. Rev. ed. 1999.

Schickel, Richard. *The Disney Version.* 3rd ed. Ivan R. Dees, Inc. 1997.

Steranko, James. *The Steranko History of Comics*, vol. I. Supergraphics. 1970.

Swan, Daniel ed. *The Best of Abbie Hoffman.* Four Walls, Eight Windows. 1989.

Tatum. Frank D. "Sandy" Jr. *A Love Affair with the Game.* The American Golfer. 2002.

Thomas, Bob. *Walt Disney: An American Original.* Simon & Schuster. 1976.

_____. *Building a Company: Roy O. Disney and the Creation of an Entertainment Empire.* Hyperion. 1998.

Von Bernewitz, Fred and Geissman, Grant. *Tales of Terror.* Gemstone Publishing and Fantagraphics Books. 2000.

Walt Disney Productions. *Animated Features and Silly Symphonies.* Abbeville Press. 1980.

_____. *Mickey Mouse.* Abbeville Press. 1978.

Watts, Steven, *The Magic Kingdom: Walt Disney and the American Way of Life.* Houghton Mifflin Co. 1997.

Waugh, Coulton. *The Comics.* University Press of Mississippi. 1994.

Wertham, Fredric, M.D. *Seduction of the Innocent.* Rinehart & Company. 1954.

Whyte, Malcolm. *The Underground Comix Family Album.* Word Play. 1998.

II. Comics,

Air Pirates. *Air Pirates Funnies.* Vol. 1, No. 1. Hell Comics. July 1971.

_____. _____. Vol. 1, No. 2. Hell Comics. Aug. 1971.

_____. *Air Pirates Funnies.* (tabloid) Vol. 1, No. 1. 1972.

Hallgren, Gary *et al. The Tortoise and the Hare.* No 1. Last Gasp Eco-Funnies. 1971.

Jackson, Jack *et al. Rip Off Comix* No. 21. Rip Off Press. 1988.

London, Bobby. *The Dirty Duck Book.* The Company and Sons. 1971.

_____ *et al. Left-Field Funnies.* Apex Novelties. 1972.

_____ et al. *Merton of the Movement.* Last Gasp Eco-Funnies. 1971.

New Mouse Liberation Front. *Air Pirates.* No year or publisher given.

O'Neill, Dan. *Comics and Stories.* Vol. 1, No. 1. No year or publisher given.

_____. Vol. 1, No. 2. No year or publisher given.

_____. Vol. 1, No. 3. No year or publisher given.

_____. Vol. 2, No. 1. Comics and Comix. 1975.

_____. Vol. 2, No. 2. Comics and Comix. 1975.

Richards, Ted *et al. Dopin' Dan.* No. 1. Rip Off Press. 1972.

_____ *et al. Dopin' Dan.* No. 2. Rip Off Press. 1973.

_____ *et al. Dopin' Dan.* No. 3. Last Gasp Eco-Funnies. Oct. 1973.

_____. *E.Z. Wolf.* No. 1. Rip Off Press. July 1977.

_____. *E.Z. Wolf's Astral Outhouse.* Last Gasp Eco-Funnies. 1977.

_____. *The Whole Forty-Year-Old Hippie Catalog.* Rip Off Press. 1978.

_____. *The Forty-Year-Old Hippie* No. 2. Rip Off Press. 1979.

Richards, Ted and Murphy, Willie. *Two Fools.* Last Gasp Eco-Funnies. 1976.

Shelton, Gilbert and Richards, Ted. *A Revised History of the American Revolution.* Rip Off Press. 1976.

III. Articles.

Abramson, Elliott M. "How Much Copying Under Copyright: Contradictions, Parodies, Inconsistencies," 61 Temp. L.Rev 133 (1988).

Babiskin, Lisa M. "Oh, Pretty Parody: Campbell v. Acuff-Rose," 8 Harv. J. of Law & Tech. 193 (1994).

Beauchamp, Monte ed. "Comments on Crumb," *Blab* #3. Kitchen Sink Press. Sept. 1988.

_____ int. "Kim Deitch," *The Comics Journal.* July 1988.

Blackbeard, Bill. "Dan O'Neill" in Horn, Maurice ed. *The World Encyclopedia of Comics.* Chelsea House Publishers. 1976.

_____. "Mickey Mouse and the Phantom Artist" in Thompson, Don & Lupoff, Dick eds.. *The Comic-Book Book.* Krause Publications, rev. ed. 1998.

Boyd, Robert int. "Sherry Flenniken," *The Comics Journal.* Nov. 1991.

Brand, Stewart. "Dan O'Neill Defies U.S. Supreme Court," *The Co-Evolution Quarterly.* Spring 1979.

_____. "Disney Sues O'Neill, Brand, and POINT." *The Co-Evolution Quarterly No. 22.* Summer 1979.

Burr, Sherri L. "Artistic Parody: A Theoretical Conduit," 14 Cardozo Arts & Ent. LJ 65 (1996).

Cooney, William. "Mickey Mouse Wins Out Over Air Pirates," *San Francisco Chronicle* Feb. 6, 1980, p. 14.

Cox, Gail Diane. "Don't Mess With the Mouse," *National Law Journal.* July 31, 1989, p.1.

Cruse, Howard. "Raising Issues," *Comics Scene* #7, 1982.

_____. "The Other Side of the Coin," *Comics Scene* #8. 1982.

Dreschler, C.T. "Extent of Doctrine of 'Fair Use' Under Federal Copyright Act," *American Law Reports.* 3d ed. 1969.

Drewes, Carolyn. "This is Stepanian the Dope Lawyer," *San Francisco Examiner-Chronicle.* Nov. 5, 1972, p.4 "Sunday Scene" c.1.

Geerdes, Clay. "Liberating Walt Disney," Los Angeles *Free Press* Aug. 13, 1971, p. 39.

_____. "Dan O'Neill and the Air Pirates," *Graphic Story World.* Dec. 1972.

Gordon, Wendy J. "Reality as Artifact," 55 *Law and Contemporary Problems* 93 (1992).

_____. "An Inquiry into the Merits of Copyright," 41 *Stanford Law Review* 1347 (1989).

_____. "A Property Right in Self-Expression," 10 *Yale Law Journal* 1533 (1993).

Groth, Gary int. "The Straight Dope from R. Crumb," *The Comics Journal.* April 1988.

_____ int. "A Walk on the Wild Side: The Spain Rodriguez Interview," *The Comics Journal.* May 1998.

_____ int. "Art Spiegelman," *The Comics Journal.* Sept. 1995.

_____ int. "Bill Griffith: Politics, Pinheads and Post-Modernism," *The Comics Journal.* March 1993.

Gunther, Marc. "Has Eisner lost the Disney Magic," *Fortune.* Jan. 7, 2002.

Jacobson, Nels. "Faith, Hope and Parody," 31 Hous. L. Rev. 955 (1994.)

King, Peter H. "Mickey, the Mouse That Roars," San Francisco *Examiner-Chronicle.* June 3, 1979, A3.

Lee, Jay. "Campbell v. Acuff-Rose," 29 USF L.Rev 279.

Light, Sheldon N. "Parody, Burlesque and the Economic Rationale for Copyright," 11 Conn. L. Rev. 615 (1979).

Loeb, Paul and Sharpe, Warren. "Mice Guys Finish Last," *New West.* July 2, 1979.

London, David. "Toon Town: Do Cartoon Crossovers Merit Fair Use Protection," 38 B.C. L. Rev. 145 (1996).

MCH. "Who Created Roger Rabbitt?" *The Comics Journal* #137 (September, 1990).

____. "Disney Comics Decimated." *The Comics Journal* #145 (October, 1991).

Milner, Richard. "Patriarch of the Underfunnies," *Gallery,* 1975 (month unknown).

Netterville, Victor S. "Copyright and Tort Aspects of Parody, Mimicry and Humerous Commentary," 35 SoCal. L. Rev. 225 (1962).

Ogar, Richard. "Inside a Lawyers' Commune," *The Berkeley Barb*, Sept. 25, 1970, p. 7.

O'Neill, Dan. "Communique #1 from the M.L.F.," *The Co-Evolution Quarterly.* Spring 1979.

Posner, Richard A. "When is Parody Fair Use?" 21 J. Legal Stud. 71 (1992).

Riggenberg, Steve int. "Robert Williams," *The Comics Journal.* Aug. 1993.

Roach, David (DAR), review of *Dan O'Neill's Comics and Stories* in Plowright, Frank ed. *The Slings and Arrows Comic Guide.* Aurum Press. 1997.

Rogow, Bruce. "The Art of Making Law from Other People's Art," 14 Cardozo Arts & Ent. LJ 127 (1966).

Romero, Artie int. "A Discussion With Ted Richards," *Cascade.* March 1978.

_____. "Larry Todd Speaks," *Cascade.* April 1978.

_____. "Dan O'Neill," *Cascade.* May 1978.

Rosen, Jeffrey. "Disney's Copyright Conquest," *The New Republic.* Oct. 28, 2002.

Saba, Arn int. "Floyd Gottfredson: Mickey's Other Master." *The Comics Journal.* March 1988.

Stack, Frank int. "Gilbert Shelton," *The Comics Journal.* May 1996.

Surridge, Matthew. "Hack's Progress, or Hogarth's Harlot and the Establishment of Creators' Rights," *The Comics Journal.* August 2001.

Tritten, Larry. "Is Mickey Mouse a Sacred Cow?" *Los Angeles Times.* Sept. 23, 1979. CAL 50.

Unattributed. "Odd Man In," *Newsweek.* March 16, 1964.

_____. "A Blow for Irony," *Daily Californian.* Nov. 25, 1969.

_____. "Pickets Protest Dropping of Chronicle Comic," *San Francisco Chronicle.* Dec. 1, 1969.

_____. "Deluge brings Bodkins back," *Editor and Publisher.* Dec. 13, 1969.

_____ . "A 50-ton Mouse is Stepping on My Fingers," *San Francisco Chronicle.* March 10, 1972, p. 5.

_____. "The Mouse Puts Dan O'Neill in Court Again," *Id.* June 27, 1979, p. 6.

_____. "Mickey Mouse Heads for Settlement," *Id.* Sept. 6, 1979, p. 66.

_____. "Sleeping Beauty Is Off Limits," *Rolling Stone.* Sept. 17, 1970, p. 9.

_____. "u.g. comix panel," *Cascade.* Feb. 1980.

Vogel, Jason M. "The Cat in the Hat's Latest Bad Trick," 20 Cardozo L.Rev. 287 (1996).

Weber, Jonathan. "Ever-Expanding, Profit-Maximizing, Cultural-Imperialist, Wonderful World of Disney." *Wired.* Feb. 2002.

Wheelwright, Kevin M. "Parody, Copyrights and the First Amendment," 10 USF L. Rev. 564 (1976).

White, Ted. "The Spawn of M.C. Gaines" in Lupoff, Dick & Thompson, Don eds. *All in Color for a Dime.* Arlington House. 1970.

_____ "The Impact of the Comics Code Authority," *The Comics Journal.* Jan. 2002.

Yonover, Geri J. "The Precarious Balance: Moral Rights, Parody and Fair Use," 14 Cardozo Arts & Ent. LJ 79 (1996).

IV. Other.

Amburg, Van. Transcript of interview of Dan O'Neill for KGO-TV news. Nov. 30, 1970.

Anonymous. "The Sky River III Story." SunsetStrip/ Palace/2534.

Beerbohm, Robert L. "Comics Reality, Part One: The Origin and Development of the Direct Sales Market." beenishboy/reality1.txt.

_____. "Comics Reality #8: The Comic Book Store Phenom — Rebirth of an Industry." Ibid.

Groth, Gary. Unpublished interview of Dan O'Neill. Undated.

Iwerks, Leslie. "The Hand Behind Mickey Mouse: The Ub Iwerks Story," documentary film. 1999.

Mann, Ron. "Comic Book Confidential," documentary film. 1988.

Riggenberg, S.C. "Bobby London and the Air Pirates Follies." Last update 5-12-98.

INDEX

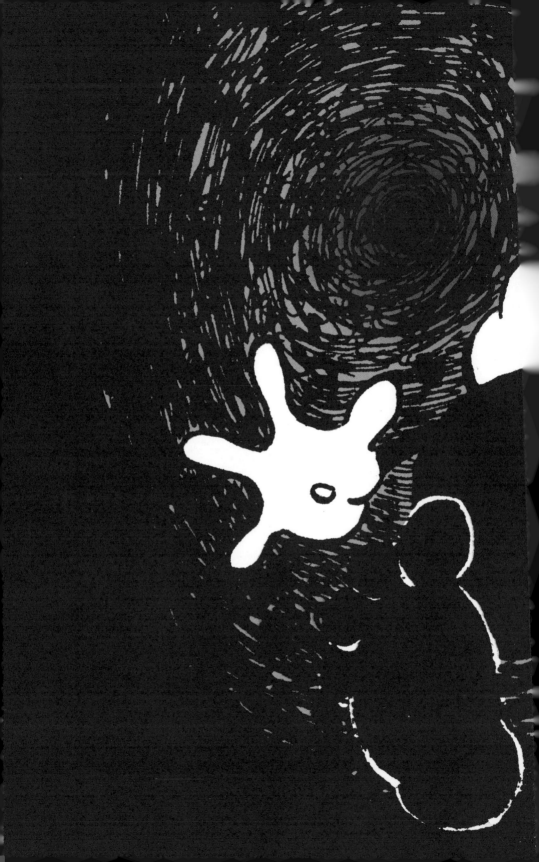